Heidi Kennedy • Katie Handing • Sarah Ince

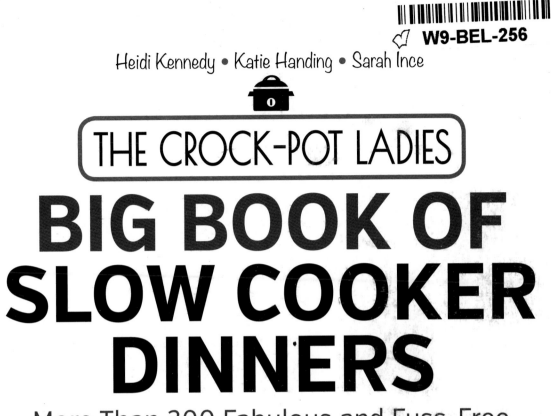

THE CROCK-POT LADIES

BIG BOOK OF SLOW COOKER DINNERS

More Than 300 Fabulous and Fuss-Free Recipes for Families on the Go

Quick-to-Fix Meals from the Ladies Who Make Slow Cooking Fun and Delicious

HARVARD COMMON PRESS

Inspiring | Educating | Creating | Entertaining

Brimming with creative inspiration, how-to projects, and useful information to enrich your everyday life, Quarto Knows is a favorite destination for those pursuing their interests and passions. Visit our site and dig deeper with our books into your area of interest: Quarto Creates, Quarto Cooks, Quarto Homes, Quarto Lives, Quarto Drives, Quarto Explores, Quarto Gifts, or Quarto Kids.

23 22 21 20 19   1 2 3 4 5

ISBN: 978-1-55832-924-9

Digital edition published in 2019
Library of Congress Cataloging-in-Publication Data available

Design and Page Layout: *tabula rasa* graphic design
Photography: Glenn Scott Photography

Printed in China

CROCK POT LADIES IS IN NO WAY ASSOCIATED WITH THE CROCK-POT BRAND OF SLOW COOKERS.

MIX
Paper from
responsible sources
FSC™ C007683

DEDICATIONS

HK—To my family, Russell, Marilyn, Joel, Parker, Liam, and Carly.

KH—This is dedicated to the two reasons I do what I do, my daughters Molly and Natalie.

SI—To my mother, who gave me a love of hassle-free, simple meals, and my Aunt Veda, who gave me a love of owning many Crock-Pots at once. I think of you both often while I'm putting large dinners together for church or school. I hope that I've made you proud. I wish you were still here.

CONTENTS

PREFACE

WE ARE THE CROCK-POT LADIES AND WE ARE HAPPY TO MEET YOU

The time is 3:30 in the afternoon. You grab your purse and keys, and rush out the door to go pick up the kids from school. Twenty minutes later everyone is safely buckled in the car, and you are off to the first of many after-school activities. Your son needs to be dropped off at Scouts, and then your daughter has to be rushed across town for swim practice. You sit on the sidelines of the pool and wait for an hour, and then you're off to go pick up your son from Scouts.

You get home, and toss your purse and keys on the table. The kids unload their backpacks and start on their homework, and you then realize that you don't have a single thing planned for dinner tonight! The pile of mail on the kitchen counter calls your name because you know there is a coupon for pizza delivery in that pile somewhere. Feeling a bit guilty, you dig through the stack of paper to find the coupon, and you call in your pizza order. It's not the healthiest option, and it's not very frugal even with a coupon. Plus, you really like serving your family a meal that you cooked at home.

But how do you get dinner cooked and on the table when it feels like all you do on some days is drive around in the car running the kids to their events, going to the post office, picking up the dry cleaning, and a million-and-one other errands?

Enter the slow cooker. With a little bit of preplanning, you can throw your ingredients in the slow cooker in the morning or early afternoon and come home from all those errands with dinner hot and ready to go!

In this book, we share our favorite slow cooker recipes. They will allow you to serve your family, your friends, and your guests delicious dinners using easy-to-shop-for ingredients. We will discover exciting flavors, and we'll put new twists on old classics!

INTRODUCTION

SLOW COOKER MAGIC

We have been cooking in our slow cookers for years now. Over the course of time, we have picked up some tips and tricks—from the best features to look for when buying a new slow cooker to the best ways to keep your slow cooker clean and shiny!

A SLOW COOKER BUYER'S GUIDE

When shopping for a new slow cooker, the first thing that you want to consider is what size will best meet the needs of your family. The choices available in the market can be overwhelming. Prices can range from $10 to $400. And then you have all the different sizes to contend with. Do you need an itty-bitty 1½-quart (1.4-L) slow cooker or a huge 9-quart (8.5-L) one? What about all the bells and whistles that slow cookers have these days? What features are worth the trouble and which ones can you skip?

Between the three of us ladies we have a combined total of fourteen slow cookers. Because this is our business, we tend to collect slow cookers in various sizes and shapes so that we can cook and test a variety of dishes. We have a good grasp on what features to look for when shopping for a new slow cooker.

Our ideal slow cooker would be a 6-quart (5.7-L), oval-shaped slow cooker with programmable settings that allow you to set your slow cooker to cook on either LOW or HIGH. It would have a programmable time range of four to twelve hours, and automatically turn the slow cooker to the WARM setting for up to two hours when the cooking time is up before turning off completely. We also think having a locking lid is wonderful if you travel with your slow cooker at any time (e.g., holidays, parties, potlucks, etc.). If there is a place on the cooker to wrap the cord for storage, it just makes us happy. The price on this slow cooker would be no more than fifty dollars.

That would be our ideal, go-to slow cooker for everyday use. Let's break it down a little further.

SIZE

The size of slow cooker that will best serve you really depends on how many people you are cooking for.

1 to 2 people	=	1- to 3-quart (946 ml to 2.8-L)
3 to 5 people	=	4- to 5-quart (3.8- to 4.7-L)
6 to 8 people	=	6- to 7-quart (5.7- to 6.6-L)
9 or more people	=	8-quart (7.6-L) or larger

We should also note that smaller dishes, such as dips, are usually cooked in a smaller cooker.

SHAPE

Slow cookers come in two basic shapes: round or oval. Both shapes are fine, but we feel that the oval shape works better if you are cooking roast cuts of meat or whole chicken. Also, there is now a rectangular slow cooker that is newer to the market. The crock liner of this slow cooker is the same as a 9- x 13-inch (23- x 33-cm) cake pan and is great for cooking casseroles, lasagnas, and cakes. They turn out looking like they were cooked in the oven.

SETTINGS

You have two options for slow cooker settings: manual or programmable. With a manual slow cooker, you have a knob that you turn to set your slow cooker on LOW or HIGH; some models also have a WARM setting. You can find manual cookers in all sizes and shapes, and they tend to be less expensive than programmable cookers. Keep in mind, you will need to set a timer and be present to turn the cooker off when your dish is cooked, otherwise you risk it burning. But if you are around the house, this option is just fine.

Programmable cookers allow you to truly "set it and forget it." You can set the cooking temperature and the time you want your dish to cook for. And most (but not all) will turn the cooker to the WARM setting when the cook time is done. We value these options because we are busy ladies taking care of our families and we don't have time to babysit our slow cookers.

Many of the smaller-sized slow cookers only come with manual controls. We have found it next to impossible to find a 3-quart (2.8 L) or smaller-sized slow cooker that is programmable. So, if you are cooking for one or two people you may not be able to find a programmable slow cooker.

BELLS AND WHISTLES

Slow cookers these days come with all sorts of bells and whistles. Some of these extras are nice to have. To sort through some of these features, we have created a list in the order of how functional they are:

- **Locking Lid:** A locking lid is a nice feature if you travel or you bring your slow cooker to events or parties. We always bring a dish in our slow cookers to family gatherings or chuck potlucks. Having a lid that locks helps keep the food from sloshing out all over the car. Locking lids almost always have a rubber gasket around the edges of the lid and a couple of latches that hold the lid onto the slow cooker while traveling. It's a great feature!

- **Dishwasher-Safe Insert:** Being able to throw the pottery crock insert in the dishwasher is always great and saves washing it by hand. Most modern slow cooker inserts are dishwasher-safe, but it is something we always look for before buying a new slow cooker just to be sure.

- **Lid Storage:** When you take the lid off a slow cooker that has been cooking away, there is always some condensation that collects on the inside of the lid. When you place the lid on the kitchen counter, that water can create a puddle on your countertop. Some slow cookers now have a place where you can set the wet lid and the liquid either collects in a reservoir or drips back in your slow cooker. It's a handy feature to have, for sure. If you don't have a slow cooker with this feature, you can just place a kitchen towel on the counter and place your lid on that. But the lid storage option is nice to have.

- **Cord Length:** Slow cookers usually come with rather short cords. The average cord length is about only 2-feet long (60 cm). Some models have cords as long as 3 feet (90 cm). Most modern kitchens have plenty of convenient outlet placements, but if you have to reach for an outlet in your kitchen, having that extra foot of cord can be very handy. And if you bring your slow cooker to parties or potlucks, you just never know how close an available outlet will be. A longer cord is nice to have. You can always use an extension cord if you absolutely have to, but make sure that the electrical rating of the cord is the same as or greater than the electrical rating of your slow cooker.

- **Cord Storage:** When not in use, appliances can be a bit of a bother if there is no place to store the cord. We do find having cord storage is a nice feature. If the slow cooker you purchase does not have this feature, you can easily find some sort of cord wrap in the organization section of your local stores. A rubber band will work just fine, too.

- **Stove Top–Safe Insert:** Newer slow cookers feature a metal insert instead of the standard pottery crock insert. These can be placed directly on the stove top, and you can sear meats or sauté vegetables right in the insert and not dirty up another pan. While this feature is nice, the slow cooker meals that require prebrowning the meat are few and far between. Using a skillet on the stove top has not been a big enough inconvenience to warrant the higher cost of a slow cooker with a stove top–safe insert.

ARE "MULTICOOKERS" SLOW COOKERS?

Multicookers are all the rage these days, and that's for good reason. They allow you to replace several kitchen appliances with just one appliance that does the work of a slow cooker, pressure cooker, rice cooker, and steamer–just to name a few. There are so many options available out there now in the realm of multicookers that it can be a little overwhelming.

To be honest with you, we don't use multicookers for our recipes. We find that a good old-fashioned slow cooker is the way to go.

But, to answer the question, multicookers are indeed slow cookers. If you have a multicooker that has a slow cooker option, you can cook the recipes in this book in your multicooker.

If your multicooker does not have a distinct slow cooker feature, the appliance is going to cook like a pressure cooker and is going to cook much faster than a slow cooker. We strongly suggest that you follow your multicooker's instruction manual for converting slow cooker recipes to pressure cooker recipes.

SLOW COOKER BASICS

Slow cooker models vary, but in general most of them have at least two settings: LOW (about 180°F, or 82°C) and HIGH (about 280°F, or 138°C). Some models also have a WARM setting that allows you to keep food hot for serving while entertaining. Most programmable slow cookers will automatically switch to the WARM setting after the set cooking time is over. This adds convenience, and it helps you avoid overcooking the food when you are away from home or otherwise occupied.

Most slow cooker recipes give a range in time to account for variables such as thickness of the meat, how full the slow cooker is, and the variation in cooking times for different slow cooker models. Always cook a dish for the lowest cooking time given in a recipe, and cook the recipe longer only if needed. For example, if a recipe calls for cooking on LOW for 6 to 8 hours, cook the dish for 6 hours, and then check to see if the dish is cooked. Cook longer only if it needs it.

Some recipes are more forgiving than others. Recipes that call for large roasts, ground beef, beef or pork stew meat, and beans are usually okay to cook for longer periods of time without risk of overcooking. But more delicate meats, such as chicken, pork chops, and seafood, can suffer from overcooking if cooked too long.

Newer models of slow cookers tend to heat up more quickly than older models. Old slow cookers can also lose their efficiency and may not achieve proper cooking temperatures. Do a simple test to make sure your slow cooker is still reaching safe cooking temperatures.

TIPS, TRICKS, AND HACKS

Invest in a well-calibrated meat thermometer and test the doneness of meats before serving. It is safe to assume that the meat is cooked to the proper temperature if the meat is falling off the bone and can be shredded easily. Important: Not all meat cooked in the slow cooker is cooked to that degree of doneness, so check the temperature just to be safe.

Be sure the lid is well-placed over the slow cooker's ceramic insert. It should not be tilted or off center. The steam created during cooking helps create a seal and keeps the heat inside the slow cooker.

Try to refrain from lifting the lid of the slow cooker to

SAFE COOKING TEMPERATURES FOR MEATS

Beef (whole cuts of roasts, steaks, chops, ribs, etc.): 145°F (63°C)

Veal (whole cuts of roasts, steaks, chops, ribs, etc.): 145°F (63°C)

Lamb (whole cuts of roasts, steaks, chops, ribs, etc.): 145°F (63°C)

Pork (whole cuts of roasts, steaks, chops, ribs, fresh ham, etc.): 160°F (71°C)

Chicken (whole or pieces): 165°F (74°C)

Ground Beef: 160°F (71°C)

Ground Turkey or Chicken: 160°F (71°C)

Precooked Ham (reheat): 140°F (60°C)

HOW TO DO A SLOW COOKER TEMPERATURE CHECK

- *Fill the slow cooker two-thirds of the way full with room-temperature water.*

- *Cover the slow cooker and turn it to the LOW setting for 8 hours.*

- *After 8 hours, quickly open the lid of the slow cooker and check the temperature of the water with a thermometer.*

- *The temperature should be at least 185°F (85°C).*

- *If the water is too hot, a recipe cooked for 8 hours will likely be overcooked. If the temperature is below 185° F (85°C), the slow cooker is not safe to use and should be discarded.*

take a peek inside while the food is cooking. Lifting the lid releases the heat that has built up inside the slow cooker. The loss of heat can mean an extra 20 to 30 minutes of cooking time each time you lift the lid. Don't open the slow cooker unless the recipe instructs you to stir or add ingredients.

If cooking at higher altitudes (3,000 feet or higher), allow extra time for cooking. It can take liquids longer to reach the simmer point. You may wish to start your slow cooker on the HIGH setting for 1 hour and then turn the cooker down to the LOW setting to finish cooking. Dishes such as whole roasts will probably need to cook an additional 1 hour. Always check your food at the lowest time range given in a recipe, and cook for additional time as needed. This is when a good meat thermometer comes into play; you want to make sure your meat is cooked to the proper safe temperature.

When food is finished cooking, remove it from the slow cooker within 1 hour. Refrigerate the leftovers.

Reheating food in a slow cooker is not recommended. The cooker can take several hours to reach proper cooking temperatures. Instead, heat up already-cooked food on the stove top or in the microwave, then place it in the slow cooker to keep food hot for serving.

Some recipes, such as meatloaf and layered dishes, are easier to remove from the slow cooker if you use foil handles. Here is how to create foil handles for your slow cooker:

- Cut three 25- × 3-inch (64- × 7½-cm) strips of heavy-duty aluminum foil.

- Crisscross the strips in the bottom of the slow cooker so that they resemble the spokes of a wheel. Make sure that the strips run up the sides of the slow cooker and hang over the edge.

- Coat the strips of foil with nonstick cooking spray.

- Place the food in the center of the strips in the insert.

- Cook according to the directions in the recipe.

- After cooking, grasp the foil strips and carefully lift the food up and out of the slow cooker.

To help with cleanup, especially when cooking sticky foods such as barbecue ribs, it may be helpful to use a slow cooker liner. These BPA-free plastic bags are designed to withstand the heat of cooking in the slow cooker, and they can be thrown away after use. You can find them in most grocery stores in the aisle where you would find aluminum foil, plastic wrap, parchment paper, and freezer bags.

Baking cakes, cobblers, and breads is something we love to do in our slow cookers because we can bake without heating up the oven. However, the moist environment in your slow cooker can leave baked goods a little bit soggy due to the condensation that collects on the lid and drips down onto your baked goods. To prevent this, simply place a clean kitchen towel or several sheets of paper toweling between the top of the ceramic insert and the lid. Make sure the towel does not touch your food.

Certain recipes, such as fruit butters, need to cook down and cook off excess liquid. If the lid on the slow cooker is completely sealed, the extra liquid can't evaporate and escape. To solve this problem, simply prop the lid up a little bit using the handle of a wooden or metal spoon. Don't use a plastic spoon as it may melt.

SLOW COOKER TROUBLESHOOTING

While slow cooker cooking is pretty simple, there are some instances when something goes wrong. It may be due to user-error or a malfunction. Regardless of the cause, here are some of our top troubleshooting tips.

Meat comes out too dry or too tough. If your meat is dried out or too tough, there probably was not enough liquid in the recipe or the cooking temperature was too high for that particular cut of meat. While you don't need a lot of liquid for slow cooking, and meat will release its own cooking liquid, you do want to make sure there is some liquid in the slow cooker. Additionally, beef and larger cuts of pork usually do best following the low-and-slow method of cooking. Thinner-cut pork chops and leaner meats like chicken do better with a high-and-fast method. Some meats have more connective tissue than others, and they should cook longer at slower temperatures. While meats with less connective tissues (such as boneless, skinless chicken breasts) should be cooked faster and at a higher temperature.

There is too much liquid in my dish. Very little evaporation occurs during slow cooking because the lid stays closed and seals the cooker. That means you will need about 50 percent less cooking liquid than is called for in stove top or oven recipes. If food appears too liquid, remove the cover for about 1 hour before it has finished cooking and cook on the HIGH setting so that the cooking liquid can evaporate.

My slow cooker does not have an automatic shutoff or timer. You have a couple of options if your slow cooker is not programmable and does not automatically turn the slow cooker off or switch to the WARM setting after cooking. The first option is to just set a timer or your smartphone to remind you of when a dish is done cooking. Or you can purchase a light timer at just about any big-box or hardware store. This is a timer that is designed to turn lights on and off while you are on vacation so that it looks like you are home when you are not. Plug your slow cooker into this timer and follow the instructions on the timer for setting it up to automatically turn your slow cooker after so many hours.

The recipes make too much food. Because we are cooking for our large families, most of our recipes are designed to serve six or more people, with some of our recipes for parties serving twelve or more. That being said, most recipes can be scaled down. The easiest recipes to scale down are soups, stews, and chilis. Meat dishes can be cut down to serve fewer people as well. Keep the cooking temperature the same as in the recipe, but cook those dishes for less time. Start with half of the cooking time and check it often to see when it is done.

The food is not cooked evenly. Certain ingredients in your food may cook faster than others for one of two reasons: Your food was not placed in the slow cooker in the proper order, or pieces of food were not cut to the same size. Certain foods, such as root vegetables (e.g., carrots, potatoes, parsnips, sweet potatoes), need to be placed on the bottom and along the sides of the slow cooker so that they are closer to the heating element. Pieces on the bottom will cook much faster than pieces on the top. Additionally, make sure your pieces are cut uniformly, as smaller pieces cook faster than larger pieces.

I'm not sure whether to use the LOW or HIGH setting to cook. It really is best to follow the recipe and cook at the temperature recommended. Most recipes have the option to cook on either LOW or HIGH, with the LOW temperature cooking for a longer time and the HIGH temperature cooking for a shorter time. If the recipe gives just one option, follow that and don't try converting the recipe. If a recipe has only a LOW cooking temperature, that means that the recipe is best cooked on LOW. This method allows plenty of time to soften beans or make the beef or pork super tender and moist. If a recipe says to cook on HIGH, this means that the recipe really will do better at that higher temperature for a shorter period of time. For instance, baked goods and certain leaner cuts of meat (such as boneless, skinless chicken breasts or boneless pork chops) will cook faster without drying out.

There are hard water or bean residue stains on the inside of slow cooker that won't come off. If you have hard water in your area, your slow cooker may show white spots or a ring of white, hard, lime scale deposits. Oftentimes beans will leave this white mark, too. It is more visible on black ceramic inserts. This white discoloring is not harmful at all, and you don't need to worry about it unless it really bothers you. To remove it, simply wash your insert with hot soapy water, rinse well, and dry. Then fill your slow cooker with water and about 1 cup (235 ml) of distilled white vinegar. Cover the slow cooker. Cook on LOW for 6 hours or so. That hot vinegar water should dissolve the white deposits.

Foods cook too fast. There are several reasons your food may cook too fast. The most common reason is that you are using a slow cooker that is too big. Slow cookers should be filled at least two-thirds of the way full. If you are not filling your slow cooker up, it may be best to purchase a smaller one. The second reason is that you are cooking the food for too long. Most slow cooker recipes give a time range. Always cook recipes for the least amount of time given in the time range, then check to see if it needs more time. For example, if the recipe says to "cover and cook on LOW for 6 to 8 hours," you should cook it on LOW for 6 hours, and cook it longer only if needed. The third most common reason is that something is wrong with your slow cooker. It's normal for the countertop under your cooker to get warm. If the surface is super hot, that is a sign that your slow cooker is overheating and it may be unsafe to use it. Contact the manufacturer of your particular make and model for assistance.

The slow cooker smokes when you turn it on. There are two common reasons your slow cooker may be smoking when you turn it on. If your slow cooker is brand-new, the smoke is probably coming from the manufacturing oil used on the heating element or metal housing. This is common and will dissipate after a couple of uses. The second cause of smoke is usually from food or liquids on the heating element or metal housing. If the source of the smoke is spilled food, unplug your slow cooker and let it cool to room temperature. Wipe off the food with a damp washcloth and a mild all-purpose cleaner. Dry with a dish towel before plugging your cooker back in and turning it on.

The slow cooker never heats up. If you plug your slow cooker in and turn it on and it never heats up, check to see if the outlet is working properly. It could be a breaker switch or a GFI (ground fault interrupter) has tripped. If your outlet is working properly, then there is something wrong with the electrical component of your slow cooker. It could be the heating element, cord, or plug, and you will need to either have it repaired or purchase a new slow cooker.

Food burns or sticks to the slow cooker. There are several reasons your food may burn or stick. The most common reason is that there is not enough liquid. With the exception of a few recipes, such as snack mix and granola, you cannot cook dry in the slow cooker. You don't need a lot of liquid, but you do need some—especially for meat dishes. Also, some dishes are more prone to sticking than others. Foods that are high in sugar or starch (e.g., barbecue sauce or rice) may stick to your slow cooker. Be sure to follow the recipe exactly.

If called for, use a disposable slow cooker liner or spray your slow cooker with nonstick cooking spray (or both!) to make cleanup easier.

The power went off or the slow cooker was accidentally unplugged while cooking. If your slow cooker lost power for less than two hours, your food should be safe to continue cooking. If it has been longer than two hours, then you should remove the food from the slow cooker and discard it as it may not be safe to eat. If you are unsure how long you have been without power, err on the side of caution, discard the food, and order pizza.

The glass lid or ceramic insert is cracked. The most common reason your slow cooker's lid or ceramic insert may crack is because it was dropped or something was dropped on it. Another reason it may crack is an extreme change in temperature, such as running cold water in a hot insert or placing the lid or insert on a cold countertop; stone countertops can be quite cold and are usually the culprit. Additionally, placing frozen or very cold food in a slow cooker that has already been heated up can cause the insert to crack. Always let your ceramic insert and lid cool to room temperature before placing them in or under water to wash or rinse. Always set your lid or base on a towel or hot pad instead of directly on the counter. And, while you can put frozen meat in your slow cooker, always start by putting the frozen meat in and then turning the slow cooker on so that the meat can slowly warm up with the slow cooker. If your slow cooker's insert or lid has broken or cracked, contact the manufacturer for replacement options.

The slow cooker has a hot spot. Some slow cookers have a certain spot that cooks hotter than the rest of the slow cooker. This hot spot tends to be on the side opposite of where the controls or knobs are. This hot spot can affect baked goods or casserole dishes more than soups and stews. The solution is to either place a small piece of foil over that hot spot area or rotate the stoneware insert a couple of times during cooking, much like you would rotate a cookie sheet in the oven while baking.

The rice or pasta in the dish is mushy. Most recipes that include rice or pasta call for it to be added near the end of the cooking time or to precook it on the stove top. There are a few exceptions to this rule, but in general add the pasta or rice at the end of cooking.

Does food really need to be browned first? Browning meat seals the juices in the meat and provides an additional flavor component. Browning meat caramelizes the naturally occurring sugars in the meat and creates a crust on the meat; this imparts some great flavors to your dish. You can safely omit this step if time is short, but the finished dish may not have the same flavor profile and may also be a bit drier.

MAINTAINING AND CLEANING YOUR SLOW COOKER

Most modern slow cookers come with a removable ceramic insert, which makes it very easy to clean and maintain. Always allow the insert to cool off to room temperature before cleaning. The rapid change in temperature of a hot insert and cool, or even warm, water can cause the insert to crack.

Our philosophy when it comes to cleaning your slow cooker is "an ounce of prevention is worth a pound of cure." That means, it is easier to prevent a dirty slow cooker than it is to clean a crusty burned-on mess. If your slow cooker dish is high in sugar and prone to sticking and burning, spray the insert with nonstick cooking spray or vegetable oil, or use a plastic slow cooker liner. Barbecue sauce is a main culprit for sticking and burning, but it's easily prevented by taking this one extra step.

Your slow cooker will never get gross and dirty if you clean it properly inside and out after every single use. Just wipe the base down inside and out after every use–most of the time all you need is a soft sponge, hot water, and standard dishwashing liquid. A little baking soda can be used as a gentle scouring powder to help you scrub off any slightly stuck-on food.

You can also put the insert in the dishwasher if your insert is dishwasher-safe. (Check the manual.) If you find that you have food stuck on the slow cooker, use some of these methods to help get your insert looking brand-new. Always start with the least toxic or time-consuming option first, then work your way down the list only as needed.

CLEANING STUCK-ON FOOD FROM YOUR SLOW COOKER INSERT

A mild abrasive scouring pad is always the first step if a regular sponge and dish soap are not cutting it. A little scrubbing here should remove most stuck-on foods.

If scrubbing does not work, try soaking your insert. Fill the insert with hot water; add a squirt of dishwashing liquid and about a quarter of a cup (60 g) of baking soda. Place the insert inside the heating base, cover the slow cooker, and turn it to the LOW setting for 3 or 4 hours. This method works for us about 90 percent of the time if there is really stuck-on burned food.

If soaking does not work, the last resort we would recommend is to spray the inside of the insert with ammonia-based oven cleaner. Let it sit for a couple of hours and then wash very well with warm, soapy water.

If your slow cooker is suffering from mineral deposits from hard water, you can easily remove those unsightly stains. Add 1 cup (235 ml) of distilled white vinegar to the insert and fill the rest of the way with water. Turn the slow cooker on to HIGH for 2 hours. Carefully pour out the hot water and let the slow cooker cool before washing as normal.

To clean the cooking base of the slow cooker, always make sure to unplug it first and let it cool to room temperature. Then, lightly spray the base with your favorite all-purpose cleaner. Wipe it down with a clean washcloth, microfiber cloth, or paper towels. For stuck-on food, make a paste of baking soda and water. Scrub that in lightly, and you should get off most of the stuck-on food on the inside and outside of the cooking base.

Sometimes when you travel with your slow cooker, food can slosh out and drip between the slow cooker insert and the cooking base. This can really get cooked on, and it can be next to impossible to clean up with normal cleaning methods. If the inside of your slow cooker base is really dirty, the one trick that we have found that works amazingly well is this: Pour about a half of a cup (120 ml) of ammonia in a small glass bowl. Place that bowl inside the base of the slow cooker. Cover the base with aluminum foil or plastic wrap to really seal in the ammonia vapors and let it sit undisturbed overnight. The fumes from the ammonia will help loosen up the burned-on food, and you should be able to easily wipe it after it has sat 8 to 12 hours.

Warning: Keep in mind that ammonia is a potent cleaning agent. You should use ammonia only in a well-ventilated room. Never mix ammonia with bleach, as the combination can cause toxic fumes that can kill you.

ADJUSTING RECIPES TO DIFFERENT SIZES

There are two basic rules to keep in mind if you want to use a different-size slow cooker than the size listed in the recipe.

- **Fill rate:** Slow cookers work best when they are filled at least two-thirds of the way full.
- **Liquid ratio:** It is important to try and keep the ratio of liquid to solids about the same.

Keep those two rules in mind when adjusting a recipe to a different-size slow cooker. Most slow cooker recipes can be scaled up or down to meet the size of your cooker.

While all three of us ladies have several slow cookers in various sizes, we realize that most people don't have the space or desire to have two, three, four, or more slow cookers. Between the three of us, we own fourteen slow cookers!

If you have a really big slow cooker, the easiest way to scale a recipe down is to use an oven-safe baking dish that fits inside your slow cooker insert. Simply add the ingredients to the dish so that it is at least two-thirds of the way full, then place the dish inside the ceramic insert. Cover with the slow cooker lid and cook as directed.

SLOW COOKING FOR THE FREEZER: TOOLS AND TECHNIQUES

We're busy mothers, and we think there is immense value in taking a few hours a week to prep up a few extra slow cooker freezer meals. These are great for when we know there is a hectic day on the schedule—because we have parent-teacher conferences or IEP meetings, or the kids have a soccer game, doctor visits, ballet practice, choir rehearsal, youth group at church, or a swim meet. We have included twenty-seven slow cooker recipes in this cookbook that can be made into freezer meals. You can quickly partially thaw out a bag, pop it in the slow cooker, and let it cook while you go about your busy day!

All our freezer meals are stored in gallon-size freezer bags. Some of the meals require a second quart-size freezer bag to hold a sauce or other ingredients that will be added later. Look for high-quality plastic bags that are designed for the freezer. Through trial and error, we have found that the best bags are the ones that you have to close by sliding your fingers across the seal rather than the ones that have a zipper type closure. The bags that have the little zipper tab have a higher tendency to leak. And no one has time for cleaning up a frozen mess in the freezer! Meals stored in freezer bags are best cooked and eaten within six months. If you want to freeze meals for a longer period of time, a food vacuum sealing system is a wise investment. Those meals can easily go one year or more in the freezer without losing quality.

The tools needed for most freezer meals are all things you probably have on hand already.

- freezer bags
- measuring cups
- measuring spoons
- cutting board
- sharp knife
- food grater or food processor
- large skillet
- small and medium mixing bowls
- large pot
- small fine-mesh strainer
- can opener
- permanent marker for labeling your freezer bags

For the most part, we like to make one or two slow cooker freezer meals at a time. If you want to do a big freezer-meal-prep day, here are ways to organize the project so that you don't get overwhelmed or end up with a kitchen that looks like a tornado hit it!

1. Start with a clean kitchen. Wash, dry, and put away all dishes. Clear as much clutter off your countertops as possible. Move the coffeemaker, toaster, and mail over to the kitchen table so that it is out of the way. Then wipe down the kitchen counters and fill up your kitchen sink with hot soapy water so that you can wash things as you go.

2. Lay out your freezer bags on the counter. Label the bags with the name of the recipe, ingredients, cooking instructions, and today's date. Set the bags aside.

3. Read through all your recipes. Pull out all the ingredients you are going to need so that you are 100 percent sure you have everything you need.

4. Start by prepping, peeling, and chopping vegetables. Add them to the appropriate bags as you go.

5. Wash and dry your cutting boards, measuring cups, and knife as you go.

6. After the vegetables, move on to any meats that are going in your freezer meal. If the meat goes in the bag raw, start with that first. Then, move on to meat that needs to be cooked first. Again, wash and dry your cutting boards, measuring cups, knife, pots, and pans as you go.

7. Finish up with any other ingredients that are needed, such as canned soups, sauces, spices, seasonings, etc.

8. When your bags are full, lay the bags flat on the counter. Seal them, pushing out as much excess air as possible.

9. We like to put the bags flat on a rimmed baking sheet and transfer them to the freezer right on the baking sheet.

10. When the meals have frozen solid, remove the baking sheet and stack the bags like books on a bookshelf or in a plastic container that you can flip through in your freezer.

SOME FREEZER-FRIENDLY RECIPES IN THE BOOK

1. *Fresh Pork Sausage Meatballs*
2. *Veggie-Loaded Minestrone Soup*
3. *Simple Garlic–Brown Sugar Chicken*
4. *Aloha Pineapple Chicken*
5. *Sweet and Zesty Honey-N-Lime Chicken*
6. *Pulled Tandoori Chicken*
7. *Healthy Turkey Apple Meatloaf*
8. *Zesty Cilantro Lime Chicken*
9. *Simple Chicken and Black Beans*
10. *So-Easy Chicken Ranch Tacos*
11. *BBQ Ranch Meatloaf*
12. *Western Beef Casserole*
13. *Savory Ground Beef Over Rice*
14. *Mouthwatering BBQ Boneless Beef Ribs*
15. *Tangy Pineapple Pulled Beef*
16. *Super Simple Beef Tips*
17. *Bold Hamburger Goulash*
18. *Venison Shawarma Bowls*
19. *Pineapple BBQ Pork Chops*
20. *Honey Dijon Pork Chops and Potatoes*
21. *Easy Italian Sausage and Pepper Sandwiches*
22. *Spicy Sausage and Rotini*
23. *Cuban Mojo Pork*
24. *Sweet Citrus Pulled Pork Burritos*

1

APPETIZERS AND DIPS

HOT AND FRESH SPINACH DIP

Serves: 8 | **Cook Time:** 2½ to 3½ hours on LOW
Slow Cooker Size: 3- to 4-quart (2.8- to 3.8-L)

Warm and gooey, this spinach dip uses all fresh ingredients, and it is perfect served with slices of crusty Italian bread or hearty pita chips. You're going to want to really pack the fresh spinach in your 3- to 4-quart (2.8- to 3.8-L) slow cooker. But don't worry, the spinach cooks down quite a bit!

8 ounces (225 g) fresh baby spinach, chopped

8 ounces (225 g) shredded mozzarella cheese

1 cup (100 g) grated Parmesan cheese

8 ounces (225 g) cream cheese, cubed

½ whole yellow onion, chopped

1 tablespoon (10 g) minced garlic

¼ teaspoon cayenne pepper

½ teaspoon sea salt

½ teaspoon ground black pepper

1. Combine all the ingredients in a large bowl and toss to combine. The mixture is going to be dry because of all the fresh spinach, almost like a salad.
2. Put the spinach mixture in the slow cooker. You may need to push it down to get it all to fit, and that's okay.
3. Cover the slow cooker. Cook on LOW for 1½ hours.
4. Open the lid and give everything a stir.
5. Cover again and cook for an additional 1 to 2 hours, till everything is creamy and the spinach has cooked down.

SPICY JALAPEÑO POPPER DIP

Serves: 12 | **Cook Time:** 1 hour on LOW
Slow Cooker Size: 3-quart (2.8-L)

This recipe is perfect for eating while watching the big game on TV. Katie likes to toss everything in the slow cooker right as the game is starting, and in about 1 hour the dip is hot and ready to serve with tortilla chips.

16 ounces (455 g) cream cheese, softened and cubed

1 cup (225 g) mayonnaise

4 ounces (115 g) canned green chilies, drained and chopped

4 ounces (115 g) canned jalapeño chilies, drained and chopped

½ cup (60 g) shredded Mexican four-cheese blend

½ cup (60 g) shredded mozzarella cheese

1 cup (50 g) panko bread crumbs

¼ cup (25 g) grated Parmesan cheese

FOR SERVING:

Chips, bread slices, or cut-up veggies

1. Add the cream cheese, mayonnaise, green chilies, jalapeño chilies, Mexican cheese, and mozzarella cheese to the slow cooker.
2. Cover the slow cooker. Cook on LOW for 1 hour, stirring once at the ½-hour mark and again at the end of the 1 hour.
3. While the dip is cooking, mix together the panko bread crumbs and Parmesan cheese in a small bowl to make the topping.
4. Sprinkle the topping over the dip after it is cooked. Serve the dip with your favorite chips, bread slices, or cut-up veggies.

WARM BROCCOLI AND CHEESE DIP

Serves: 20 | **Cook Time:** 3 hours on LOW | **Slow Cooker Size:** 5-quart (4.7-L)

The combination of cheese and broccoli is always a big hit in Sarah's house. It happens to be her son's favorite food combination. She hadn't made a dip with broccoli before and, as expected, he loved it. While the rest of the family ate it as a dip, he spooned into it like it was a soup. Needless to say, it was a big hit!

3 cups (213 g) fresh broccoli florets

2 cups (460 g) sour cream

1 can (10.75 oz, or 305 g)
condensed Cheddar cheese soup

8 ounces (225 g) shredded
Cheddar cheese

8 ounces (225 g) cream
cheese, softened

1 medium onion, shredded
or finely chopped

1 tablespoon (15 ml) olive oil

1 tablespoon (16 g)
Worcestershire sauce

1 teaspoon garlic powder

½ teaspoon dried basil
(or 1 teaspoon basil paste
or 1 teaspoon fresh finely
minced basil)

FOR SERVING:

Pita chips, tortilla chips, sliced
crusty bread, or cut-up vegetables

1. Steam the broccoli, until slightly tender but still crisp.
2. Place all the ingredients in the slow cooker and mix well to combine.
3. Cover the slow cooker. Cook on LOW for 3 hours, stirring every 30 minutes to make sure the dip does not burn.
4. The dip is done when all the cheese is melted and gooey.
5. Set the slow cooker to the WARM setting before serving the dip with your favorite chips, slices of bread, or cut-up vegetables.

NOTES: *Because Sarah's children do not like chopped onions, she shredded them using a cheese grater instead. The onion cooks very quickly and removes the harsh onion flavor they don't like, and they can't detect that she's included them.*

MEXICAN MARGARITA CHICKEN DIP

Serves: 12 | **Cook Time:** 2 hours on LOW
Slow Cooker Size: 5-quart (4.7-L)

Tequila and fresh lime bring a ton of flavor and zip to this delicious and easy recipe. A rotisserie chicken from the deli department at your local grocery store makes it easy to have cooked chicken ready to go in this amazing dip. Serve with your favorite tortilla or pita chips!

12 ounces (340 g) cream cheese, softened and cubed

2 cups (280 g) cooked chicken

2 cups (230 g) shredded Monterey Jack cheese

¼ cup (60 ml) freshly squeezed lime juice

¼ cup (60 ml) tequila (optional)

2 tablespoons (30 ml) orange juice

1 tablespoon (6 g) lime zest

1 tablespoon (18 g) salt

1 teaspoon ground cumin

2 cloves garlic, minced

1. Add all the ingredients to the slow cooker and stir to combine.
2. Cover the slow cooker. Cook on LOW for 2 hours, stirring occasionally.
3. Set the slow cooker to the WARM setting before serving.

MEXICAN BLACK BEAN AND CORN DIP

Serves: 10 | **Cook Time:** 2 to 3 hours on HIGH
Slow Cooker Size: 5-quart (4.7-L)

This Mexican-inspired dip is filled with black beans, corn, and great flavors. Serve it with some nice sturdy tortilla chips.

14.5 ounces (411 g) canned black beans, drained and rinsed

14.5 ounces (411 g) canned yellow corn (or 4–5 ears of fresh corn removed from the cob)

10 ounces (280 g) canned diced tomatoes with green chilies, drained

8 ounces (225 g) cream cheese, softened and cubed

1 teaspoon chili powder

½ teaspoon garlic salt

½ teaspoon ground cumin

⅛ teaspoon ground cayenne pepper

1 cup (115 g) shredded Mexican four-cheese blend

1. Add the black beans, corn, tomatoes with green chilies, cream cheese, and spices to the slow cooker.
2. Stir to combine.
3. Cover the slow cooker. Cook on HIGH for 2 to 3 hours, stirring occasionally.
4. About 30 minutes before the dip is done cooking, add in the Mexican cheese. Stir the dip. Allow the cheese to melt before serving.

CHEESY MEXICAN BLACK BEAN TACO DIP

Serves: 8 | **Cook Time:** 2 hours on HIGH | **Slow Cooker Size:** 5-quart (4.7-L)

This is a nice spicy and cheesy black bean dip that is great for serving with chips, and this recipe is full of Mexican flavors. You can use a packet of low-sodium taco seasoning mix or try our homemade taco seasoning mix (page 317).

1 tablespoon (15 ml) vegetable or olive oil

1 medium onion, diced

1 package (28 g) low-sodium taco seasoning, store-bought or homemade (page 317)

14.5 ounces (411 g) canned diced tomatoes (or 2 cups fresh diced tomatoes with the juices)

2 tablespoons (2 g) chopped fresh cilantro

15 ounces (425 g) canned black beans, drained and rinsed

2–3 whole jalapeño peppers, seeds and membrane removed, diced (or a 4-ounce [115 g] can of jalapeños)

1 cup (115 g) shredded Cheddar cheese

1 cup (115 g) shredded mozzarella cheese

1 cup (115 g) shredded Mexican four-cheese blend

FOR SERVING:

Tortilla chips

1. In a medium skillet set over medium heat, add the oil. Heat until hot but not smoking. Add the onions and sauté until the onion is translucent and starting to turn brown.
2. Transfer the cooked onions to the slow cooker and add the remaining ingredients. Stir well to combine.
3. Cover the slow cooker. Cook on HIGH for 2 hours. Stir once more before serving.
4. Set the slow cooker to the WARM setting for serving and serve with tortilla chips.

EVERYTHING YOU LOVE ABOUT PIZZA DIP

Serves: 8 | **Cook Time:** 1 to 2 hours on HIGH | **Slow Cooker Size:** 3-quart (2.8-L)

This warm and gooey dip has all the flavors of pizza in a delicious dip. Use your favorite pizza toppings to make the dip your own. Heidi likes pepperoni, bell peppers, and Italian sausage. If you like pineapple, onions, olives, or whatever on your pizza, go ahead and add them in! For dipping, slice up some nice, crusty Italian bread and dig on in.

½ pound (225 g) Italian sausage

1 medium bell pepper, seeded and diced

16 ounces (455 g) mozzarella cheese, shredded

¾ cup (75 g) grated Parmesan cheese

8 ounces (225 g) cream cheese, softened

1 teaspoon Italian seasoning, store-bought or homemade (page 319)

8 ounces (225 g) jarred pizza sauce, store-bought or homemade (page 314)

¼ cup (35 g) sliced pepperoni, each slice cut in half or quarters (or use mini pepperoni slices)

1. Heat up a medium-size skillet on the stove top set on medium-high heat.
2. Add the Italian sausage and bell pepper to the skillet, and cook and crumble the sausage until no longer pink. Drain off the excess fat from the sausage and add the cooked sausage and peppers to the slow cooker.
3. Add the remaining ingredients to the slow cooker and stir to mix everything together.
4. Cover the slow cooker. Cook on HIGH for 1 to 2 hours, or until everything is hot and bubbly.

NOTES: *If you don't use Italian sausage and peppers in this dip, you can omit the stove top cooking part of the recipe. But if you want to use raw peppers or onions or any other raw meat, you will need to cook it ahead of time.*

BUBBLY ITALIAN LASAGNA DIP

Serves: 8 | **Cook Time:** 3 to 4 hours on LOW | **Slow Cooker Size:** 3-quart (2.8-L)

Whenever Heidi makes lasagna, she always serves it with plain Italian bread or garlic bread. And her favorite part of eating lasagna is spooning a little of the lasagna onto her slice of bread and taking a big bite. This dip re-creates that moment of bliss because all the flavors of lasagna are there in this warm and gooey dip: zesty tomato sauce, creamy ricotta cheese, stringy mozzarella cheese, and all the other classic Italian spices like basil, oregano, and garlic. Set out a basket of sliced, crusty Italian bread, and your guests will go crazy over this warm dip!

½ pound (225 g) Italian sausage

¼ cup (25 g) chopped yellow onion

4 tablespoons minced garlic

15 ounces (425 g) canned crushed tomatoes

1 tablespoon (5 g) dried basil

1 tablespoon (3 g) dried oregano

1 teaspoon salt

1½ cups (375 g) ricotta cheese

½ cup (50 g) grated Parmesan cheese

1 cup (115 g) shredded mozzarella cheese

1. Heat up a medium-size skillet on the stove top set on medium-high heat.
2. Add the Italian sausage, onion, and garlic to the skillet, and cook and crumble the sausage until it is no longer pink.
3. Drain off excess fat from sausage and add the cooked sausage to the slow cooker.
4. Add the crushed tomatoes, basil, oregano, and salt to the slow cooker and stir to combine.
5. In a medium mixing bowl, stir together the ricotta cheese and Parmesan cheese.
6. Spoon the ricotta cheese mixture over the sauce mixture in the slow cooker.
7. Sprinkle the mozzarella cheese over the top of everything in the slow cooker.
8. Cover the slow cooker. Cook on LOW for 3 to 4 hours, or until everything is hot and bubbly.

SWEET-AND-SPICY HONEY BUFFALO MEATBALLS

Serves: 8 | **Cook Time:** 4 to 6 hours on LOW or 2 to 4 hours on HIGH
Slow Cooker Size: 4-quart (3.8-L)

Even though hot sauce is listed as a main ingredient in this recipe, these meatballs are not actually very spicy. Instead, what you get is a meaty turkey meatball with a lovely sweetness followed by just the right amount of spicy heat.

24 ounces (680 g) frozen turkey meatballs

¼ cup (60 g) light or dark brown sugar

¼ cup (60 ml) bottled hot sauce

¼ cup (85 g) honey

¼ cup (80 g) apricot preserves

2 tablespoons (30 ml) low-sodium soy sauce

1½ tablespoons (23 g) cornstarch

1. Add the frozen meatballs to the slow cooker.
2. In a small mixing bowl, mix together the remaining ingredients until combined to create the sauce.
3. Pour the sauce mixture over the meatballs and stir to coat.
4. Cover the slow cooker. Cook on LOW for 4 to 6 hours or on HIGH for 2 to 4 hours.
5. Set the slow cooker to the WARM setting to keep the meatballs warm while serving.

ASIAN KUNG PAO MEATBALLS

Serves: 8 | **Cook Time:** 4 to 6 hours on LOW or 2 to 4 hours on HIGH | **Slow Cooker Size:** 5-quart (4.7-L)

These can be served either as an appetizer or as a main dish. To serve as a main dish, cook up some white or brown rice and steam or stir-fry a bag of frozen stir-fry vegetables. Mix the cooked vegetables into the meatballs right before serving, and then spoon the meatballs and vegetables over the rice.

24 ounces (680 g) frozen meatballs (can use chicken, turkey, beef, or pork meatballs)

½ cup (125 g) hoisin sauce

¼ cup (60 ml) unseasoned rice vinegar

¼ cup (85 g) honey

¼ cup (60 ml) low-sodium soy sauce

3 cloves garlic, minced

2 tablespoons (18 g) cornstarch

¼ to 1 teaspoon crushed red pepper flakes, to taste

1 cup (100 g) sliced green onions (for garnish)

1. Place the frozen meatballs in the bottom of the slow cooker.

2. In a small mixing bowl, mix together the hoisin sauce, rice vinegar, honey, soy sauce, garlic, and cornstarch. Pour the sauce mixture over the meatballs and stir to coat the meatballs.

3. Cover the slow cooker. Cook on LOW for 4 to 6 hours or on HIGH for 2 to 4 hours, until the meatballs are hot and the sauce has thickened a little bit and coats the meatballs nicely.

4. Toss the green onions with the meatballs or sprinkle them over right before serving.

HAWAIIAN PINEAPPLE MEATBALLS

Serves: 8 | **Cook Time:** 4 to 6 hours on LOW or 3 to 4 hours on HIGH | **Slow Cooker Size:** 4-quart (3.8-L)

With just five ingredients these sweet pineapple meatballs are a big hit with everyone who samples them. This is another meatball recipe that is easily transformed from an appetizer for parties to a main dish to serve your family. This one is a big hit with the kids just spooned over some steamed rice.

32 ounces (905 g) frozen meatballs (can use chicken, turkey, beef, or pork meatballs)

3 whole bell peppers (1 red, 1 yellow, and 1 orange), chopped

18 ounces (510 g) pineapple preserves

8 ounces (225 g) hoisin sauce

2 cloves garlic, minced

1. Place the frozen meatballs and bell peppers in the bottom of the slow cooker.

2. In a small bowl, mix together the pineapple preserves, hoisin sauce, and minced garlic until combined to create the sauce.

3. Pour the sauce over the meatballs and peppers in the slow cooker. Stir to coat.

4. Cover the slow cooker. Cook on LOW for 4 to 6 hours or on HIGH for 3 to 4 hours, until the meatballs are warmed through and the bell peppers are tender.

FRESH PORK SAUSAGE MEATBALLS

Serves: 6 | **Cook Time:** 3 to 4 hours on LOW or 1 to 2 hours on HIGH plus 30 to 45 minutes on LOW
Slow Cooker Size: 6-quart (5.7-L)

This is a fun appetizer for a party, or just enjoy it for dinner. If you are having a large gathering, you may want to make more than one batch or use two crocks at once. Sarah used her largest 6½- and 6-quart (6.2- and 5.7-L) crocks, as you need the space when they are cooking. You can use a hot or mild sausage. One trick Sarah always does with meatballs or meatloaf is line the metal mixing bowl with press-and-seal plastic wrap. When she's done mixing, she pulls the wrap off and it's much easier to clean.

1 pound (455 g) pork sausage (mild or spicy)

4 ounces (115 g) cream cheese

½ cup (58 g) shredded sharp Cheddar cheese

16 ounces (455 g) bottled barbecue or buffalo sauce

Nonstick cooking spray

1. Spray the slow cooker with nonstick cooking spray to prevent sticking.
2. In a large mixing bowl, mix together the sausage, cream cheese, and Cheddar cheese with your hands.
3. Form the meat mixture into approximately 12 meatballs and place the meatballs in the slow cooker.
4. Cover the slow cooker. Cook on LOW for 3 to 4 hours or on HIGH for 1 to 2 hours, turning the meatballs several times while they are cooking.
5. When the meatballs are cooked through, remove them carefully from the slow cooker and place on a baking sheet covered in paper towels. Pat with a paper towel to remove excess cooking fat.
6. Drain the cooking liquid from the meatballs from the slow cooker and discard. Wash and dry your slow cooker before proceeding.
7. Place the sausage meatballs back in the slow cooker and pour barbecue sauce over the meatballs. Stir to coat.
8. Cover the slow cooker. Continue to cook on LOW for 30 to 45 minutes, until the sauce is warm and bubbly.
9. Set the slow cooker to the WARM setting to keep the meatballs warm while serving.

FREEZER MEAL INSTRUCTIONS: *Follow steps 1 and 2 above. Place the meatballs in a gallon-size zippered freezer bag and squish out as much air as possible before zipping closed. Label your bag with the name of the dish and cooking instructions.*

TO COOK THE FREEZER MEAL: *Place the frozen meal in the refrigerator to thaw. Cook the recipe per the directions beginning at step 3.*

ITALIAN PARMESAN-BASIL-GARLIC CHICKEN WINGS

Serves: 6 | **Cook Time:** 1 to 2 hours on HIGH | **Slow Cooker Size:** 5-quart (4.7-L)

Wings are a common appetizer that can be made in the crock-pot, but this recipe is unique because these do not use a hot, buffalo-, or barbecue-type sauce. This is a great recipe for when you need an appetizer, but it can also be used for the main dish for your family meal as well. Sarah's family likes that the wings are extremely flavorful but not overly spicy.

The first few steps take very little time, then you'll need to stir the dish every 45 minutes or so to make sure the wings are well coated, cooked through, and do not burn. The last step takes about 10 minutes all together as we crisp the skin under the broiler and coat the wings in some grated Parmesan cheese.

The hardest part is likely finding the correct sauce. The bottle of Parmesan garlic wing sauce looks like a yellow ranch sauce. Sarah went to the local grocery store and found it next to the normal spicy hot wing sauce. If you cannot find this particular kind of wing sauce at your local grocery store, use Parmesan ranch salad dressing and garlic butter instead of regular butter (or a teaspoon or two of garlic powder).

3 pounds (1.4 kg) chicken wings

2 cups (475 ml) Parmesan garlic wing sauce

1 cup (225 g) salted butter

2 teaspoons (10 g) basil paste (or fresh minced basil or 1 teaspoon dried basil)

1 cup shredded Parmesan cheese

2 teaspoons (5 g) ground paprika

Salt and pepper, to taste

1. Place the chicken wings, wing sauce, butter, and basil in the slow cooker.
2. Cover the slow cooker. Cook on HIGH for 1 to 2 hours, stirring the wings every 30 minutes so that the wings cook evenly and do not burn.
3. Use a meat thermometer to check the wings. Make sure they have reached an internal temperature of 165°F (74°C).
4. Cover a large rimmed baking sheet with aluminum foil. Turn your oven on to the broil setting and allow it to reach temperature.
5. Carefully remove each chicken wing with tongs and spread the wings on the prepared cookie sheet.
6. Sprinkle with salt and pepper.
7. Broil for 3 minutes under the broiler, flip the cookie sheet around, and cook an additional 2 to 3 minutes until the wings are crispy and browned.
8. While the wings are broiling, mix together the Parmesan cheese and paprika in a large shallow bowl or container.
9. Remove the wings from the oven. Use tongs to place each wing carefully in the bowl and coat with the cheese mixture. Repeat with each wing.
10. Place the cheese-coated wings back on the cookie sheet and return them to the broiler. Broil for an additional 2 to 3 minutes, until the cheese is melted and bubbly.

HOLIDAY ORANGE-CRANBERRY TURKEY MEATBALLS

Serves: 12 | **Cook Time:** 4 to 6 hours on LOW or 2 to 3 hours on HIGH
Slow Cooker Size: 5-quart (4.7-L)

This simple appetizer recipe is perfect for serving to your guests during the winter holiday season. It has all the great flavors that you crave during the holidays. Bright cranberries and zesty orange are the perfect combination with savory turkey meatballs. To bring the sugar content down a little bit, look for a low-sugar orange marmalade fruit spread.

32 ounces (905 g) frozen turkey meatballs

14 ounces (397 g) whole-berry cranberry sauce

17.25 ounces (489 g) orange marmalade (look for low-sugar if possible)

12 ounces (355 ml) chili sauce

1 large navel orange (zested and juiced)

1. Place the frozen turkey meatballs in the slow cooker.
2. Mix together the remaining ingredients in a small bowl to create the sauce and pour over meatballs.
3. Stir to coat.
4. Cover the slow cooker. Cook on LOW for 4 to 6 hours or on HIGH for 2 to 3 hours, stirring the meatballs halfway through the cooking time.
5. Turn the slow cooker to the WARM setting to serve.

WARM MAPLE BACON-WRAPPED LITTLE SMOKIES

Serves: 8 | **Cook Time:** 2 to 3 hours on LOW
Slow Cooker Size: 6½-quart (6.2-L) or larger

Sarah served this dish to dinner guests, and they were ecstatic as it had been years since they had eaten Little Smokies. They were amazed by how good they could taste! Bacon and real maple syrup with the brown sugar give these meaty bites a touch of sweetness. If you are serving a large group, you can easily do two crocks at once with double the smokies. A 6½-quart (6.2-L) slow cooker works well, as you want to try and get these in one flat layer. A casserole slow cooker would work great, too!

16 ounces (455 g) bacon (not thick-cut)

14 ounces (397 g) Little Smokies sausage links

⅓ cup (107 g) real maple syrup

1 cup (150 g) brown sugar

1. Spray the slow cooker with nonstick cooking spray or lightly coat with butter.
2. Cut each slice of bacon into thirds.
3. Individually wrap each Little Smokie with a piece of the cut bacon and secure with a toothpick to hold the bacon in place while it cooks.
4. Lay the bacon-wrapped Little Smokies in a single layer, packing them in as necessary.
5. Pour the maple syrup over the Little Smokies.
6. Sprinkle the brown sugar over the Little Smokies.
7. Cover the slow cooker. Cook on LOW for 2 to 3 hours, until the bacon is cooked through.
8. Set the slow cooker to the WARM setting if you wish to keep these appetizers warm while serving.

EASY SAUCY LITTLE SMOKIES

Serves: 10 | **Cook Time:** 3 to 4 hours on LOW
Slow Cooker Size: 3-quart (2.8-L)

With just five ingredients, these easy-to-make Little Smokies are a great appetizer to serve your guests at your next party. The sauce is both sweet and tangy, and it really sets off the flavor of the smoky little cocktail sausages!

28 ounces (794 g) Little Smokies sausage links

¾ cup (180 g) ketchup

⅔ cup (152 g) barbecue sauce

⅔ cup (150 g) brown sugar

1½ teaspoons Worcestershire sauce

1. Add all the ingredients to the slow cooker and stir to coat all the Little Smokies in the sauce mixture.
2. Cover the slow cooker. Cook on LOW for 3 to 4 hours, or until the sausages are hot and the sauce is bubbly.
3. Set the slow cooker to the WARM setting to keep them warm for serving.
4. Set out fun and colorful toothpicks to allow your guests to pluck sausage links straight from the slow cooker.

SWEET-AND-SOUR PINE-APPLE LITTLE SMOKIES

Serves: 24 | **Cook Time:** 2 to 3 hours on HIGH
Slow Cooker Size: 5-quart (4.7-L)

Everyone loves these sweet-and-sour Little Smokies. Brown sugar brings the sweet while pineapple and vinegar bring the sour to this fun appetizer.

2 pounds (about 1 kg) Little Smokies sausage links

20 ounces (567 g) canned pineapple chucks, undrained

1 cup (225 g) brown sugar, packed

½ cup (120 ml) vinegar

3 tablespoons (24 g) all-purpose flour

2 teaspoons (6 g) dried mustard

1½ teaspoons soy sauce

1. Add the Little Smokies to the slow cooker.
2. In a bowl, combine the pineapple with the juice, brown sugar, vinegar, flour, mustard, and soy sauce. Stir to create the sauce mixture.
3. Pour the sauce over the Little Smokies in the slow cooker.
4. Cover the slow cooker. Cook on HIGH for 2 to 3 hours, or until the sausages are hot and the sauce is nice and bubbly and has thickened.
5. Set the slow cooker to the WARM setting to keep the sausages warm while serving.

NOTES: *If you prefer this without the pineapple chunks, substitute 1¼ cups (295 ml) pineapple juice for the 20-ounce (567-g) can of pineapple chunks.*

CLASSIC PARTY SNACK MIX

Serves: 15 | **Cook Time:** 1½ hours on HIGH plus 20 to 30 minutes on LOW
Slow Cooker Size: 5-quart (4.7-L) or larger

Everyone loves to dig into this classic party snack mix. It's pretty much the traditional recipe only cooked in the slow cooker. Of course, you can adapt and adjust the recipe to suit your needs, too. If you are gluten intolerant, use gluten-free cereals. Can't have nuts? Omit them. Want to add some dried fruit like cranberries or raisins? Go for it. Feel free to add candy-coated chocolates or chocolate chips after the mix is done cooling. They bring some sweetness to complement the salty!

3 cups (90 g) rice Chex cereal

3 cups (90 g) corn Chex cereal

3 cups (90 g) chocolate Chex cereal

3 cups (80 g) Kix cereal

3 cups (120 g) pretzels

1 cup (236 ml) vegetable oil

14 ounces (397 g) lightly salted and roasted cashews

2 tablespoons (32 g) Worcestershire sauce

1½ teaspoons seasoned salt

¾ teaspoon garlic powder

1. Optional: Line the slow cooker with a slow cooker liner to make clean-up easier.
2. Pour the dry cereals, nuts, and pretzels into the slow cooker.
3. In a small bowl, mix together the remaining ingredients and pour over everything in the slow cooker. Stir to coat each piece.
4. Cook uncovered for 1½ hours on HIGH, stirring the mixture every 15 minutes to keep the bottom from burning.
5. After 1½ hours, turn the slow cooker to LOW. Continue to cook for an additional 20 to 30 minutes, stirring the mixture every 5 to 10 minutes until it is no longer soggy and is crispy.
6. When it is done cooking, carefully pour the contents of the slow cooker onto a parchment paper–lined rimmed cookie sheet.
7. Allow to cool completely before serving.
8. Party mix can be saved in an airtight plastic bag or container for up to 1 week.

SAVORY RANCH PARMESAN PARTY MIX

Serves: 24 | **Cook Time:** 2 to 3 hours on HIGH | **Slow Cooker Size:** 6-quart (5.7-L) or larger

Everyone loves a good party mix. This mix is perfect for something to nibble on while mingling or to snack away on while watching the big game on TV. This recipe combines the classic ingredients of a good party mix with the flavors of ranch dressing mix (either store-bought or homemade) and freshly grated Parmesan cheese. Beware . . . this stuff is addictive!

1 cup (225 g) unsalted butter, sliced

2 tablespoons (32 g) Worcestershire sauce

4 cups (120 g) rice Chex cereal

4 cups (120 g) corn Chex cereal

4 cups (160 g) pretzel sticks

16 ounces (455 g) lightly salted mixed nuts

½ cup (50 g) freshly grated Parmesan cheese

2 ounces (55 g) ranch dressing mix, store-bought or homemade (page 318)

1. Melt the butter in a small saucepan on the stove over medium heat. Turn off the heat, add the Worcestershire sauce, and stir to combine.

2. Dump the cereals, pretzel sticks, and nuts in the slow cooker and gently mix together.

3. Pour half of the butter mixture over the cereal mixture.

4. Sprinkle half of the Parmesan cheese over the cereal mixture.

5. Carefully stir the cereal mixture together to coat with the butter mixture and Parmesan cheese, being as careful as possible not to break up the cereal and pretzel pieces.

6. Repeat with the remaining butter mixture and Parmesan cheese.

7. Cook uncovered for 2 to 3 hours on HIGH, stirring the mixture every half hour or so until the party mix is glazed and no longer soggy from the butter.

8. Line a rimmed baking sheet with parchment paper. Pour the party mix out on the prepared baking sheet.

9. Sprinkle the dry ranch dressing mix powder over everything while it is still warm. Stir and toss to lightly coat each piece with a little of the ranch dressing mix.

10. Allow to cool completely before storing in an airtight container for up to 1 week.

NOTES: *If you are allergic to nuts, omit the nuts and increase either the cereal or pretzels by 1 cup.*

2

SOUPS, BROTHS, CHILIS, AND STEWS

HEARTY POTATO AND KIELBASA SAUSAGE CHOWDER

Serves: 8 | **Cook Time:** 8 to 10 hours on LOW or 5 to 6 hours on HIGH | **Slow Cooker Size:** 6-quart (5.7 L)

This lovely chowder recipe is packed with tons of flavor. Kielbasa sausage and tender potato chunks are simmered away in a cheesy broth that is not too thick. We like to serve this soup with fresh pretzel dinner rolls from our local bakery. They are perfect for sopping up the soup!

1 medium yellow onion, chopped

1 clove garlic, minced

32 ounces (946 ml) chicken broth, store-bought or homemade (page 310)

6 medium Yukon gold potatoes, peeled and diced

2 cups (328 g) frozen corn kernels

16 ounces (455 g) kielbasa sausage, sliced into ¼-inch (6-mm) slices

1 whole bay leaf

½ teaspoon dried thyme

½ teaspoon freshly ground black pepper

8 ounces (225 g) sharp Cheddar cheese, shredded

1 cup (235 ml) heavy whipping cream

1. Add all the ingredients except the Cheddar cheese and cream to the slow cooker.

2. Stir to combine.

3. Cover the slow cooker. Cook on LOW for 8 to 10 hours or on HIGH for 5 to 6 hours, or until the potatoes are fork-tender.

4. Remove the lid, and remove and discard the bay leaf.

5. Add the Cheddar cheese and cream to the soup, and stir to combine and let the cheese melt.

6. Ladle the soup in bowls and serve.

CREAMY CHICKEN POTPIE SOUP

Serves: 6 | **Cook Time:** 6 to 7 hours on LOW | **Slow Cooker Size:** 6-quart (5.7-L)

This creamy soup has all the flavors of your favorite chicken potpie but in soup form. Serve with slices of nice crusty bread for dipping. If you are feeling fancy, you can take a store-bought pie crust and cut cute little shapes and bake them up as dippers. This recipe uses cooked chicken, a great way to use up leftover chicken or a store-bought rotisserie chicken.

1–1½ pounds (455–680 g) cooked chicken, diced or shredded

2 cups (260 g) chopped carrots

1 cup (130 g) frozen peas

1 small onion, diced

¼ cup (55 g) unsalted butter

⅛ teaspoon salt

⅛ teaspoon freshly ground black pepper

¼ teaspoon garlic powder

¼ teaspoon dried thyme

2 low-sodium chicken bouillon cubes

4 cups (940 ml) milk

1 cup (235 ml) low-sodium chicken broth, store-bought or homemade (page 310)

½–¾ cup (64–94 g) all-purpose flour

1. Add all the ingredients except the flour to the slow cooker.
2. Cover the slow cooker. Cook on LOW for 5 to 6 hours, or until the chicken is cooked through and the carrots are tender.
3. Open the lid of the slow cooker and slowly whisk the flour into the soup to prevent lumps. Add more or less flour depending on how thick you want the final soup to be.
4. Cover the slow cooker. Cook for 1 more hour on LOW to allow the soup to thicken.

NOTES: *To make this soup gluten-free, use a gluten-free all-purpose flour mix to thicken the soup. Make sure to use a brand of bouillon cubes that is gluten-free as well.*

VEGGIE-LOADED LENTIL SOUP

Serves: 6 to 8 | **Cook Time:** 6¼ to 7¼ hours on LOW | **Slow Cooker Size:** 5-quart (4.7-L)

This vegetarian soup really hits the spot on a cold evening. Brown lentils are cooked in a veggie-loaded broth for a warm and satisfying soup that leaves you not missing the meat at all.

8 cups (1.9 L) vegetable stock

14.5 ounces (411 g) canned fire-roasted diced tomatoes

2 large white potatoes, peeled and diced

2 large carrots, peeled and diced

2 stalks celery, diced

1 large white onion, diced

16 ounces (455 g) brown lentils

½ teaspoon salt

½ teaspoon freshly ground black pepper

2 cups (110 g) fresh kale, washed, stems removed and chopped

1. Add all the ingredients except for the kale to the slow cooker.
2. Cover the slow cooker. Cook on LOW for 6 to 7 hours, or until the potatoes and carrots are cooked through.
3. Open the lid and stir the kale into the soup.
4. Cover the slow cooker and cook for an additional 15 minutes to allow the kale to slightly wilt and cook into the soup.

CHUNKY CHICKEN AND KIELBASA SAUSAGE STEW

Serves: 6 | **Cook Time:** 6 to 8 hours on LOW or 3 to 4 hours on HIGH
Slow Cooker Size: 6-quart (5.7-L) or larger

This healthy recipe really hits the spot on a cold winter day. It is the perfect recipe to use up leftover cooked chicken or turkey, and it is full of your favorite root vegetables. You can use any combination of root vegetables you want or just stick to one depending on what you have on hand.

1 medium yellow onion, chopped

1 medium carrot, sliced

1 stalk celery, sliced

2 cloves garlic, minced

29 ounces (858 ml) low-sodium chicken broth, store-bought or homemade (page 310)

2 cups (weight will vary) cubed root vegetables (such as butternut squash, parsnips, potatoes, or sweet potatoes)

14.5 ounces (411 g) canned diced tomatoes, undrained

8 ounces (225 g) canned tomato sauce

1 tablespoon (3 g) dried Italian seasoning, store-bought or homemade (page 316)

½ teaspoon freshly ground black pepper

8–10 ounces (225–280 g) cooked chicken, cut into bite-size pieces (from a deli rotisserie chicken, refrigerated cooked chicken strips, or leftover cooked chicken)

8 ounces (225 g) turkey kielbasa sausage, sliced

FOR SERVING:

Crusty bread

1. Prepare all the ingredients and add them to the slow cooker.
2. Cover the slow cooker. Cook on LOW for 6 to 8 hours or on HIGH for 3 to 4 hours, or until the root vegetables are tender.
3. Ladle hot soup into bowls and serve with crusty bread.

CREAMY NEW ENGLAND CLAM CHOWDER

Serves: 6 to 8 | **Cook Time:** 3½ to 4½ hours on HIGH | **Slow Cooker Size:** 6-quart (5.7-L)

A creamy New England clam chowder recipe that will rival just about any clam chowder you will find in some of the best restaurants on the East Coast. This creamy chowder is a thick broth (but not too thick) that is flavored with bacon and special seasonings and loaded with tender chunks of potatoes and clams. Serve with traditional oyster crackers for a hearty dinner or lunch.

6 slices thick-cut bacon, chopped

1 medium yellow onion, chopped

5 medium potatoes, peeled and diced into ½-inch (1-cm) cubes

12 ounces (340 g) canned whole baby clams

8 ounces (235 ml) bottled clam juice

1 clove garlic, minced

2 bay leaves

1½ teaspoons freshly ground black pepper

½ teaspoon bay seasoning

¼ teaspoon dried thyme, crushed

¼ teaspoon crushed red pepper flakes

¼ cup (32 g) all-purpose flour

3½ cups (835 ml) half-and-half

FOR SERVING (OPTIONAL):

Oyster crackers

1. In a large skillet on the stove top set on medium heat, add the bacon. Slowly cook the bacon until crispy. Remove the cooked bacon with a slotted spoon. Set aside on a plate lined with paper towels to drain.

2. Pour off the bacon fat from the skillet except for about 2 tablespoons (30 ml) and add the onion to the skillet. Cooked the onion over medium-high heat until the onion becomes translucent and starts to just turn brown.

3. Add the cooked bacon, onion, potatoes, clams, clam juice, garlic, bay leaves, black pepper, bay seasoning, thyme, and red pepper flakes to the slow cooker. Stir to combine.

4. Cover the slow cooker. Cook on HIGH for 3 to 4 hours, until the potatoes are tender.

5. During the last half hour of cooking, whisk together the flour and half-and-half in a bowl until there are no lumps. Slowly stir this mixture into your soup.

6. Cover and continue cooking for the additional 30 minutes of the cooking time.

7. Ladle hot soup into bowls and serve with oyster crackers (if desired).

MEATY NO-BEAN CHILI

Serves: 16 | **Cook Time:** 8 to 10 hours on LOW or 4 to 5 hours on HIGH | **Slow Cooker Size:** 6-quart (5.7-L)

If you don't like beans in your chili, this is the recipe for you. The dish is warm and hearty and full of great flavors from warm spices such as cumin, oregano, red pepper flakes, and the secret ingredient—cocoa powder! Yellow and red onion adds great flavor, and you can add additional spice if you like it spicy by adding in some peppers.

3 pounds (1.4 kg) ground beef

1 large red onion, chopped

1 large yellow onion, chopped

3 cloves garlic, minced

1 cup sliced celery

2 tablespoons (18 g) cornmeal

1 tablespoon (7 g) ground cumin

1 tablespoon (4 g) crushed red pepper flakes

1 tablespoon (5 g) unsweetened cocoa powder

2 teaspoons (5 g) chili powder

1 teaspoon kosher salt

1 teaspoon freshly ground black pepper

1 teaspoon dried oregano

28 ounces (794 g) canned diced tomatoes

14 ounces (397 g) canned tomato sauce

6 ounces (170 g) canned tomato paste

3 cups (705 ml) beef broth, store-bought or homemade (page 311)

1. In a medium skillet on the stove top, crumble and brown the ground beef with the red and yellow onions. Drain off the excess fat from the skillet and add the cooked beef and onions to the slow cooker.

2. Add the remaining ingredients to the slow cooker and mix well to combine.

3. Cover the slow cooker. Cook on LOW for 8 to 10 hours or on HIGH for 4 to 5 hours.

NOTES: *Top bowls of chili with your favorite chili toppings such as cheese, sour cream, tortilla chips, or diced avocado.*

ALL-AMERICAN BISON CHILI

Serves: 16 | **Cook Time:** 10 to 12 hours on LOW or 5 to 6 hours on HIGH | **Slow Cooker Size:** 6-quart (5.7-L)

Here in Wyoming, bison meat is very popular as a healthy alternative to traditional beef. Bison has less fat and more nutrients than regular beef, and we are lucky enough to be able to get locally raised, grass-fed bison meat right in our grocery store. This chili recipe is out-of-this-world full of flavor. There is just the right amount of kick and spice to make your taste buds say "hello!" without it being so spicy that it burns your mouth!

2 pounds (about 1 kg) ground bison (can also use ground beef if you cannot find bison meat)

1 large yellow onion, chopped

5 cloves garlic, minced

1 large poblano pepper, seeded and chopped

1 large red bell pepper, seeded and chopped

1 large orange bell pepper, seeded and chopped

1 large yellow bell pepper, seeded and chopped

15.5 ounces (439 g) white hominy, drained

15.5 ounces (439 g) canned red kidney beans, undrained

15 ounces (425 g) canned black beans, undrained

14.5 ounces (411 g) canned fire-roasted tomatoes, undrained

8 ounces (225 g) canned tomato sauce

6 ounces (170 g) canned tomato paste

2 teaspoons (5 g) ground cumin

1 teaspoon ground coriander

1 teaspoon ground cayenne pepper

1½ teaspoons chili powder

1 teaspoon kosher salt

1 teaspoon freshly ground black pepper

¼ teaspoon crushed red pepper flakes

1. In a medium skillet on the stove top, crumble and brown the ground bison. Then add the cooked meat to the slow cooker (no need to drain).

2. Add all the remaining ingredients to the slow cooker and stir well to combine.

3. Cover the slow cooker. Cook on LOW for 10 to 12 hours or on HIGH for 5 to 6 hours.

NOTES: *Top your bowls of chili with your favorite toppings. You can keep it simple with just shredded sharp Cheddar cheese and a dollop of sour cream. A piece of corn bread on the side—or crumbled into the chili—makes it perfect!*

HEARTY STEAK AND BEAN CHILI

Serves: 12 | **Cook Time:** 8 to 10 hours on LOW | **Slow Cooker Size:** 6-quart (5.7-L)

Tender steak is transformed into a hearty chili. You can use any type of steak that you have on hand, but cheaper cuts of steak are perfect for this bean-and-meat filled recipe. We like to use cubed steak, flank steak, flat iron steak, or tri-tip as these are generally inexpensive if you watch for sales at your local grocery store.

2 pounds (about 1 kg) beef steak

1 medium yellow onion, diced

2 stalks celery, thinly sliced

29 ounces (822 g) canned diced tomatoes, undrained

15 ounces (425 g) canned black beans, drained

15 ounces (425 g) canned kidney beans, drained

6 ounces (170 g) canned tomato paste

2 teaspoons (5 g) ground chili powder

1 teaspoon garlic powder

1 teaspoon ground cumin

1 teaspoon granulated sugar

¼ teaspoon dried oregano

Salt and pepper, to taste

1. Cut the steak into bite-size cubes and place in the bottom of the slow cooker.
2. Add the onion and celery to the slow cooker with the beef.
3. Add the remaining ingredients except for the salt and pepper to the slow cooker.
4. Cover the slow cooker. Cook on LOW for 8 to 10 hours, or until the onions and celery are tender.
5. Season with salt and pepper to taste.

NOTES: *To add more spice to this recipe, you can add 1 or 2 jalapeño peppers diced small. You can also use canned ranch-style beans instead of the black or kidney beans (or both).*

CREAMY CHICKEN WILD RICE SOUP

Serves: 8 to 10 | **Cook Time:** 8 to 9 hours on LOW or 4 to 5 hours on HIGH
Slow Cooker Size: 6-quart (5.7-L)

Tender shredded chicken, wild rice, and plenty of herbs and aromatics make this creamy soup stand out from the crowd. We served this soup with pretzel rolls from the bakery, and they were the perfect bread to sop up the soup!

1 cup uncooked (180 g) wild rice blend

1 pound (455 g) boneless skinless chicken breast (about 2 to 3 breast halves)

1 medium yellow onion, chopped

2 cups chopped carrots (about 4 to 5 medium carrots)

1 cup chopped celery (about 2–3 stalks celery)

5 cloves garlic, minced

8 cups (1.9 L) low-sodium chicken broth, store-bought or homemade (page 310)

2 bay leaves

2 tablespoons salt-free seasoning blend (such as Mrs. Dash Original Blend)

1 teaspoon poultry seasoning

1 teaspoon dried thyme, crushed

1 teaspoon dried rosemary, crushed

1 teaspoon dried tarragon, crushed

1 teaspoon salt

1 teaspoon black pepper

4 tablespoons (55 g) butter

½ cup (68 g) all-purpose flour

2 cups (475 ml) half-and-half

1. Place the uncooked rice, chicken breasts, onion, carrots, celery, garlic, chicken broth, and spices in the slow cooker.

2. Cover the slow cooker. Cook on LOW for 7 to 8 hours or on HIGH for 3 to 4 hours.

3. During the last half hour of cooking remove the chicken breasts from the soup and place on a plate to cool.

4. While the chicken is cooling, add the butter to a small saucepan and allow the butter to melt completely.

5. Add the flour to the butter and stir to combine the flour into the melted butter. Allow the butter-and-flour mixture to cook for 1 minute.

6. Slowly add the half-and-half while whisking with a wire whisk into the butter-and-flour mixture until no lumps appear. Allow mixture to cook until thick and creamy.

7. Add the mixture to the soup in the slow cooker.

8. Shred the chicken and add it back into the soup.

9. Cover the slow cooker and cook for 1 additional hour on HIGH, until the soup is nice and thick.

SOUTHWESTERN CREAMY WHITE CHICKEN CHILI

Serves: 6 to 8 | **Cook Time:** 6½ to 8½ hours on LOW | **Slow Cooker Size:** 5-quart (4.7-L) or larger

This chili recipe is a creamy twist on a classic, and it's the perfect meal for a cold fall or winter day. It really hits the spot with a side of freshly baked corn bread!

1–1½ pounds (455–680 g) boneless skinless chicken breasts

3 cups (705 ml) low-sodium chicken broth, store-bought or homemade (page 310)

1 medium yellow onion, diced

2 cloves garlic, minced

31 ounces (879 g) canned great northern beans, drained and rinsed

14.5 ounces (411 g) canned whole-kernel corn, drained

8 ounces (225 g) canned diced mild green chilies

1 teaspoon ground cumin

¾ teaspoon dried oregano

½ teaspoon chili powder

½ teaspoon salt

¼ teaspoon ground cayenne pepper

¼ cup (60 ml) half-and-half

4 ounces (115 g) cream cheese, softened and cubed

1. Add all the ingredients except for the half-and-half and the cream cheese to the slow cooker.
2. Cover the slow cooker. Cook on LOW for 6 to 8 hours, or until the chicken is cooked through and the onions are soft.
3. Remove the chicken from the slow cooker and shred the meat with two forks.
4. Add the shredded chicken back into the slow cooker.
5. Stir in the half-and-half and the cream cheese.
6. Cover the slow cooker. Cook for an additional 30 minutes on LOW, or until the chili is creamy and cream cheese is melted and mixed in well.

CHICKEN, BUTTERNUT SQUASH, AND QUINOA SOUP

Serves: 6 to 8 | **Cook Time:** 3 to 4 hours on HIGH | **Slow Cooker Size:** 5-quart (4.7-L)

This hearty soup is full of butternut squash, chicken, corn, quinoa—and flavor! The cumin and coriander add a nice Latin American flavor. We like to top this soup with a little sour cream and Cheddar cheese right before serving.

1–2 pounds (455 g to about 1 kg) boneless skinless chicken breasts, cut into bite-size pieces

1 cup (173 g) quinoa, uncooked

4 cups (560 g) cubed butternut squash

14.5 ounces (411 g) canned kidney beans, drained and rinsed

14.5 ounces (411 g) canned corn, drained, or 2 cups fresh corn kernels

14.5 ounces (411 g) canned petite diced tomatoes, undrained

2 cloves garlic, minced

5 cups (1.4 L) low-sodium chicken broth, store-bought or homemade (page 310)

1 teaspoon ground cumin

1 teaspoon ground coriander

½ teaspoon crushed red pepper flakes

½ teaspoon ground paprika

Salt and pepper, to taste

FOR SERVING (OPTIONAL):

Sour cream

Cheddar cheese

1. Place the quinoa in a fine-mesh strainer and rinse under cool water to remove the coating.
2. Add all the ingredients to the slow cooker and stir to combine.
3. Cover the slow cooker. Cook on HIGH for 3 to 4 hours, until the squash and quinoa are cooked through.
4. With a slotted spoon remove half of the cubed squash and mash it into a pulp. Add the mashed squash back in the soup and stir.
5. Ladle soup into bowls. Top with sour cream and Cheddar cheese (if desired).

DECADENT LOBSTER BISQUE

Serves: 6 | **Cook Time:** 4 to 6 hours on LOW or 2 to 3 hours on HIGH plus 45 minutes on LOW
Slow Cooker Size: 4-quart (3.8-L) or larger

This decadent soup is perfect for any special occasion (think Valentine's Day). It is fancy enough to be served as part of an elegant meal, but easy enough to make any day you want something that tastes amazing!

2 whole shallots, finely minced

1 clove garlic, finely minced

29 ounces (822 g) canned petite diced tomatoes, with the juice

32 ounces (946 ml) low-sodium chicken broth, store-bought or homemade (page 310)

1 tablespoon (7 g) Old Bay seasoning

1 teaspoon dried dill

¼ cup (15 g) chopped fresh parsley

1 teaspoon freshly ground black pepper

½ teaspoon ground paprika

4 whole lobster tails

1 pint (473 ml) heavy whipping cream

NOTES: *You may substitute half of a mild onion for the shallots if you cannot find shallots. You may also use less cream or substitute half-and-half for the cream for less fat.*

1. Place the shallots and garlic in a microwave-safe bowl and microwave on high for 2 to 3 minutes, or until the shallots are wilted and starting to turn translucent. If you don't have a microwave, cook them in a small skillet on the stove top.

2. Add the shallot-and-garlic mixture to the slow cooker.

3. Add the tomatoes, chicken broth, Old Bay seasoning, dill, parsley, pepper, and paprika to the slow cooker.

4. Use a sharp knife to cut off the fan part of the very end of the lobster tail and add the fans of the lobster tails to the slow cooker.

5. Place the remaining part of the lobster in the refrigerator until later.

6. Stir everything in the slow cooker to combine.

7. Cover the slow cooker. Cook on LOW for 4 to 6 hours or on HIGH for 2 to 3 hours.

8. Fish the lobster tail fans out of the soup and discard.

9. Use a blender or immersion blender to puree the soup mixture to your desired chunkiness. We like to puree half of the soup until smooth and the other half of the soup just to a light puree.

10. Add the pureed soup back in the slow cooker.

11. Remove the lobster tails from the refrigerator and add them to the soup. Cover the slow cooker. Cook on LOW for about 45 minutes, or until the shells of the lobster turn red and the meat is opaque, firm, and white.

12. Remove the lobster tails from the soup and set on a plate to allow them to cool slightly.

13. While the lobster is cooking, add the cream to the soup and stir to combine.

14. Use a sharp knife to cut each lobster tail in half length-wise and remove the lobster flesh from the shells.

15. Discard the shells. Roughly chop the lobster meat and add it back in the soup.

KID-FRIENDLY MEATBALL BEEF STEW

Serves: 6 to 8 | **Cook Time:** 6 hours on LOW or 5 hours on HIGH | **Slow Cooker Size:** 5-quart (4.7-L)

For some reason our kids are more apt to eat anything if there are meatballs in it. In this easy recipe, we replaced beef stew meat with frozen meatballs and everyone gobbles it up!

28 ounces (794 g) frozen Italian-style meatballs

6 medium carrots, peeled and sliced

5 medium potatoes, peeled and diced into ½- to ¾-inch (1- to 2-cm) chunks

1 medium yellow onion, diced

32 ounces (946 ml) low-sodium beef stock, store-bought or homemade (page 311)

1 packet (2 ounces, or 55 g) low-sodium dry onion soup mix, store-bought or homemade (page 319)

2 cloves garlic, minced

2 whole bay leaves

1 teaspoon dried oregano, crushed

1 teaspoon dried rosemary, crushed

⅛ teaspoon freshly ground black pepper

⅛ teaspoon salt

½ cup (68 g) all-purpose flour

1½ cups (355 ml) cold water

1. Add the meatballs, carrots, potatoes, onion, beef stock, onion soup mix, garlic, bay leaves, oregano, rosemary, pepper, and salt.

2. In a bowl or measuring cup, mix together the all-purpose flour and cold water together with a fork until you have a slurry with no lumps of flour in it.

3. Add the slurry mixture to the slow cooker and stir to combine and mix everything together.

4. Cover the slow cooker. Cook on LOW for 6 hours or on HIGH for 5 hours, or until the potatoes and carrots are cooked through.

5. Remove the bay leaves from the stew and discard.

NOTES: Serve this delicious stew with rolls or bread for sopping up the stew juices or try it spooned over rice or egg noodles.

FULLY LOADED BAKED POTATO SOUP

Serves: 6 to 8 | **Cook Time:** 6 to 8 hours on LOW or 3 to 4 hours on HIGH plus 30 minutes on LOW
Slow Cooker Size: 5-quart (4.7-L)

If you like a baked potato with everything on it, then you are going to love this creamy potato soup filled with bacon, cheese, sour cream, onions, and then topped with chives. This soup is a meal in itself.

6 slices thick-cut bacon, diced

1 medium yellow onion, diced

32 ounces (946 ml) low-sodium chicken stock, store-bought or homemade (page 310)

4–5 medium russet potatoes, peeled and diced into ½-inch (1-cm) cubes

2 stalks celery, diced

1 medium carrot, peeled and diced

2 cloves garlic, minced

2 bay leaves

1 teaspoon dried thyme, crushed

½ teaspoon freshly ground black pepper

1 cup (230 g) sour cream

1 cup (235 ml) half-and-half

¼ cup (32 g) all-purpose flour

1 cup (120 g) grated extra-sharp Cheddar cheese

Chives (for garnish)

1. In a large skillet on the stove top set on medium heat, add the diced bacon and slowly cook the bacon until crispy. Remove the cooked bacon with a slotted spoon and set aside on a plate lined with paper towels to drain.

2. Pour off the bacon fat from the skillet except for about 2 tablespoons (30 ml) and add the onion. Cook the onion over medium-high heat until the onion becomes translucent and starts to just turn brown.

3. Add half of the bacon, the onion, chicken stock, potatoes, celery, carrot, garlic, bay leaves, thyme, and pepper to the slow cooker. Stir to combine.

4. Cover the slow cooker. Cook on LOW for 6 to 8 hours or on HIGH for 3 to 4 hours, or until the potatoes and carrots are soft.

5. During the last half hour of cooking whisk together the sour cream, half-and-half, and flour until there are no lumps of flour.

6. Remove and discard the bay leaves.

7. Add the cream mixture and shredded Cheddar cheese to the soup and stir to combine.

8. Cover and continue cooking on LOW for the remaining 30 minutes, until the soup is thickened.

9. Ladle the hot soup into bowls. Garnish with chopped chives and a sprinkle of the reserved bacon.

SUMMER ZUCCHINI AND CORN CHOWDER

Serves: 6 to 8 | **Cook Time:** 7½ to 8½ hours on LOW | **Slow Cooker Size:** 5-quart (4.7-L)

This soup is summer goodness in a bowl! Fresh sweet corn and zucchini are highlighted with just the right amount of spices and jalapeño peppers. This soup is lovely served with corn bread or warm French bread for dipping!

3 medium russet potatoes, peeled and diced into ½-inch (1-cm) cubes

4 ears of fresh corn, kernels removed from cob (or 29 ounces canned or frozen corn)

1 medium zucchini, diced

2–4 strips thick sliced bacon, cooked and chopped

1 medium yellow onion, diced

1 medium carrot, peeled and diced

2 stalks celery, diced

2 cloves garlic, minced

½ teaspoon dried thyme

4 cups (940 ml) water

1 bay leaf

Pinch of salt and pepper

1 cup (235 ml) half-and-half

FOR SERVING (OPTIONAL):
Cayenne pepper
Fresh parsley

1. Add all the ingredients except for the half-and-half to the slow cooker.
2. Cover the slow cooker. Cook on LOW for 7 to 8 hours, or until the potatoes are tender.
3. Remove the bay leaf and discard.
4. Stir in the half-and-half and cook for an additional 30 minutes on LOW.
5. Ladle the hot soup into bowls. Garnish with a dash of cayenne pepper and fresh parsley (if desired).

HEARTY CHICKEN AND POTATO STEW

Serves: 6 | **Cook Time:** 6 to 7 hours on LOW or 4 to 5 hours on HIGH | **Slow Cooker Size:** 6½-quart (6.2-L)

This recipe is a creamy chicken and garden veggie stew using mashed potato flakes (i.e., instant mashed potatoes) as a thickener for the soup. Use whatever vegetables your family prefers, and turkey can be used instead of chicken.

3–4 tablespoons (42–55 g) unsalted butter

1 medium yellow onion, diced

2 medium russet potatoes, peeled and diced

3 medium carrots, peeled and diced

2 stalks celery, diced

1 cup (100 g) fresh green beans, trimmed

1 cup (235 ml) low-sodium chicken broth, store-bought or homemade (page 310)

3–4 pounds (1.4–1.8 kg) boneless skinless chicken breasts

¼ teaspoon salt

¼ teaspoon freshly ground black pepper

¼ teaspoon ground paprika

2 bay leaves

1 packet (28 g) dry ranch dressing mix, store-bought or homemade (page 318)

12 ounces (355 ml) canned evaporated milk

¾ cup (173 g) sour cream

¼–½ cup (13–26 g) mashed potato flakes, divided and to taste

1. Set the slow cooker on the HIGH temperature. Add the butter, onion, potatoes, carrots, celery, and green beans to the slow cooker as you prepare them. You want the butter to melt and coat the vegetables.

2. When the butter has melted and has coated the vegetables, add the chicken broth.

3. Place the chicken on top of the vegetables in the slow cooker.

4. Sprinkle the salt, pepper, and paprika over the chicken.

5. Add the bay leaves and ranch dressing mix.

6. Cover the slow cooker. Cook on LOW for 6 to 7 hours or on HIGH for 4 to 5 hours.

7. If you are cooking on HIGH at the 4-hour mark, remove the chicken from the slow cooker and shred the meat into bite-size pieces. Add the chicken back into the slow cooker and add the evaporated milk and sour cream along with the chicken. If you are cooking on LOW, do the same with the chicken, evaporated milk, and sour cream at the 6-hour mark.

8. Remove the bay leaves and discard.

9. Add ¼ cup (13 g) of the mashed potato flakes to the soup and stir to combine. Cover the slow cooker. Cook for an additional 10 to 20 minutes to thicken up the soup. If you feel that the soup is still too thin for your liking, feel free to add an additional ¼ cup (13 g) of potato flakes and cook for an additional 10 minutes.

NOTES: *You can use either fresh or frozen chicken in this recipe. The chicken will cook just fine either way without needing to adjust the cooking time range given.*

SAVORY CHICKEN AND SQUASH SOUP

Serves: 6 | **Cook Time:** 7 to 8 hours on LOW or 4 to 5 hours on HIGH | **Slow Cooker Size:** 6½-quart (6.2-L)

This soup is a great recipe for the abundance of zucchini and yellow squash growing in your garden that you may be struggling to find ways to use up. The butternut squash I used was already precut and found in the produce section of my local grocery store. If you have access to whole squash, feel free to peel and dice up your own. The butternut squash adds just the right amount of sweetness to please everyone with this hearty soup.

2–3 frozen chicken breasts (see note)

4 strips of bacon, cooked and chopped

2 stalks celery, chopped

16 ounces (455 g) butternut squash, diced

2 medium zucchini, sliced

1 medium yellow squash, sliced

1 large yellow onion, diced

2 medium carrots, peeled and diced

14.5 ounces (411 g) canned whole corn kernels, drained (may also use fresh or frozen corn)

1 tablespoon (1 g) dried parsley flakes

1 teaspoon dried basil

2 bay leaves

5 cups (1.4 L) low-sodium chicken broth, store-bought or homemade (page 310)

Salt and pepper, to taste

1. Place all the prepared ingredients except for the salt and pepper in the slow cooker. Make sure to leave enough room to close the lid when you add the chicken broth.

2. Cover the slow cooker. Cook on LOW for 7 to 8 hours or on HIGH for 4 to 5 hours, or until the internal temperature of the chicken reaches 165°F (74°C) on an instant-read meat thermometer.

3. Remove the chicken from the slow cooker and shred the meat into bite-size pieces. Add the shredded meat back in the soup.

4. Remove the bay leaves and discard.

5. Taste the soup and season with salt and pepper as needed.

NOTES: *You can use fresh or frozen chicken in this recipe. Turkey works well, too!*

HEARTY VEGETABLE BEEF SOUP

Serves: 8 | **Cook Time:** 6 to 8 hours on LOW | **Slow Cooker Size:** 4-quart (3.8-L)

This easy recipe for vegetable beef stew has only five ingredients—making it super simple to throw together in the morning and have dinner ready later with zero fuss.

1 pound (455 g) ground beef

46 ounces (1.4 L) canned vegetable juice

14.5 ounces (411 g) canned whole corn kernels, drained

16 ounces (455 g) frozen mixed vegetables (peas, carrots, and green beans)

14.5 ounces (411 g) canned diced potatoes

1. In a medium skillet over medium-high heat, crumble and brown the ground beef until no longer pink. Drain off the excess grease and add the meat to the slow cooker.

2. Add the remaining ingredients to the slow cooker.

3. Cover the slow cooker. Cook on LOW for 6 to 8 hours.

NOTES: *You can use 1 or 2 fresh potatoes (peeled and diced) instead of the canned potatoes. You may, however, need to cook the soup for an additional hour.*

GREEK LEMON CHICKEN AND RICE SOUP

Serves: 6 | **Cook Time:** 7 to 8 hours on LOW or 3 to 4 hours on HIGH | **Slow Cooker Size:** 6½-quart (6.2-L)

This Greek-inspired soup recipe is based on a Mediterranean sauce known as avgolemono, which is an egg yolk and lemon juice–based sauce. It is often served over vegetables such as steamed artichokes. This soup has a very deep lemon flavor when using all four lemons, so feel free to use less lemon juice depending on how lemony you want your soup to be.

2 pounds (about 1 kg) boneless skinless chicken breasts

2 medium carrots, peeled and diced

½ cup (93 g) uncooked long-grain white rice

2 stalks celery, diced

1 large yellow onion, minced

1 clove garlic, minced

32 ounces (946 ml) low-sodium chicken broth, store-bought or homemade (page 310)

10.5 ounces (298 g) canned low-fat canned cream of chicken soup

1–4 small lemons, juiced

Salt and pepper, to taste

Green onion or fresh parsley (optional)

1. Add all the ingredients except for the salt, pepper, green onion, and parsley (if desired) to the slow cooker. Stir to combine.

2. Cover the slow cooker. Cook on LOW for 7 to 8 hours or on HIGH for 3 to 4 hours, or until the chicken is fully cooked and reaches 165°F (74°C) on a meat thermometer.

3. Remove the chicken from the slow cooker and shred the meat into bite-size pieces. Add the chicken back in the soup.

4. Season the soup with salt and pepper to taste. Keep in mind that lemony dishes need less salt, so go easy at first.

5. Ladle the soup into bowls. Garnish with chopped green onion or fresh parsley (if desired).

SIMPLE CORNED BEEF AND CABBAGE SOUP

Serves: 8 | **Cook Time:** 6 to 7 hours on LOW | **Slow Cooker Size:** 6-quart (5.7-L)

Corned beef and cabbage is the ultimate peasant food because it is inexpensive and easy to make. This soup combines all the flavors of this classic dish into a comforting bowl of soup.

1–2 pounds (455 g to about 1 kg) corned beef brisket with the spice packet, cut into bite-size pieces

32 ounces (946 ml) low-sodium chicken broth, store-bought or homemade (page 310); see Notes

1 pound (455 g) potatoes, peeled and diced into ½-inch (1-cm) pieces

1 pound (455 g) carrots, peeled and diced

1 medium yellow onion, diced

2 cloves garlic, minced

½ head green cabbage, roughly chopped

1. Add the corned beef brisket including the spices, chicken broth, potatoes, carrots, onion, and garlic to the slow cooker.
2. Cover the slow cooker. Cook on LOW for 4 hours.
3. Add the roughly chopped cabbage and cover the slow cooker. Continue to cook for an additional 2 to 3 hours, or until the potatoes, carrots, and beef are tender.
4. Taste the soup. Add salt and pepper to your liking; keep in mind corned beef is usually pretty salty, so go easy on the salt.

NOTES: *This soup pairs well with crusty bread or rolls to sop up the broth.*

Most store-bought corned beef briskets these days come with a spice packet. However, if your brisket does not come with it, you can easily make your own spice blend by using 1 teaspoon mustard seeds, 1 teaspoon coriander seeds, 1 crushed bay leaf, 1 teaspoon peppercorns, 2 to 3 whole cloves, and 1 teaspoon fennel seeds.

CHEESY TORTELLINI SPINACH SOUP

Serves: 6 to 8 | **Cook Time:** 5 hours on LOW | **Slow Cooker Size:** 6½-quart (6.2-L)

This is a very easy recipe to put together, and to make it go even quicker, you can precook the ground beef when you make another recipe earlier in the week. Just put that in the refrigerator and set it aside for this recipe. Thinking ahead can make slow cooker cooking even easier! This recipe has a nice smooth flavor, and the tortellini pasta adds great texture and flavor.

29 ounces (822 g) canned Italian-style diced tomatoes

19 ounces (539 g) frozen tortellini pasta

1 pound (455 g) lean ground beef, crumbled, browned, and drained

4–5 ounces (115–142 g) frozen spinach

4 cups (940 ml) low-sodium beef broth, store-bought or homemade (page 311)

3 cloves garlic, minced

1 teaspoon ground cumin

1 teaspoon dried oregano

8 ounces (225 g) cream cheese

1 cup (100 g) freshly grated Parmesan cheese (plus more for garnish)

Salt and pepper, to taste

FOR SERVING:

Crusty bread

1. Add the tomatoes, tortellini, cooked ground beef, spinach, beef broth, garlic, cumin, and oregano.
2. Cover the slow cooker. Cook on LOW for 4 hours.
3. Add the cream cheese and Parmesan cheese, cover the slow cooker, and cook for an additional 1 hour on LOW. Stir to distribute the melted cream cheese throughout the soup.
4. Taste the soup and season with salt and pepper as needed.
5. Ladle the hot soup into bowls. Garnish with additional freshly grated Parmesan cheese. Serve with crusty bread for dipping in the creamy broth.

NOTES: *If you need this soup to cook longer, add the first eight ingredients to the slow cooker and cook it for up to 8 hours. Add the cream cheese and Parmesan cheese during the last hour of cooking. Cook the tortellini pasta on the stove top according to the package directions and add the cooked pasta to the soup at the last minute to avoid mushy pasta.*

VEGGIE-LOADED MINESTRONE SOUP

Serves: 8 | **Cook Time:** 6 to 8 hours on LOW | **Slow Cooker Size:** 6-quart (5.7-L)

This Italian-style soup is jam-packed with vegetables and beans and FLAVOR! Everyone in the family is going to love this recipe!

28 ounces (794 g) canned crushed tomatoes

15 ounces (425 g) canned kidney beans, drained and rinsed

15 ounces (425 g) canned black beans, drained and rinsed

14.5 ounces (411 g) canned diced tomatoes, undrained

2 cups (180 g) fresh green cabbage, cut into ½-inch (1-cm) strips

2 stalks celery, diced

1 medium yellow onion, diced

1 medium carrot, peeled and diced

½ teaspoon fresh basil, minced

½ teaspoon dried oregano

2–4 cups (475–940 ml) low-sodium vegetable broth, store-bought or homemade (page 312; start with 2 cups and use more as needed)

12 ounces (340 g) cooked rotini pasta

Salt and pepper, to taste

Parmesan cheese (optional)

1. Add all the ingredients—except for the pasta, salt, pepper, and Parmesan cheese—to the slow cooker.

2. Cover the slow cooker. Cook on LOW for 6 to 8 hours, or until the vegetables are tender.

3. Taste the soup and season with salt and pepper to your preference.

4. On the stove top, cook the pasta in boiling water according to the directions on the package until the pasta is al dente.

5. Drain the pasta and add it to the hot soup in the slow cooker.

6. Ladle the soup into bowls and garnish with shredded Parmesan cheese (if desired).

FREEZER MEAL INSTRUCTIONS: Label the freezer bag with the name of the recipe, ingredients, and cooking instructions. Add all the ingredients except for the pasta, vegetable broth, salt, pepper, and Parmesan cheese to a gallon-size freezer bag. Carefully lay the freezer bag flat, push out as much air as possible, and zip the bag closed. Freeze the bag flat in the freezer. When it is frozen, you can stand it upright if you desire. Set aside the vegetable broth and pasta in your pantry for when you are ready to cook this freezer meal.

TO COOK THE FREEZER MEAL: Thaw the freezer meal bag in the refrigerator. Pour the contents of the bag into the cooker and cook the recipe per the directions beginning at step 1.

CREAMY CHICKEN GNOCCHI SOUP

Serves: 4 to 6 | **Cook Time:** 7 hours on LOW | **Slow Cooker Size:** 5-quart (4.7-L)

There is a popular chain restaurant that offers an amazing chicken gnocchi soup, and this is our version of that recipe . . . but made in the slow cooker, of course. And it is AMAZING. Creamy soup is loaded with chicken, veggies, and tender pillows of gnocchi dumplings. This recipe calls for cooked chicken, not raw, so use up some leftover cooked chicken or grab a rotisserie chicken from the deli at your grocery store. In a pinch you can even use canned chicken.

1–2 pounds (445 g to about 1 kg) cooked chicken, diced or shredded

4 cups (940 ml) low-sodium chicken stock, store-bought or homemade (page 310)

5 stalks celery, sliced

3 medium carrots, peeled and sliced

1 medium yellow onion, diced

1 tablespoon (3 g) dried Italian seasoning, store-bought or homemade (page 316)

2 tablespoons (18 g) cornstarch

1 tablespoon (15 ml) cold water

16 ounces (455 g) fresh or frozen potato gnocchi

14.5 ounces (411 g) canned evaporated milk

1 tablespoon (15 ml) olive oil

3 cloves garlic, minced

8 ounces (225 g) fresh or frozen spinach, chopped

FOR SERVING:

Bread, bread sticks, or crackers

1. Add the cooked chicken, chicken stock, celery, carrots, onion, and Italian seasoning to the slow cooker.

2. Cover the slow cooker. Cook on LOW for 6 hours, or until the vegetables are tender.

3. In a small bowl, mix together the cornstarch and cold water to create a slurry, which will be used to thicken the soup. Add the slurry, gnocchi, and evaporated milk to the soup and stir to combine. Cover and continue to cook while you prepare the remaining ingredients.

4. In a medium skillet set over medium-high heat, heat the olive oil and add the garlic and spinach. Sauté until the garlic is lightly golden-brown and the spinach is wilted (if using fresh spinach).

5. Stir the garlic-and-spinach mixture into the slow cooker. Cover the cooker and cook for 1 additional hour.

6. Ladle the hot soup into bowls and serve with bread, bread sticks, or crackers.

NOTES: *If using frozen spinach in this recipe, thaw the spinach and place the thawed spinach inside a clean flour sack towel. Wring out as much liquid as possible before adding it to the pan with the olive oil and garlic.*

ITALIAN SAUSAGE TUSCAN BEAN AND KALE SOUP

Serves: 8 | **Cook Time:** 6 to 8 hours on LOW | **Slow Cooker Size:** 6-quart (5.7-L)

Sweet Italian sausage gives this soup a ton of flavor, and the chopped kale added near the end of the cooking time packs a healthy punch. We like to brown the sausage and chop the vegetables the night before. In the morning we can just dump everything in the slow cooker and go about our day knowing that when we get home, dinner is going to be just about done.

2 pounds (about 1 kg) sweet Italian sausage (bulk not links)

1 small yellow onion, diced

45 ounces (1.3 kg) canned cannellini beans, drained

28 ounces (794 g) canned no-salt-added crushed tomatoes

28 ounces (794 g) canned no-salt-added diced tomatoes

2 cups (475 ml) water

3 cloves garlic, minced

½ teaspoon fennel seeds

½ teaspoon dried oregano, crushed

½ teaspoon dried basil, crushed

2 cups (110 g) kale, stems removed and roughly chopped (You can also use a bag of prepared kale found in the salad section of your local grocery store.)

Parmesan cheese (optional)

1. In a large skillet on the stove top, brown and crumble the Italian sausage along with the onion until the sausage is browned and the onions are translucent, about 20 minutes.

2. Drain off excess fat from the cooked sausage and add the sausage and onions to the slow cooker.

3. Add the remaining ingredients except for the kale and Parmesan (if desired) to the slow cooker and stir to combine.

4. Cover the slow cooker. Cook on LOW for 6 to 8 hours.

5. During the last 30 minutes of cooking, stir the kale into the soup. Cover the slow cooker. Continue cooking for the remaining 30 minutes, or until the kale is slightly wilted.

6. Ladle the hot soup into bowls. Top with shredded Parmesan cheese (if desired).

ITALIAN TOMATO SOUP WITH GNOCCHI

Serves: 6 to 8 | **Cook Time:** 6½ hours on LOW | **Slow Cooker Size:** 5-quart (4.7-L)

Everyone loves this homemade, creamy tomato soup with fluffy potato gnocchi dumplings. Serve with a grilled cheese or a panini sandwich or toasted French bread for a meal that really satisfies.

28 ounces (794 g) canned whole plum tomatoes, undrained

14.5 ounces (411 g) canned tomato sauce

1 large yellow onion, diced

5 cloves garlic, minced

3½ cups (825 ml) low-sodium chicken stock, store-bought or homemade (page 310)

2 tablespoons (9 g) dried basil, crushed

1 teaspoon granulated sugar

1 teaspoon kosher salt

½ teaspoon freshly ground black pepper

1 cup (235 ml) half-and-half

¼ cup (55 g) unsalted butter

3 tablespoons (24 g) all-purpose flour

½ cup (120 ml) milk

1 cup (80 g) shredded Parmesan cheese, plus more for optional garnish

16 ounces (455 g) fresh or frozen potato gnocchi

1. Add the tomatoes, tomato sauce, onion, garlic, chicken stock, basil, sugar, salt, pepper, and half-and-half to the slow cooker.

2. Cover the slow cooker. Cook on LOW for 6 hours.

3. Transfer the soup to the jar of a blender or use an immersion blender right in the stoneware crock. Carefully blend until the soup is smooth. Be careful as the soup is hot!

4. On the stove top, prepare a roux to thicken the soup by melting the butter in a small pan. When the butter is melted, slowly whisk the flour into the butter. Cook for 1 to 2 minutes. Next, slowly whisk the milk into the butter-and-flour mixture until there are no lumps and the mixture is thick.

5. Add the roux to the slow cooker and mix well.

6. Add the Parmesan cheese and the uncooked gnocchi to the soup. Cover the slow cooker. Continue to cook for 30 minutes on LOW, or until the gnocchi is cooked. Be careful not to overcook as the gnocchi will get sticky if cooked too long.

7. Serve immediately in bowls garnished with additional Parmesan cheese (if desired).

ITALIAN BEEF STEW WITH RED WINE

Serves: 6 to 8 | **Cook Time:** 8 to 10 hours on LOW | **Slow Cooker Size:** 6-quart (5.7-L)

Tender morsels of beef are simmered away all day in a delicious broth that has a little red wine added to it. Onion, carrots, celery, and mushrooms add plenty of vegetables, and the garlic, oregano, thyme, marjoram, and basil give this hearty stew tons of flavor!

2½ pounds (1.1 kg) beef stew meat

⅓ cup (42 g) all-purpose flour

1 teaspoon salt

½ teaspoon freshly ground black pepper

2 tablespoons (30 ml) olive oil, divided

4 cups (940 ml) low-sodium beef broth, store-bought or homemade (page 311), divided

1½ pounds (680 g) russet potatoes, peeled and diced into ½-inch (1-cm) cubes

4 medium carrots, peeled and diced

4 cloves garlic, minced

2 stalks celery, diced

1 large yellow onion, diced

30 ounces (850 g) canned diced tomatoes, undrained

8 ounces (225 g) baby portabella mushrooms, sliced

¼ cup (60 ml) dry red wine

1 tablespoon (5 g) dried basil, crushed

1 teaspoon dried oregano, crushed

1 teaspoon dried thyme, crushed

¾ teaspoon dried rosemary, crushed

½ teaspoon dried marjoram, crushed

FOR SERVING (OPTIONAL):

Parmesan cheese

1. Place the beef stew meat in a large zippered plastic bag and add the flour, salt, and pepper. Seal the bag and toss to evenly coat the beef in flour.
2. Heat 1 tablespoon (15 ml) of olive oil in a large skillet over medium-high heat. When the oil is hot, add half of the beef and cook tossing occasionally until the beef has browned, about 5 to 6 minutes. Transfer the browned beef to a plate.
3. Add the other 1 tablespoon (15 ml) of olive oil to the skillet and cook the other half of the floured beef until browned. Remove the beef and add it to the same plate with the first batch of browned beef.
4. Keeping your skillet on medium-high heat, slowly add 1 cup (235 ml) of the beef broth and the red wine. Cook while stirring frequently and scraping the bottom of the pan to loosen the browned bits on the bottom. Remove from the heat and add the liquid to the slow cooker.
5. Add the remaining ingredients except for the Parmesan cheese to the slow cooker.
6. Cover the slow cooker. Cook on LOW for 8 to 10 hours, or until the beef is very tender.
7. Spoon the hot stew into bowls and sprinkle with freshly grated Parmesan cheese (if desired).

SIMPLE CHICKEN ENCHILADA SOUP

Serves: 6 to 8 | **Cook Time:** 8 hours on LOW or 4 hours on HIGH | **Slow Cooker Size:** 5-quart (4.7-L)

Canned or homemade enchilada sauce brings a ton of Mexican flavor to this creamy chicken soup. We like to serve this soup with tortilla chips and extra cheese to make it extra yummy.

2 whole boneless skinless chicken breasts

16 ounces (455 g) frozen corn kernels

15 ounces (425 g) canned black beans, drained and rinsed

5 ounces (140 g) canned tomato sauce

1 medium yellow onion, diced

1 can (10.75 ounces, or 305 g) cream of chicken soup

10 ounces (280 g) canned enchilada sauce

1½ cups (355 ml) milk

1 cup (115 g) shredded cheese (such as Cheddar, pepper jack, or Colby jack), plus more for optional garnish

Tortilla chips (optional)

1. Add the chicken, corn, black beans, tomato sauce, and onion to the slow cooker.

2. In a separate bowl, whisk together the cream of chicken soup, enchilada sauce, and milk. Pour the mixture over everything in the slow cooker.

3. Cover the slow cooker. Cook on LOW for 8 hours or on HIGH for 4 hours, or until the chicken is cooked though.

4. Carefully remove the chicken from the slow cooker and shred the meat. Add the shredded meat back to the slow cooker and stir.

5. Add 1 cup of shredded cheese and stir.

6. Ladle the hot soup into bowls. Garnish the soup with additional shredded cheese and tortilla chips (if desired).

TEX-MEX CHICKEN TACO SOUP

Serves: 6 to 8 | **Cook Time:** 6 to 8 hours on LOW | **Slow Cooker Size:** 6-quart (5.7-L)

This recipe can be easily adapted to what your family likes by omitting and adding what your family prefers. Beans can be replaced with other beans such as kidney beans or garbanzo beans, and you can easily add celery, bell peppers, black olives, cabbage, spinach, and mushrooms. You can also use turkey instead of chicken, and have fun with what you add to the soup, like chips, cheese, avocado, sour cream, and cilantro.

3 whole boneless skinless chicken breasts

16 ounces (455 g) canned chili beans, undrained

15 ounces (425 g) canned black beans, drained

15 ounces (425 g) canned corn kernels, drained

15 ounces (425 g) canned diced tomatoes, undrained

8 ounces (225 g) canned tomato sauce

1 small yellow onion, diced

1 package (28 g) low-sodium taco seasoning mix, store-bought or homemade (page 317)

FOR SERVING (OPTIONAL):

Sour cream

Shredded cheese

Tortilla chips

1. Place all the ingredients in the slow cooker except for the toppings and the taco seasoning and stir well.
2. Cover the slow cooker. Cook on LOW for 6 to 8 hours.
3. Remove the cooked chicken and shred. Add the shredded chicken back to the soup and stir.
4. Ladle the hot soup into bowls. Top with tortilla chips, shredded cheese, and sour cream (if desired).

3

GRAIN DISHES, PASTA DISHES, AND CASSEROLES

CREAMY CHICKEN AND WILD RICE HOT DISH

Serves: 6 to 8 | **Cook Time:** 6 to 8 hours on LOW or 3 to 4 hours on HIGH
Slow Cooker Size: 3½-quart (3.3-L) casserole OR 6-quart (5.7-L) oval

This recipe is a little bit labor-intensive because you need to sauté onions and then create a roux to thicken a homemade cream sauce. But if you can brown ground beef in a frying pan, then you can easily make the sauce, too. I really wanted to avoid using canned "cream of" whatever soup, so thus the little extra steps. I also cooked this casserole in my 3½-quart (3.3-L) casserole slow cooker because I wanted it to look more like a traditional oven-baked casserole. But if you don't have one, a 6-quart (5.7-L) oval slow cooker will work just as well.

1 small onion, diced

1 clove garlic, finely minced

⅓ cup (75 g) unsalted butter

½ cup (68 g) all-purpose flour

1½ teaspoons salt

½ teaspoon freshly ground black pepper

1 teaspoon dried thyme

½ teaspoon poultry seasoning

2½ cups (570 ml) low-sodium chicken broth

2 cups (475 ml) half-and-half

2 boneless skinless chicken breasts, cubed

2 cups (360 g) uncooked wild rice blend

6 ounces (170 g) white button mushrooms, sliced

4 ounces (115 g) jarred pimientos, drained

⅓ cup (37 g) pecans, finely chopped

1. In a large saucepan, sauté the onion and garlic in the butter until tender.
2. Stir in the flour, salt, pepper, thyme, and poultry seasoning until blended.
3. Slowly stir in the broth and bring to a boil.
4. Boil and stir for 2 minutes, or until bubbly and thickened.
5. Stir in the cream. Set aside.
6. Add the cubed chicken, wild rice blend, mushrooms, and pimentos to the slow cooker.
7. Pour the creamy sauce mixture over everything and gently stir to combine.
8. Sprinkle the top of the casserole with pecans.
9. Cover the slow cooker. Cook on LOW for 6 to 8 hours or 3 to 4 hours on HIGH, until the chicken and rice are cooked through.

NOTES: If you really want to skip making your own roux and cream sauce, you can use two cans of your favorite cream soup (cream of mushroom, cream of celery, cream of chicken) and skip the flour and half-and-half.

SPICY BUFFALO CHICKEN PASTA

Serves: 8 | **Cook Time:** 6 hours on LOW | **Slow Cooker Size:** 6-quart (5.7-L)

If you like spicy buffalo chicken wings, then you are going to adore this creamy and slightly spicy sauce and chicken. It's is cooked right in the slow cooker and served over pasta.

10.5 ounces (298 g) canned cream of chicken soup

¾ cup (175 ml) bottled buffalo wing sauce

3 whole boneless skinless chicken breasts, cut into bite-size pieces

2 cups (460 g) sour cream

½ cup (120 ml) bottled ranch salad dressing

1 cup (115 g) shredded mozzarella cheese, plus more for optional garnish

16 ounces (455 g) cooked penne pasta

1. In a small mixing bowl, mix together the cream of chicken soup and buffalo wing sauce.
2. Place the cut-up chicken in the slow cooker, pour the sauce mixture over the chicken, and toss to coat the chicken in the sauce.
3. Cover the slow cooker. Cook on LOW for 6 hours, stirring once in the middle of the cooking time if you can.
4. To the slow cooker add the sour cream, ranch dressing, and mozzarella cheese. Stir well.
5. Add pasta to the slow cooker and mix it into the sauce.
6. Spoon sauce-coated pasta onto plates and top with additional cheese (if desired).

NOTES: *Feel free to use low-fat ingredients to make this recipe a little healthier. Low-fat cream of chicken soup, sour cream, ranch dressing, and cheese will all work fine. Don't use fat-free as they don't cook up quite the same.*

HEARTY POTATO AND KIELBASA SAUSAGE CASSEROLE

Serves: 6 to 8 | **Cook Time:** 3 to 4 hours on HIGH | **Slow Cooker Size:** 6-quart (5.7-L)

If you are looking for good, old-fashioned, comfort food then this casserole recipe really fits the bill. Frozen hash browns, kielbasa sausage, and a few other key ingredients make this hearty, stick-to-your ribs casserole perfect for dinner any night of the week. We have even been known to eat leftovers (if there are any) for breakfast the next day.

32 ounces (905 g) frozen diced hash brown potatoes, defrosted

14 ounces (397 g) kielbasa smoked sausage, diced

1 small yellow onion, diced

1 clove garlic, minced

1 cup (115 g) shredded sharp Cheddar cheese

10.5 ounces (298 g) canned low-sodium cream of chicken soup

1 cup (235 ml) water

½ teaspoon poultry seasoning

1. Lightly butter or spray the insert of your slow cooker with nonstick cooking spray.
2. Place the hash browns, kielbasa, onion, garlic, and cheese in the slow cooker, and mix them together.
3. In a small bowl, mix together the can of cream of chicken soup, water, and poultry seasoning. Pour over everything in the slow cooker.
4. Cover the slow cooker. Cook on HIGH For 3 to 4 hours, or until the potatoes are cooked and sausages are hot.

NOTES: *You can add a can of drained diced tomatoes and/or some diced canned green chilies to change up the recipe into a different flavor profile. Heidi's husband even likes canned diced jalapeño peppers to really bring some spice to this dish.*

SOUR CREAM CHICKEN NOODLE CASSEROLE

Serves: 6 to 8 | **Cook Time:** 6 to 8 hours on LOW or 3 to 4 hours on HIGH plus 30 minutes on LOW
Slow Cooker Size: 3½-quart (3.3-L) casserole or 6-quart (5.7-L) oval

Crushed potato chips top this creamy chicken noodle casserole that is always a hit with the kids and adults alike in Heidi's family. Feel free to throw in some broccoli or cauliflower to add some veggies to the dish, too. I find if I cut up cauliflower really small, I can sneak it into dishes with a cream sauce, and my kids hardly notice it is in there! Mom win!

1 pound (455 g) boneless skinless chicken breasts or thighs

2½ cups (570 ml) low-sodium chicken stock, store-bought or homemade (page 310)

1 teaspoon dried Italian seasoning, store-bought or homemade (page 316)

½ cup (120 ml) sour cream

12 ounces (340 g) uncooked spaghetti noodles, broken in half

1 cup (34 g) low-salt potato chips, crushed

6 ounces (168 g) sharp Cheddar cheese, shredded

1. Add the chicken, stock, and Italian seasoning to the slow cooker.
2. Cover the slow cooker. Cook on LOW for 6 to 8 hours or on HIGH for 3 to 4 hours.
3. Shred the cooked chicken with two forks.
4. Stir in the sour cream and add the spaghetti noodles, pressing the noodles into the broth to allow them to cook.
5. Cover the slow cooker and turn on to HIGH. Cook for about 30 minutes, or until the noodles are done, stirring the noodles once or twice to make sure they cook evenly.
6. Top the casserole with crushed potato chips and shredded cheese and cover once more. Let cook for about 5 minutes so that the cheese can melt.

NOTES: *If you want to add vegetables to this casserole, steam a bag of frozen veggies in the microwave and add them to the crock-pot when you add the noodles.*

PIEROGI AND CHICKEN SAUSAGE BAKE

Serves: 6 to 8 | **Cook Time:** 5 to 6 hours on LOW or 2 to 3 hours on HIGH | **Slow Cooker Size:** 6-quart (5.7-L)

This recipe has a lot of ingredients, but it is very easy to put together and comes out nice and creamy. Chicken sausage is a healthy alternative to beef or pork kielbasa, but you can use those in this recipe, too.

30 ounces (850 g) frozen pierogi

1 cup (100 g) grated
Parmesan cheese

1 small zucchini or yellow
squash, sliced

10 ounces (280 g) frozen peas

12 ounces (340 g) smoked
chicken sausage, thinly sliced
and browned on the stove top

3 cloves garlic, minced

1 tablespoon (15 g) basil paste,
or ¼ cup minced fresh basil, or
1 teaspoon dried basil (see Notes)

4 cups (940 ml) low-sodium chicken
broth, store-bought or homemade
(page 310)

8 ounces (225 g) cream cheese

1½ cups (173 g) shredded
Cheddar cheese, plus more
for optional garnish

Salt and pepper, to taste

1. Add the frozen pierogi to the slow cooker.
2. Add the Parmesan cheese, zucchini, and peas.
3. On the stove top, brown the sliced chicken sausage.
4. Add the sausage, garlic, basil paste, and chicken broth to the slow cooker.
5. Cut the cream cheese into chunks and add to the slow cooker.
6. Sprinkle Cheddar cheese over everything.
7. Cover the slow cooker. Cook on LOW for 5 to 6 hours or on HIGH for 2 to 3 hours, stirring once or twice during the cooking time to help distribute the cream cheese throughout the dish.
8. Add salt and pepper to suit your tastes and serve topped with additional shredded cheese (if desired).

NOTES: Watch your cooking time on this recipe as the pierogi can turn mushy if overcooked. Always cook a recipe for the shortest amount of time given first and cook longer only if needed.

Basil paste can be found in most major grocery stores in the produce section. It is fresh basil turned into a paste and comes in an easy-to-squeeze tube.

KID-FRIENDLY CHEESY BACON RANCH PASTA

Serves: 6 | **Cook Time:** 6 to 8 hours on LOW or 3 to 4 hours on HIGH | **Slow Cooker Size:** 4-quart (3.8-L) or larger

The flavors of cheese, bacon, and ranch are combined in a cheesy pasta dish that the kids love!

1 pound (455 g) boneless skinless chicken breasts, cubed

1 can (10.75 ounces, or 305 g) condensed Cheddar cheese soup

1 packet (28 g) ranch dressing mix, store-bought or homemade (page 318)

½ cup (120 ml) sour cream

2.5 ounces (70 g) real bacon bits

16 ounces (455 g) pasta, such as macaroni, rotini, penne, or cavatappi

FOR SERVING (OPTIONAL):

Bacon bits

Shredded Cheddar cheese

Sliced green onions

1. Add the chicken, Cheddar cheese soup, ranch dressing mix, sour cream, and bacon bits to the bottom of the slow cooker. Mix to combine.

2. Cover the slow cooker. Cook on LOW for 6 to 8 hours or on HIGH for 3 to 4 hours.

3. About 30 minutes before the end of the cooking time for the chicken, cook the pasta on the stove top according to the directions on the package until al dente. Drain the pasta.

4. Serve the chicken and sauce over cooked pasta garnishing with additional bacon bits, Cheddar cheese, or green onions (if desired).

STUPID CHICKEN

Serves: 8 | **Cook Time:** 6 to 8 hours on LOW
Slow Cooker Size: 6-quart (5.7-L)

This recipe has a silly name, but that is just because it is stupidly easy to make. Just five ingredients tossed in the slow cooker and you have dinner on the table!

3–4 (1.4–1.6 kg) pounds boneless skinless chicken breasts

29 ounces (822 g) canned petite diced tomatoes, undrained

1 packet (34 g) savory herb with garlic soup mix, store-bought or homemade (page 318)

16 ounces (455 g) bow-tie pasta

1 cup shredded Parmesan cheese

1. Place the chicken in the slow cooker.

2. Pour in the tomatoes and savory herb with garlic soup mix, stirring the soup mix into the tomatoes.

3. Cover the slow cooker. Cook on LOW for 6 to 8 hours, until the chicken is done.

4. During the last 30 minutes of cooking time, prepare the pasta according to the package directions until al dente. Drain and set aside.

5. Remove the chicken pieces from the slow cooker and shred the chicken into bite-size pieces. Place the shredded meat back to the slow cooker.

6. Add the cooked pasta and cheese to the slow cooker. Mix well and serve.

NOTES: *We like to serve this pasta dish with the pasta mixed into the chicken and sauce right in the slow cooker. But if your family likes the sauce on top of the pasta, go ahead and serve it that way.*

SIMPLE CHICKEN AND SQUASH CASSEROLE

Serves: 6 | **Cook Time:** 4 to 6 hours on LOW | **Slow Cooker Size:** 5-quart (4.7-L) or larger

If you are a gardener, then you know the real struggle of what to do with that abundance of squash and zucchini that you are growing. Even just one or two squash plants yield way more vegetables than you know what to do with. This yummy recipe was invented when Sarah had a bunch of yellow squash that needed to get used up, and she rooted around in her pantry to find the ingredients. Living in a rural area, it is not always easy to just get in the car and drive to the grocery store, so having a well-stocked pantry is essential.

1 medium yellow onion, diced, divided

10.5 ounces (298 g) canned cream of chicken soup

10.5 ounces (298 g) canned cream of mushroom soup

10.5 ounces (298 g) canned cream of celery soup

1 cup (185 g) long-grain or brown rice

4–6 boneless skinless chicken breasts

1 teaspoon garlic and herb seasoning, store-bought or homemade (page 318)

1 small yellow squash (or zucchini), thinly sliced

1. Add half of the chopped onion, canned soups, and uncooked rice in the bottom of the slow cooker.

2. Place the chicken breasts on top of mixture and season with garlic and herb seasoning.

3. Add the other half of the chopped onion and the sliced squash on top of the chicken.

4. Cover the slow cooker. Cook on LOW for 4 to 6 hours, or until the chicken is fully cooked.

NOTES: If you need to stretch this meal out to serve more people, cook more rice on the stove top and serve the chicken and sauce over the rice.

AMERICAN BEEF GOULASH

Serves: 12 to 14 | **Cook Time:** 6 hours on LOW or 3 hours on HIGH | **Slow Cooker Size:** 6-quart (5.7-L)

Don't confuse this goulash recipe with the traditional Hungarian one because this recipe is all-American! Ground beef, corn, some jarred marinara sauce, and seasonings are cooked in the slow cooker, and then cooked pasta and cheese are added at the end. Just like mom used to make!

2 pounds (about 1 kg) lean ground beef, browned and drained

1 medium yellow onion, diced

3 cloves garlic, minced

10 ounces (280 g) canned diced tomatoes with green chilies, undrained

12 ounces (340 g) canned corn kernels, drained

72 ounces (2 kg) jarred marinara sauce, store-bought or homemade (page 313)

2 tablespoons (6 g) Italian seasoning, store-bought or homemade (page 316)

1½ pounds (680 g) macaroni noodles

2 cups (230 g) shredded Cheddar cheese

Salt and pepper, to taste

1. In a medium skillet on the stove top, cook the ground beef, onion, and garlic until the ground beef is cooked through and crumbled. Drain off the excess cooking fat.

2. Add the cooked ground beef mixture to the slow cooker.

3. Add the tomatoes with green chilies, corn, marinara sauce, and Italian seasoning.

4. Give everything a quick stir and cover the slow cooker. Cook on LOW for 6 hours or on HIGH for 3 hours.

5. About 30 minutes before the end of the cooking time (or before you are ready to serve), bring a large pot of water to boil on the stove top. Cook the macaroni pasta according to the package directions until al dente, about 7 minutes.

6. Drain the pasta and carefully add the cooked pasta to the slow cooker. Stir to coat all the pasta with the sauce mixture.

7. Season with salt and pepper to taste.

8. Add the shredded Cheddar cheese right before serving.

NOTES: *This recipe serves a lot of people. But the leftovers can be reheated in the microwave for lunches, and they taste great the next day!*

CLASSIC SLOW COOKER MACARONI AND CHEESE

Serves: 4 | **Cook Time:** 2 to 2½ hours on LOW | **Slow Cooker Size:** 4-quart (3.8-L)

How can you go wrong with macaroni and cheese? Make it as a side dish to serve alongside a meat or as the star of the meal for lunch or dinner. Homemade always tastes better, and because you made it yourself, you know exactly what the ingredients are!

2 cups (186 g) uncooked macaroni pasta

2½ cups (300 g) grated sharp or extra-sharp Cheddar cheese, plus more for optional topping

½ cup (120 g) sour cream

1 can (10.75 ounces, or 305 g) condensed Cheddar cheese soup

1 cup (235 ml) milk

¼ cup (55 g) unsalted butter

3 cloves garlic, finely minced

½ teaspoon ground mustard

½ teaspoon salt

½ teaspoon freshly ground black pepper

1. In a pot on the stove top, cook the macaroni noodles following the directions on the package, until the noodles are slightly undercooked. Drain and set aside.
2. Spray the slow cooker with nonstick cooking spray or line with a slow cooker liner to prevent sticking.
3. Add the Cheddar cheese, sour cream, Cheddar cheese soup, milk, butter, garlic, mustard, salt, and pepper to the slow cooker. Mix everything together.
4. Add the drained pasta to the slow cooker and stir to coat all pasta in the cheese sauce mixture.
5. Cover the slow cooker. Cook on LOW for 2 to 2½ hours, stirring occasionally.
6. Top with additional shredded Cheddar cheese before serving (if desired).

NOTES: *This recipe serves four. You can easily double the ingredients and cook it in a 6-quart (5.7-L) slow cooker for 3 to 3½ hours on LOW.*

HEARTY CHILI MAC

Serves: 4 to 6 | **Cook Time:** 6 to 7 hours on LOW | **Slow Cooker Size:** 5-quart (4.7-L)

Katie was introduced to chili mac back when she was in high school. The mother of one of her friends made it for dinner. She had several teenagers to feed and said that chili mac was an easy yet frugal way to feed all those hungry mouths. Since then, this has been one of her favorites, and it is a recipe she serves her own hungry family on a regular basis.

1 pound (455 g) lean ground beef, cooked and drained

1 medium yellow onion, diced

4 cloves garlic, minced

29 ounces (822 g) canned chili beans in chili sauce

14.5 ounces (411 g) canned diced tomatoes

14.5 ounces (411 g) canned crushed tomatoes

2 cups (475 ml) low-sodium beef broth, store-bought or homemade (page 311)

1 tablespoon (8 g) chili powder

½ teaspoon ground cumin

¼ teaspoon kosher salt

¼ teaspoon freshly ground black pepper

16 ounces (455 g) uncooked macaroni pasta

Shredded Cheddar or Monterey Jack cheese (optional)

1. Add all the ingredients except for the macaroni pasta to the slow cooker and stir well to combine.

2. Cover the slow cooker. Cook on LOW for 6 to 7 hours.

3. Add in the uncooked pasta and stir to coat all the macaroni in the chili sauce mixture.

4. Cover the slow cooker. Cook for an additional 30 minutes on LOW, or until the pasta is al dente.

5. Top individual servings of chili mac with Cheddar or Monterey Jack cheese (if desired).

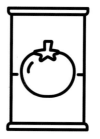

CREAMY CHEESY CHICKEN AND BROCCOLI BAKE

Serves: 4 | **Cook Time:** 6 to 8 hours on LOW | **Slow Cooker Size:** 6-quart (5.7-L)

This simple recipe can be added to your list of super easy and tasty slow cooker dishes that your family will love. The ingredients are simple, and you can serve this tasty chicken over rice or noodles.

20 ounces (567 g) canned cream of chicken soup

¾ cup (175 ml) milk

½ teaspoon garlic powder

1–2 pounds (455 g to about 1 kg) boneless skinless chicken breasts

16 ounces (455 g) frozen broccoli

1 cup shredded Cheddar cheese

1 pound (16 ounces) uncooked pasta or 1 to 2 cups uncooked rice

Salt and pepper, to taste

1. Mix the soup, milk, and garlic powder in a medium mixing bowl to create a sauce.
2. Add half of the sauce to the slow cooker.
3. Add the chicken and frozen broccoli on top of the sauce and cover with the remaining sauce mixture.
4. Sprinkle the top with the shredded cheese.
5. Cover the slow cooker. Cook on LOW for 6 to 8 hours, or until the chicken is cooked through.
6. About 30 minutes at the end of the cooking time, prepare your rice or noodles on the stove top according to the package directions.
7. Season with salt and pepper to taste.
8. Serve the creamy chicken on top of the rice or noodles.

NOTES: *You can use other types of frozen vegetables in this easy dish. Feel free to change the recipe up to use what you have in your freezer.*

ITALIAN STUFFED PASTA SHELLS WITH SPINACH

Serves: 4 to 6 | **Cook Time:** 6 to 8 hours on LOW or 3 to 4 hours on HIGH | **Slow Cooker Size:** 5-quart (4.7-L)

Stuffed shells can be made a variety of ways. This is the classic recipe made with ricotta and spinach and topped with marinara sauce. Pair with a side of steamed vegetables or fresh garden salad, and serve it with garlic bread for a family favorite.

12 ounces (340 g) frozen chopped spinach, thawed and squeezed of excess liquid

12 ounces (340 g) ricotta cheese

3 cups (345 g) shredded mozzarella cheese, divided

½ cup shredded or grated Parmesan cheese

2 cloves garlic, minced

1 tablespoon (3 g) Italian seasoning, store-bought or homemade (page 316)

28 jumbo uncooked pasta shells

48 ounces (1.4 kg) jarred marinara sauce, store-bought or homemade (page 313)

1. In a medium mixing bowl, mix together the spinach, ricotta cheese, 2 cups of the mozzarella cheese, Parmesan cheese, garlic, and Italian seasoning.
2. Fill each jumbo pasta shell with the ricotta mixture. Each shell should hold about 1 heaping tablespoon of the ricotta cheese mixture.
3. Pour half of the marinara sauce in the bottom of the slow cooker.
4. Add half of the stuffed shells to the slow cooker in a single layer.
5. Spoon half of the remaining marinara sauce on top of the first layer of shells.
6. Add another layer of stuffed shells and top that layer with the last of your marinara sauce.
7. Cover the slow cooker. Cook on LOW for 6 to 8 hours or on HIGH for 3 to 4 hours, or until the shells are cooked and tender.
8. Top with the remaining 1 cup of mozzarella cheese and serve.

EASY PEASY BAKED SPAGHETTI

Serves: 8 | **Cook Time:** 3 hours on LOW | **Slow Cooker Size:** 5-quart (4.7-L) or larger

Ground beef is simmered away with your favorite store-bought marinara sauce along with some additional seasonings. Then add in al dente pasta along with some mozzarella and cream cheese. Let it cook just a little bit more for an amazing crock-pot baked spaghetti recipe everyone in the family will adore!

32 ounces (905 g) marinara sauce, store-bought or homemade (page 313)

3 cloves garlic, minced

½ teaspoon dried parsley

½ teaspoon dried rosemary

1 pound (455 g) lean ground beef, cooked and drained

16 ounces (455 g) cooked al dente spaghetti pasta

4 ounces (115 g) cream cheese, cubed

2 cups (225 g) shredded mozzarella cheese

Grated Parmesan cheese (optional)

Fresh chopped parsley (optional)

1. Add the sauce, garlic, spices, and cooked hamburger to the slow cooker. Stir to combine.
2. Cover the slow cooker. Cook on LOW for 2 hours.
3. Add in the cooked spaghetti noodles and stir well to coat all the noodles evenly with the sauce.
4. Place the cream cheese cubes on top of the spaghetti noodles and sauce and cover the slow cooker. Cook for an additional 30 minutes on LOW.
5. Stir well to evenly distribute the melted cream cheese throughout the pasta.
6. Add the mozzarella cheese on top of the pasta and cover the slow cooker. Cook for another 30 minutes, or until the cheese is melted.
7. Serve and enjoy! Garnish with some Parmesan cheese and parsley (if desired).

SIMPLE RAVIOLI CASSEROLE

Serves: 6 to 8 | **Cook Time:** 6½ to 7¾ hours on LOW | **Slow Cooker Size:** 5-quart (4.7-L) or larger

Many grocery stores now carry different flavors of frozen ravioli, and you can switch up the flavors of this casserole a little bit depending on what flavor of ravioli you choose. Cheese-stuffed ravioli is going to work great, too!

1 pound (455 g) lean ground beef

1 medium yellow onion, diced

1 clove garlic, minced

14.5 ounces (411 g) canned tomato sauce

14.5 ounces (411 g) canned stewed tomatoes

1 teaspoon dried oregano

1 teaspoon Italian seasoning, store-bought or homemade (page 316)

¼ teaspoon kosher salt

¼ teaspoon freshly ground black pepper

12 ounces (340 g) frozen chopped spinach, thawed

16 ounces (455 g) frozen ravioli

½ cup shredded Parmesan cheese

1½ cups (175 g) shredded mozzarella cheese, divided

1. In a medium frying pan set over medium-high heat on the stove top, brown and crumble the ground beef along with the onion and garlic. Drain and add to the slow cooker.

2. Add the tomato sauce, stewed tomatoes, oregano, Italian seasoning, salt, and pepper.

3. Cover the slow cooker. Cook on LOW for 6½ to 7¾ hours.

4. Add the spinach, ravioli, Parmesan cheese, and 1 cup (115 g) of the mozzarella cheese and stir to combine.

5. Cover and cook for an additional 30 to 45 minutes, or until the ravioli is cooked through.

6. Top with the remaining ½ cup (60 g) of mozzarella cheese and serve.

ITALIAN TOMATO AND SPINACH PASTA

Serves: 6 | **Cook Time:** 3 hours on LOW plus 30 minutes on HIGH | **Slow Cooker Size:** 6-quart (5.7-L)

Ground beef and Italian sausage combine together in this creamy pasta dish that is healthy for you. Spinach and tomatoes give it great flavor, too!

1 pound (455 g) lean ground beef

1 pound (455 g) Italian sausage

1 medium yellow onion, diced

1 clove garlic, minced

28 ounces (794 g) canned diced tomatoes

1 teaspoon Italian seasoning, store-bought or homemade (page 316)

¼ teaspoon kosher salt

10 ounces (280 g) frozen spinach, thawed

16 ounces (455 g) cooked al dente rotini pasta

2 cups (225 g) shredded mozzarella cheese

8 ounces (225 g) cream cheese, cubed

1. In a large skillet set on medium-high heat on the stove top, cook and crumble the ground beef and Italian sausage along with the onion and garlic, until the meat is cooked through and no longer pink. Drain and add to the slow cooker.

2. Add the diced tomatoes, Italian seasoning, and salt.

3. Cover the slow cooker. Cook on LOW for 3 hours.

4. Thirty minutes before serving, add in the spinach, cooked pasta, mozzarella cheese, and cream cheese. Stir to combine.

5. Cover the slow cooker. Cook on HIGH for 30 minutes.

CHEESY MOZZARELLA PESTO CHICKEN PASTA

Serves: 4 to 6 | **Cook Time:** 5¼ to 6¼ hours on LOW | **Slow Cooker Size:** 5-quart (4.7-L) or larger

The whole family will love this easy and tasty dish. The pesto adds a ton of flavor to the chicken and pasta. Pair it with a side dish of your favorite steamed vegetables or a salad for a complete meal!

1 pound (455 g) boneless skinless chicken breasts or thighs

½ teaspoon salt

¼ teaspoon freshly ground black pepper

1 cup (260 g) pesto, store-bought or homemade (page 315)

½ fresh lemon, squeezed

¼ cup (55 g) unsalted butter

16 ounces (455 g) cooked al dente rotini pasta

2 cups (225 g) shredded mozzarella cheese

½ cup shredded Parmesan cheese

1. Add the chicken to the slow cooker and season with salt and pepper.
2. Spread the pesto over the chicken and squeeze the juice of one-half of a lemon over the chicken and pesto.
3. Cut the butter into pats and place on top of the chicken.
4. Cover the slow cooker. Cook on LOW for 5 to 6 hours.
5. When the chicken is cooked, shred the meat with two forks into bite-size pieces. Add the chicken back to the slow cooker.
6. Add the cooked rotini pasta, mozzarella cheese, and Parmesan cheese to the slow cooker. Stir to combine.
7. Cover the slow cooker. Cook for an additional 15 minutes, or until the mozzarella is melted.

EASY CHICKEN SPAGHETTI

Serves: 6 | **Cook Time:** 6 to 8 hours on LOW or 4 to 6 hours on HIGH | **Slow Cooker Size:** 6-quart (5.7-L)

Seasoned chicken and frozen broccoli is simmered away for hours in a jar of your favorite marinara sauce. For this dish, you can also use cauliflower or a combination of broccoli and cauliflower. Serve it over spaghetti noodles for a dinner the whole family will adore.

4 boneless skinless chicken breasts

¼ teaspoon garlic powder

¼ teaspoon kosher salt

¼ teaspoon freshly ground black pepper

24 ounces (680 g) chunky marinara sauce, store-bought or homemade (page 313)

16 ounces (455 g) frozen broccoli and/or cauliflower

1 large yellow onion, diced

16 ounces (455 g) cooked spaghetti pasta

1 cup (115 g) shredded mozzarella cheese

1. Place the chicken breasts in the slow cooker.
2. Season the chicken with garlic powder, salt, and pepper.
3. Layer the frozen vegetables and onion on top of the chicken.
4. Pour the marinara sauce over everything.
5. Cover the slow cooker. Cook on LOW for 6 to 8 hours or on HIGH for 4 to 6 hours.
6. Thirty minutes before the end of the cooking time, prepare the spaghetti pasta on the stove top according to the directions on the package.
7. While the pasta is cooking, shred the chicken with two forks.
8. Serve the chicken and sauce over cooked pasta, topping each serving with shredded cheese.

NOTES: *Feel free to use other frozen vegetables to switch things up.*

CREAMY ALFREDO CHICKEN LASAGNA

Serves: 6 to 8 | **Cook Time:** 2½ to 3 hours on LOW
Slow Cooker Size: 3½-quart (3.3-L) casserole or 6-quart (5.7-L) oval

This lovely Alfredo casserole takes advantage of jarred Alfredo sauce and rotisserie chicken from your deli. You can either buy a whole rotisserie chicken and pull the meat off the bones yourself or look for packages of rotisserie chicken meat that the deli department has already pulled for you. (If you prepare your own, reserve the bones to make your own homemade chicken broth or stock.)

15 ounces (425 g) ricotta cheese

3 cups (345 g) shredded mozzarella cheese, divided

1 cup (100 g) grated Parmesan cheese

1 large egg

30 ounces (850 g) jarred Alfredo sauce

½ cup (120 ml) water

1 teaspoon Italian seasoning, store-bought or homemade (page 316)

1 clove garlic, minced

9–12 uncooked oven-ready lasagna noodles

2–3 cups (280–420 g) store-bought rotisserie chicken, cubed

1. In a medium mixing bowl, mix together the ricotta cheese, 2 cups (230 g) of the mozzarella cheese, Parmesan cheese, and egg.
2. In another bowl, mix together the Alfredo sauce, water, Italian seasoning, and garlic.
3. In the bottom of the slow cooker, spread ¼ of the Alfredo sauce.
4. Arrange 3 to 4 lasagna noodles on top of the sauce, breaking noodles to fit if needed.
5. Spread ⅓ of the diced rotisserie chicken on top of the lasagna noodles.
6. Spread ⅓ of the ricotta cheese mixture on top of the chicken.
7. Repeat the layers two more times, making sure the Alfredo sauce covers the edges of the noodles so that they don't dry out while cooking.
8. The top layer should be Alfredo sauce.
9. Sprinkle the remaining 1 cup (115 g) of mozzarella cheese over the top.
10. Cover the slow cooker. Cook on LOW for 2½ to 3 hours, or until the noodles are tender.

NOTES: *Garlic bread and a side salad make this creamy lasagna a complete meal.*

CHEESY RICOTTA STUFFED LASAGNA ROLL-UPS

Serves: 4 to 6 | **Cook Time:** 4 to 6 hours on LOW | **Slow Cooker Size:** 5- to 6-quart (4.7- to 5.7-L)

Cooked lasagna noodles are rolled up with a filling of cheesy ricotta and then simmered away in your favorite marinara sauce. Top with even more cheese for a dish that is full of flavor!

1 pound (455 g) uncooked lasagna noodles (about 14 to 15 noodles)

3 cups (345 g) shredded mozzarella cheese, divided

15 ounces (425 g) ricotta cheese

½ cup shredded Parmesan cheese

2 large eggs

48 ounces (1.4 kg) jarred marinara sauce, store-bought or homemade (page 313)

1. On the stove top, cook the lasagna noodles until they are slightly undercooked according to the directions on the package.

2. Drain the noodles and then rinse in cool water to stop the cooking. Set aside.

3. In a medium mixing bowl, mix together 2 cups (230 g) of mozzarella cheese, ricotta cheese, Parmesan cheese, and eggs until combined. Set aside.

4. Take one noodle at a time and lay it flat. Spoon 1 heaping tablespoon full of the ricotta cheese mixture onto the bottom half of the noodles and roll the noodles around the cheese mixture.

5. Pour half of the marinara sauce in the bottom of the slow cooker.

6. Layer the rolled lasagna noodles on top of the marinara sauce until you have no more noodles left.

7. Pour the other half of the marinara sauce over the noodles.

8. Cover the slow cooker. Cook on LOW for 4 to 6 hours.

9. Thirty minutes before serving, sprinkle the remaining 1 cup (115 g) of mozzarella cheese on top. Cover and cook for 30 minutes and serve.

TRADITIONAL LAYERED LASAGNA

Serves: 10 | **Cook Time:** 6 to 8 hours on LOW
Slow Cooker Size: 3½-quart (3.3-L) casserole OR 6-quart (5.7-L) oval or larger

This traditional lasagna is the same recipe Heidi's Italian step-grandmother taught her how to make. It is filled with ricotta and mozzarella cheese, sweet Italian sausage, and a ton of love! I usually serve this with a nice fresh garden salad along with some homemade bread sticks or garlic bread.

2 pounds (about 1 kg) sweet Italian sausage

1 medium yellow onion, diced

3 cloves garlic, minced

15 ounces (425 g) ricotta cheese

1 teaspoon dried oregano, crushed

1 teaspoon dried basil, crushed

1 teaspoon dried parsley

1 large egg

1 cup (100 g) grated Parmesan cheese

48 ounces (1.4 kg) marinara sauce, store-bought or homemade (page 313)

9 ounces (255 g) no-cook lasagna noodles

4 cups (460 g) shredded mozzarella cheese

1. In a large skillet on the stove top over medium-high heat, cook and crumble the Italian sausage, onion, and garlic until the sausage is no longer pink. Drain and set aside.

2. In a medium mixing bowl, stir together the ricotta cheese, oregano, basil, parsley, egg, and Parmesan cheese with a sturdy spoon or spatula until the egg is incorporated. Set aside.

3. Add 1½ cups (368 g) of the marinara sauce to the bottom of the slow cooker. Spread it to completely cover the bottom of the dish.

4. Lay down a single layer of the uncooked lasagna noodles.

5. On top of the lasagna noodles, spread half of the ricotta cheese mixture, making sure it is evenly distributed.

6. Sprinkle a layer of mozzarella cheese on top of the ricotta cheese.

7. Add a layer of the sausage, onion, and garlic mixture.

8. Add a layer of marinara sauce.

9. Repeat the layers: noodles, ricotta cheese, mozzarella cheese, sausage, sauce, ending with a layer of sauce and then a light layer of mozzarella cheese.

10. Cover the slow cooker. Cook on LOW for 6 to 8 hours, or until the noodles are cooked through.

NOTES: *This recipe is best cooked in one of the new casserole slow cookers because it comes out looking just like traditional oven-baked lasagna. But you can cook it in a large 6-quart (5.7-L) or larger oval slow cooker, too. You will just need to break up the lasagna noodles to fit the slow cooker.*

CHEESE-STUFFED BEEFY MANICOTTI

Serves: 4 to 6 | **Cook Time:** 2¼ to 3¼ hours on HIGH | **Slow Cooker Size:** 5-quart (4.7-L) or larger

Cooking pasta in the crock-pot is possible! These manicotti shells are stuffed with a cheesy filling, and they make a great meal when served with crusty bread and vegetables or a salad.

2½ cups (675 g) cottage cheese or ricotta cheese

2½ cups (290 g) shredded mozzarella cheese, divided

1½ cups shredded Parmesan cheese

2 teaspoons (2 g) Italian seasoning, store-bought or homemade (page 316)

¼ teaspoon kosher salt

¼ teaspoon freshly ground black pepper

1 pound (455 g) lean ground beef, browned and drained

48 ounces (1.4 kg) jarred marinara sauce, store-bought or homemade (page 313)

8 ounces (225 g) uncooked manicotti pasta

14.5 ounces (411 g) diced tomatoes, drained

1. In a medium mixing bowl, mix together the cottage cheese, 1½ cups (175 g) of mozzarella cheese, Parmesan cheese, Italian seasoning, salt, and pepper. Set aside.

2. Place the cheese filling mixture in a piping bag (or a gallon-size zippered freezer bag with one corner cut off).

3. Pour half of the marinara sauce in the bottom of the slow cooker.

4. Pipe each manicotti noodle with the cheese mixture and place in the slow cooker, nestling each noodle in the sauce.

5. Cover the filled noodles with the remaining half of the marinara sauce, drained tomatoes, and browned ground beef.

6. Cover the slow cooker. Cook on HIGH for 2 to 3 hours, or until the pasta is cooked through.

7. Top with the remaining 1 cup (115 g) of mozzarella cheese, cover, and cook for an additional 15 minutes until the cheese is melted.

VEGETARIAN MEXICAN QUINOA CASSEROLE

Serves: 8 to 10 | **Cook Time:** 2½ to 3 hours on HIGH | **Slow Cooker Size:** 6-quart (5.7-L)

Healthy quinoa and yummy Mexican flavors combine in this healthier-for-you casserole. Red, yellow, and green bell peppers add pretty colors to this yummy dish. Spoon some of the casserole into bowls and top with fresh salsa or avocado—or both!

2¼ cups (530 ml) vegetable broth, store-bought or homemade (page 312)

1 cup (173 g) uncooked quinoa

14.5 ounces (411 g) canned diced tomatoes, undrained

15 ounces (425 g) canned black beans, drained and rinsed

15 ounces (425 g) canned corn kernels, drained

1 small to medium red bell pepper, seeded and chopped

1 small to medium yellow bell pepper, seeded and chopped

1 small to medium green bell pepper, seeded and chopped

1 small yellow onion, diced

3 cloves garlic, minced

1 tablespoon (8 g) chili powder

¼–½ teaspoon crushed red pepper flakes

1 teaspoon kosher salt

1 teaspoon freshly ground black pepper

1 teaspoon ground cumin

1 teaspoon dried oregano, crushed

1 cup (115 g) shredded Mexican cheese

TOPPINGS:

Salsa fresca

Diced avocado

Sour cream

Fresh cilantro

1. Add the vegetable broth, quinoa, and diced tomatoes to the slow cooker. Stir to combine.

2. Add the remaining ingredients except for the cheese and stir to mix together.

3. Cover the slow cooker. Cook on HIGH for 2½ to 3 hours, or until the quinoa is cooked and the casserole is very thick.

4. Add the shredded Mexican cheese to the top of the casserole. Cover and cook for an additional 5 to 10 minutes, or until the cheese is melted.

5. Top bowls of casserole with your favorite toppings, such as salsa fresca, avocados, sour cream, cilantro, etc.

FIESTA CHICKEN, BEAN, AND RICE CASSEROLE

Serves: 6 to 8 | **Cook Time:** 7½ to 8½ hours on LOW | **Slow Cooker Size:** 6-quart (5.7-L)

This Southwestern casserole is full of great flavors! My family loves to have multiple taco-type toppings so that they can individualize their plates with diced avocado, sour cream, sliced black olives, salsa, shredded lettuce, cilantro . . . . It all tastes good on this fun casserole!

1½ pounds (680 g) boneless skinless chicken breasts

29 ounces (822 g) canned diced tomatoes

15 ounces (425 g) canned tomato sauce

14.5 ounces (411 g) canned whole kernel corn

15 ounces (425 g) canned black beans, drained and rinsed

1 packet (28 g) low-sodium taco seasoning mix, store-bought or homemade (page 317)

2 cups (475 ml) water

1½ cups (278 g) long-grain rice, boiled on the stove top for 5 minutes before adding

Shredded Cheddar cheese

FOR SERVING:

Tortilla chips

1. Spray the slow cooker with nonstick cooking spray, if desired, to help clean up later.
2. Add the chicken, tomatoes, tomato sauce, corn, black beans, and taco seasoning mix to the slow cooker. Mix together to combine.
3. Cover the slow cooker. Cook on LOW for 7 to 8 hours, or until the chicken is cooked through. Pull the chicken out and shred with two forks. Place the shredded meat back in the slow cooker.
4. About 30 minutes before the end of the cooking time, place the water and rice in a large saucepan. Bring to a boil, simmer for 5 minutes, and then drain off the excess water. Fluff the rice with a fork, add it to the slow cooker, and stir to combine.
5. Cover the slow cooker and continue cooking on LOW for 30 additional minutes.
6. Top with cheese and serve with tortilla chips.

NOTES: *You can also skip the tortilla chips and use the casserole as a yummy burrito filling in flour tortillas.*

4

CHICKEN, TURKEY, AND GAME BIRDS

MAPLE SMOKEHOUSE CHICKEN

Serves: 8 to 10 | **Cook Time:** 6 to 7 hours on LOW or 3 to 4 hours on HIGH
Slow Cooker Size: 6-quart (5.7-L) or larger

This chicken recipe has a unique and smoky flavor that comes from a little bit of liquid smoke. (Liquid smoke can be found in most grocery stores near the spices and seasonings.) Apple cider vinegar tenderizes the chicken legs, and it imparts great flavor and tang. You can broil the chicken legs after they are done cooking in the slow cooker to get them a little bit crispy. If you don't have the time or patience to do this extra step, you can just skip it!

5 pounds (2.3 kg) chicken drumsticks and/or bone-in chicken thighs.

1 teaspoon roasted garlic and herb seasoning

1 cup (235 ml) apple cider vinegar

1 tablespoon (15 ml) hot sauce

1 tablespoon (20 g) real maple syrup

½ teaspoon liquid smoke

¼ cup (38 g) brown sugar

1 tablespoon (18 g) salt

1 tablespoon (7 g) ground paprika

1 teaspoon freshly ground black pepper

1. Spray the bottom of the slow cooker with nonstick cooking spray, if desired, to help with cleanup later.
2. Season the chicken pieces with the roasted garlic and herb seasoning on all sides and place them in the bottom of the slow cooker.
3. In a medium mixing bowl, mix together the apple cider vinegar, hot sauce, maple syrup, and liquid smoke.
4. Add the brown sugar, salt, paprika, and black pepper. Stir to create the sauce.
5. Pour the sauce mixture over the chicken.
6. Cover the slow cooker. Cook on LOW for 6 to 7 hours or on HIGH for 3 to 4 hours, or until the chicken is cooked through.
7. The chicken is ready to eat as is, but you can broil the chicken to impart a bit of extra browning and crispiness to the skin.

TO BROIL:

1. Set your oven to the broil setting.
2. Carefully remove the chicken from the slow cooker with tongs and place it on a rimmed baking sheet covered in parchment paper or aluminum foil.
3. Place the chicken under the broiler for about 3 minutes per side, turning the baking sheet halfway during cooking to make sure it cooks evenly and doesn't burn.
4. Remove the chicken and serve.

PERFECT SLOW-ROASTED HERBED CHICKEN

Serves: 4 | **Cook Time:** 2 to 3 hours on HIGH | **Slow Cooker Size:** 5-quart (4.7-L) or larger

No one will believe that this easy recipe was cooked in the slow cooker! It's healthy, flavorful, and moist! Serve the roasted chicken for dinner with your favorite sides, or use the cooked meat in any recipe that calls for cooked rotisserie chicken!

1 tablespoon (15 ml) olive oil

1 teaspoon ground paprika

1 teaspoon garlic powder

½ teaspoon seasoned salt

½ teaspoon dried thyme

½ teaspoon dried basil

½ teaspoon freshly ground black pepper

½ teaspoon liquid browning (optional)

4 whole boneless skinless chicken breasts

1. In a small bowl, mix together the olive oil, spices, and liquid browning sauce (if desired).

2. Rub the spice mixture all over the chicken. Place the seasoned chicken in the slow cooker.

3. Cover the slow cooker. Cook on HIGH for 2 to 3 hours, or until the chicken is cooked through.

NOTES: *Liquid browning can be found in most grocery stores near the spices, herbs, and other seasonings. This ingredient is optional, but it does impart a nice roasted brown color to the chicken as well as a little bit of extra flavor.*

WHOLE ROASTED ROSEMARY CHICKEN

Serves: 6 to 8 | **Cook Time:** 7 to 8 hours on LOW | **Slow Cooker Size:** 6-quart (5.7-L) or larger

With the amazing aroma of fresh rosemary and thyme, this moist, tender whole chicken will be a fantastic meal. Be sure to pick a chicken that will fit in your slow cooker!

SPECIAL EQUIPMENT:

Heavy-duty aluminum foil

Twine

1 whole (4–5 pound, or 1.8–2.3 kg) young whole chicken, defrosted

2 small yellow onions, quartered

1½ cups (195 g) baby carrots

1½ tablespoons garlic and herb seasoning, store-bought or homemade (page 318)

1 tablespoon (15 g) kosher salt

2 teaspoons (4 g) freshly ground black pepper

2 teaspoons (5 g) ground paprika

1–2 teaspoons olive oil

4 fresh rosemary sprigs

2 fresh thyme sprigs

NOTES: *If you want crispy chicken skin, you can place your whole chicken under the broiler for about 4 to 5 minutes just to brown it up a little bit. However, the paprika in the herb rub does give the chicken a nice color, so you may not find this step necessary.*

1. Cut two pieces of heavy-duty aluminum foil to approximately 26 inches (66 cm) long. Fold each piece of foil several times until you have strips that are about 3 inches (7.5 cm) wide. Place the strips in the bottom of the slow cooker making sure that the ends protrude out the top. These strips will be used to help you lift the roasted chicken out of the slow cooker.

2. Place the onions and baby carrots in the bottom of the slow cooker on top of the foil strips, pushing the onions around the edges so there is room for your whole chicken.

3. Remove the neck and giblets from inside of the chicken. Dispose of them or reserve them to make broth for another recipe.

4. Tie the legs together with the twine.

5. Place the chicken in the slow cooker with the legs at the top of the slow cooker.

6. In a small bowl, mix together the roasted garlic and herb seasoning, salt, pepper, and paprika to create a rub.

7. With your hands massage the olive oil into the skin of the chicken and then rub the spice mixture all over the skin of the chicken.

8. Add the rosemary and thyme sprigs on top of the chicken, placing them as flat as possible on the skin of the chicken, and tucking them in the wings to hold them in place if necessary.

9. Cover the slow cooker. Cook on LOW for 7 to 8 hours, or until the chicken is cooked and the internal temperature of the breast meat reads 165°F (74°C) on an instant-read meat thermometer.

10. Carefully remove the sprigs of herbs and discard them.

11. Place a serving platter next to your slow cooker. Using the foil handles to help, lift the whole chicken out of the slow cooker and place it on your serving platter.

12. Lift out the onions and carrots from the slow cooker with a slotted spoon and place them around the chicken on the platter.

13. Remove the twine from the legs and serve.

SIMPLE GARLIC–BROWN SUGAR CHICKEN

Serves: 6 | **Cook Time:** 2 to 4 hours on LOW | **Slow Cooker Size:** 5-quart (4.7-L) or larger

This delicious recipe marries the savory flavors of garlic and chicken with the sweetness of brown sugar. It comes out moist and tender. Serve the chicken straight out of the slow cooker over rice for an easy dinner that is full of flavor the whole family will love! Just four simple ingredients!

2 tablespoons (30 ml) olive oil

4 cloves garlic, minced

½ cup (75 g) brown sugar

2 pounds (about 1 kg) boneless skinless chicken breasts, cut into bite-size pieces

FOR SERVING:

Cooked white or brown rice

1. In a large skillet, heat the olive oil and minced garlic. Cook for a minute or two, just until the garlic starts to turn translucent but not browned.
2. Add in brown sugar and heat until the brown sugar has melted.
3. Add the chicken to a bowl and pour the garlic–brown sugar mixture over it.
4. Add the chicken and cover the slow cooker. Cook on LOW for 2 to 4 hours.
5. Serve over hot cooked white or brown rice.

FREEZER MEAL INSTRUCTIONS: Follow steps 1 through 3 above. Place everything in a gallon-size zippered freezer bag, and squish out as much air as possible before zipping closed. Label your bag with the name of the dish and cooking instructions.

TO COOK THE FREEZER MEAL: Place the frozen meal in the refrigerator to thaw. Pour the contents of the bag into the cooker and cook the recipe per the directions beginning at step 4.

SWEET AND ZESTY HONEY-N-LIME CHICKEN

Serves: 6 | **Cook Time:** 4 to 5 hours on LOW | **Slow Cooker Size:** 6-quart (5.7-L)

This yummy recipe is one that Sarah's family really enjoys a lot, and she has found multiple ways to use the chicken meat in different kinds of meals. Because this recipe can be made into a freezer meal, you can make up several batches at once and have them ready to go on days where you know you are going to have a busy day. Just pop the freezer meal in the slow cooker early in the day and come home to the main part of dinner done and ready to go. All you have to do is shred the chicken and decide how to serve it. Sarah's family really likes it served over steamed brown or white rice, or try using it for tacos, burritos, or quesadillas.

4–5 boneless skinless chicken breasts

15 ounces (425 g) canned black beans, drained and rinsed

½ cup (170 g) honey

¼ cup (60 ml) low-sodium chicken broth, store-bought or homemade (page 310)

2 fresh limes, juiced and zested

3 cloves garlic, minced

½ teaspoon salt

1. Add the chicken and the black beans to the slow cooker.
2. In a small bowl, pour the honey, chicken broth, lime zest, lime juice, garlic, and salt. Whisk until combined. Pour over the chicken and beans.
3. Cover the slow cooker. Cook on LOW for 4 to 5 hours.
4. Remove the chicken pieces from the slow cooker and shred the meat. Add the shredded meat back to the slow cooker and mix to combine.

FREEZER MEAL INSTRUCTIONS: Add the chicken and beans to a gallon-size freezer bag. Mix together the sauce mixture and add it to the bag. Squish the contents of the bag to mix everything together a little bit. Lay the bag flat, remove as much excess air as possible, and seal the bag. Label the bag with the name of the recipe, ingredients, date, and cooking instructions.

TO COOK THE FREEZER MEAL: Thaw the freezer meal bag in the refrigerator. Pour the contents of the bag into the cooker and cook the recipe per the directions beginning at step 2.

CHICKEN AND MUSHROOMS WITH FRESH THYME

Serves: 4 to 6 | **Cook Time:** 6 to 7 hours on LOW or 3 to 4 hours on HIGH | **Slow Cooker Size:** 6-quart (5.7-L)

A little slicing and dicing of the mushrooms and vegetables are all this easy yet elegant recipe needs. We used a combination of our favorite mushrooms in this recipe, but feel free to use your favorite. This chicken is perfect served over pasta for a dinner that is simple and satisfying.

4–6 ounces (115–168 g) white button mushrooms, sliced

4–6 ounces (115–168 g) shiitake mushrooms, sliced

4–6 ounces (115–168 g) crimini mushrooms, sliced

4–6 ounces (115–168 g) oyster mushrooms, sliced

1 medium onion, diced

1 medium carrots, peeled and diced

¼ cup (14 g) sundried tomatoes

¾ cup (175 ml) low-sodium chicken stock, store-bought or homemade (page 310) ¼ cup (60 ml) dry white wine or chicken broth

3 tablespoons (30 g) quick-cooking tapioca

1½ teaspoons minced fresh thyme leaves

½ teaspoon garlic salt

½ teaspoon freshly ground black pepper

3 pounds (1.4 kg) skinless, bone-in chicken thighs or drumsticks

FOR SERVING:

Cooked pasta

Parmesan cheese

1. Place all the ingredients except the chicken in the slow cooker. Stir to combine.
2. Place the chicken on top of the mushroom mixture.
3. Cover the slow cooker. Cook on LOW for 6 to 7 hours or on HIGH for 3 to 4 hours.
4. Serve the chicken over cooked pasta and garnish with Parmesan cheese.

HONEY GARLIC CHICKEN AND VEGGIES

Serves: 4 to 6 | **Cook Time:** 6½ to 7½ hours on LOW
Slow Cooker Size: 3½-quart (3.3-L) casserole or 6-quart (5.7-L) oval

This simple recipe is a complete meal cooked right in your slow cooker. Chicken thighs come out tender and the potatoes, carrots, and green beans provide healthy vegetables. It is all simmered in a delicious honey garlic sauce. So good!

4–6 whole bone-in skin-on chicken thighs

6–8 baby red potatoes, halved

6 medium carrots, peeled and cut into 1-inch (2.5-cm) chunks

1 pound (455 g) fresh green beans, ends trimmed

½ cup (120 ml) low-sodium soy sauce

½ cup (170 g) honey

¼ cup (60 g) ketchup

2 cloves garlic, minced

1 teaspoon dried basil

¼ teaspoon crushed red pepper flakes

¼ teaspoon freshly ground black pepper

1. Place the chicken thighs, potatoes, and carrots in the slow cooker.
2. In a small mixing bowl, mix together the remaining ingredients to create the sauce.
3. Pour the sauce mixture over everything in the slow cooker.
4. Cover the slow cooker. Cook on LOW for 6 to 7 hours, or until the potatoes and carrots are tender.
5. Add the green beans and mix them into the slow cooker.
6. Cover the slow cooker. Cook for an additional 30 minutes, until they are cooked yet still slightly crisp.

BROWN SUGAR AND BALSAMIC GLAZED CHICKEN

Serves: 4 to 6 | **Cook Time:** 4 to 6 hours on LOW | **Slow Cooker Size:** 5-quart (4.7-L) or larger

Whole chicken breasts are simmered away in the slow cooker in a sauce that turns into a glaze right in the cooker. In this easy no-fuss recipe, the balsamic vinegar adds tang and the brown sugar adds sweetness, while the onion and garlic round out the flavors.

4–6 boneless skinless chicken breasts or thighs

¼ cup (60 ml) balsamic vinegar

¼ cup (38 g) brown sugar

¼ cup (60 ml) water

1 small yellow onion, minced

2–3 cloves garlic, minced

1 teaspoon ground mustard powder

1 tablespoon (8 g) cornstarch

Salt and pepper, to taste

1. Spray the slow cooker with nonstick cooking spray or line with a slow cooker liner, if desired, to help with cleanup later.

2. Place the chicken in the bottom of the slow cooker.

3. In a small bowl, mix together the balsamic vinegar, brown sugar, water, onion, garlic, mustard powder, and cornstarch until combined and the cornstarch is dissolved. Pour over the chicken.

4. Cover the slow cooker. Cook on LOW for 4 to 6 hours, stirring occasionally to distribute the glaze.

5. Season with salt and pepper to taste before serving.

NOTES: Some brands of chicken contain more water, so when they cook, they tend to make a dish a little bit watery. If you find that your chicken has released a lot of excess liquid and the sauce is not turning into a glaze, simply remove the chicken from the slow cooker and pour the cooking liquid in a saucepan. Whisk together another tablespoon of cornstarch with a ¼ cup (60 ml) of cold water to make a slurry. Whisk the slurry into the cooking liquid in the pan and simmer on medium heat until the sauce thickens.

ALOHA PINEAPPLE CHICKEN

Serves: 6 | **Cook Time:** 4 to 6 hours on LOW | **Slow Cooker Size:** 6-quart (5.7-L)

Make this delicious recipe in your slow cooker today or prep ahead for a quick-and-easy crock-pot freezer meal. Your family will love the sweet and tangy chicken served over rice!

3 whole boneless skinless chicken breasts

10 ounces (280 g) canned pineapple chunks, drained

½ cup (120 ml) pineapple juice

½ cup (100 g) granulated sugar

½ cup (120 ml) white vinegar

3 cloves garlic, minced

2 tablespoons (30 ml) low-sodium soy sauce

FOR SERVING:
Steamed white or brown rice

1. Add all the ingredients to the slow cooker and stir to combine.
2. Cover the slow cooker. Cook on LOW for 4 to 6 hours, or until the chicken is cooked through.
3. Remove the chicken and pineapple out of the slow cooker and place it in a serving bowl.
4. Shred the chicken meat with two forks, adding some of the cooking juices from the slow cooker to keep the chicken moist.
5. Serve over steamed white or brown rice.

FREEZER MEAL INSTRUCTIONS: Place all the ingredients in a gallon-size zippered freezer bag. Lay flat and seal the bag, removing any excess air as much as possible. Label the freezer bag with the name of recipe, ingredients, date, and cooking instructions.

TO COOK THE FREEZER MEAL: Thaw the freezer meal bag in the refrigerator. Pour the contents of the bag into the cooker and cook the recipe per the directions beginning at step 1.

EASY CHICKEN DINNER PIE

Serves: 4 to 6 | **Cook Time:** 6 to 8 hours on LOW
Slow Cooker Size: 3½-quart (3.3-L) casserole or 6-quart (5.7-L) oval

If you have some leftover chicken (or turkey), this recipe is super easy to make and everyone in the family will love it. Sarah cooked this in a 3½-quart (3.3-L) rectangular casserole slow cooker. You can also use a 6-quart (5.7-L) or larger oval cooker, and the recipe will come out just great. Feel free to add your favorite veggies to the recipe to change it up and adapt it to suit your family's preferences.

1 pound (455 g) cooked chicken (or turkey)

¾ teaspoon kosher salt, divided

1½ cups shredded Cheddar or Colby Jack cheese

2 large eggs

1 cup (235 ml) milk

¾ cup (94 g) all-purpose flour

2 teaspoons (5 g) ground paprika

¾ teaspoon baking powder

½ teaspoon garlic powder

½ tablespoon (8 ml) vegetable oil

1. Spray the bottom and sides of the slow cooker with nonstick cooking spray.

2. Add the cooked chicken to the bottom of the slow cooker and season with ¼ teaspoon salt.

3. Cover the chicken with the shredded cheese.

4. In a medium mixing bowl, mix together the eggs, milk, flour, paprika, baking powder, ½ teaspoon of salt, garlic powder, and oil until combined.

5. Pour the mixture evenly over the chicken and cheese.

6. Place a layer of paper towels or a clean flour-sack kitchen towel between the lid and stoneware crock to absorb any condensation that collects on the lid while cooking so that it won't drip down onto the crust of your pie.

7. Cook on LOW for 6 to 8 hours, until a toothpick inserted in the middle of the crust comes out clean.

GARLIC LOVERS' CHICKEN WITH 40 CLOVES OF GARLIC

Serves: 8 | **Cook Time:** 4 to 5 hours on LOW | **Slow Cooker Size:** 6-quart (5.7-L)

If you are a garlic lover, then you are going to ADORE this easy fix-it-and-forget it recipe that is full of great garlic flavor. The garlic in this recipe is slow-cooked and roasted with the chicken, and it is not overwhelming at all. This recipe starts in a frying pan on the stove, and then finishes slow cooking for 4 to 5 hours in the slow cooker where the garlic is allowed to roast and get mellow. Serve the chicken and creamy sauce over hot pasta or rice for dinner.

2 pounds (about 1 kg) boneless skinless chicken breasts

¼ teaspoon kosher salt

¼ teaspoon freshly ground black pepper

¼ cup (59 ml) olive oil

1 small yellow onion, finely diced

40 cloves of garlic, peeled (about 3–4 heads of garlic)

¼ cup (32 g) all-purpose flour

½ cup (120 ml) white wine (or chicken stock plus a splash of vinegar)

1 cup (235 ml) low-sodium chicken stock, store-bought or homemade (page 310)

1 tablespoon (2 g) fresh thyme, minced

1 tablespoon (4 g) fresh parsley, minced

FOR SERVING:

Cooked pasta or rice

1. Pat the chicken breasts dry with paper towels and season with salt and pepper.
2. In a large skillet set over medium-high heat, heat the oil until hot.
3. Working in batches, brown the chicken for 3 to 4 minutes per side until golden-brown.
4. Transfer the seared chicken to the bottom of the slow cooker and set aside.
5. Sauté the onion and whole garlic cloves in the remaining pan drippings until lightly gold and caramelized.
6. Reduce the heat to medium. Stir in the flour and cook for 1 minute.
7. Slowly whisk the wine and chicken broth until the sauce is smooth.
8. Bring the sauce to a simmer over medium heat, stirring until thickened.
9. Taste the sauce and season with salt and pepper if needed.
10. Pour the sauce over the chicken in the slow cooker and sprinkle with fresh thyme and parsley.
11. Cover the slow cooker. Cook on LOW for 4 to 5 hours, or until the chicken is tender and reads 165°F (74°C) on an instant-read meat thermometer.
12. Serve the chicken and sauce over hot pasta or rice.

NOTES: *Look for large jars of already-peeled whole cloves of garlic. They're ready for you to use in this recipe. It saves so much time and stinky garlic hands!*

SO GOOD MAPLE DIJON CHICKEN

Serves: 8 | **Cook Time:** 5 to 6 hours on LOW or 3 to 4 hours on HIGH
Slow Cooker Size: 3½-quart (3.3-L) casserole or 6-quart (5.7-L) oval

This recipe is perfect for dinner any day of the week, but it comes off fancy enough to serve to dinner guests. The combination of tender chicken thighs, tangy stone-ground mustard, and real maple syrup is out of this world.

2 cups (250 g) all-purpose flour

1 teaspoon salt

1 teaspoon freshly ground black pepper

8 whole bone-in or boneless skin-on chicken thighs

Vegetable oil

SAUCE:

1 cup (322 g) real maple syrup

¼ cup (60 g) grainy Dijon mustard

1 teaspoon roughly chopped fresh sage

1 teaspoon roughly chopped fresh rosemary

1. Add the flour, salt, and pepper to a gallon-size zippered food storage bag. Mix to combine.

2. Place 2 chicken thighs in the bag with the flour and zip close the bag. Shake the bag to coat the chicken with the flour. Shake off any excess flour and place chicken on a larger platter. Set aside.

3. Heat 1 inch (2.5 cm) of vegetable oil in a large skillet on the stove top on medium heat until hot.

4. With tongs carefully place 2 to 3 pieces of chicken in the hot oil and cook for about 3 minutes on each side until the chicken is a light golden-brown. The chicken will not be fully cooked inside.

5. Transfer the chicken to the slow cooker and proceed with cooking the remaining chicken in the oil.

TO MAKE THE SAUCE

1. In a small bowl, mix together the maple syrup, Dijon mustard, and fresh herbs.

2. Spoon over the chicken in the slow cooker.

3. Cover the slow cooker. Cook on LOW for 5 to 6 hours or on HIGH for 3 to 4 hours, or until the chicken is cooked through.

NOTES: *If you do not have access to fresh herbs, you can use ½ teaspoon dried sage and rosemary in this recipe.*

BOURBON STREET CHICKEN

Serves: 6 | **Cook Time:** 6⅓ to 8⅓ hours on LOW or 3⅓ to 4⅓ hours on HIGH
Slow Cooker Size: 6-quart (5.7-L)

The name of this recipe is a little bit deceiving. It's named after a street in New Orleans, "Bourbon Street," and not because it contains bourbon, the barrel-aged whiskey . . . . Oh, darn! But regardless of the lack of booze in this recipe, you'll still want to make this mouthwatering dish for dinner. Served over rice, it makes a fantastic dinner any day of the week!

4 whole boneless skinless chicken breasts, cut into bite-size pieces

1 clove garlic, minced

1 teaspoon grated fresh ginger

¼ cup (120 ml) frozen apple juice concentrate, thawed

¼ cup (60 g) light brown sugar, packed

¼ cup (60 g) ketchup

1 tablespoon (15 ml) red wine vinegar

⅓ cup (80 ml) low-sodium soy sauce

¼ cup (32 g) cornstarch

1. Place the chicken in the bottom of the slow cooker.
2. In a small bowl, combine the garlic, ginger, apple juice concentrate, brown sugar, ketchup, vinegar, and soy sauce. Stir.
3. Pour the sauce over chicken.
4. Cover the slow cooker. Cook on LOW for 6 to 8 hours or on HIGH for 3 to 4 hours.
5. During the last 20 minutes of cooking time, stir the chicken pieces in the sauce to break them up a bit. Ladle out about ½ cup (120 ml) of the cooking liquid into a small bowl.
6. Whisk the ¼ cup (32 g) of cornstarch into the reserved cooking liquid until there are no lumps to create a slurry.
7. Pour the cornstarch slurry in the slow cooker and stir to combine.
8. Cover and cook for an additional 20 minutes on LOW, or until the sauce in the slow cooker has thickened.

NOTES: *Serve this moist and full-of-flavor chicken over rice or pasta for a quick-and-easy dinner the whole family will enjoy! While this recipe is alcohol-free as is, you can add ¼ cup (60 ml) of your favorite brand of bourbon whiskey to the sauce mixture if you want.*

FANCY MERLOT CHICKEN WITH MUSHROOMS

Serves: 6 | **Cook Time:** 5 to 6 hours on LOW | **Slow Cooker Size:** 6-quart (5.7-L)

Tender chicken thighs and mushrooms are simmered in a merlot-infused sauce. This is perfect served over hot fettuccine or rice and sprinkled with freshly grated Parmesan cheese.

5–6 cups fresh button mushrooms, sliced

1 medium yellow onion, diced

3 cloves garlic, minced

3 pounds (1.4 kg) boneless skinless chicken thighs

6 ounces (168 g) tomato paste

¾ cup (175 ml) chicken broth

½ cup (120 ml) merlot wine

2 tablespoons (6 g) quick-cooking tapioca

2 teaspoons (9 g) granulated sugar

2 teaspoons (1 g) dried basil

½ teaspoon kosher salt

¼ teaspoon freshly ground black pepper

FOR SERVING:

Cooked pasta or rice

Grated Parmesan cheese

1. Place the mushrooms, onion, and garlic in the bottom of the slow cooker.
2. Add the chicken to the top of the mushrooms.
3. In a small bowl, combine the tomato paste, broth, wine, tapioca, sugar, basil, salt, and pepper to create the sauce.
4. Pour the sauce over the chicken.
5. Cover the slow cooker. Cook on LOW for 5 to 6 hours, or until the chicken is tender.
6. Serve over hot pasta or rice, sprinkled with Parmesan cheese over top.

NO-FUSS CHICKEN MARSALA

Serves: 4 to 6 | **Cook Time:** 5 to 6 hours on LOW plus 30 minutes on HIGH
Slow Cooker Size: 5-quart (4.7-L) or larger

Chicken, garlic, mushrooms, and Marsala wine make for a slow cooker dinner that is simple but tasty! Marsala is a white wine fortified with brandy, and it brings an amazing flavor to this tender chicken. Most of the alcohol cooks off during the slow-cooking process; however, if you want to make this nonalcoholic, you can use ¾ cup (175 ml) white grape juice and ¼ cup (60 ml) sherry vinegar.

4–6 boneless skinless chicken breasts

1 cup white mushrooms, sliced

1 cup (235 ml) sweet Marsala wine

2–3 cloves garlic, minced

½ cup (120 ml) water

¼ cup (32 g) cornstarch

1. Add the chicken, mushrooms, wine, and garlic to the slow cooker.
2. Cover the slow cooker. Cook on LOW for 5 to 6 hours, or until the chicken is cooked through.
3. Remove the chicken from the slow cooker and set aside.
4. In a small bowl, mix together the cold water and cornstarch. Whisk until there are no lumps to create a slurry.
5. Add the slurry and whisk it into the liquid in the slow cooker.
6. Add the chicken back to the slow cooker.
7. Cover the slow cooker. Cook for an additional 30 minutes on HIGH, or until the sauce has thickened.

NOTES: *Serve the chicken and sauce over egg noodles, mashed potatoes, or rice.*

ASIAN CHICKEN TERIYAKI BOWLS

Serves: 4 to 6 | **Cook Time:** 4 to 6 hours on LOW | **Slow Cooker Size:** 4-quart (3.8-L) or larger

Everyone in Katie's family loves homemade teriyaki chicken bowls, just like you get in the restaurant. The flavor is amazing, and you can get a lot of healthy, steamed vegetables into the kids when they're paired with this yummy chicken. For even more flavor, marinate the chicken in the sauce in the refrigerator overnight, then cook in the slow cooker the next day!

4–6 boneless skinless
chicken breasts

1 cup (235 ml) low-sodium
chicken broth, store-bought
or homemade (page 310)

½ cup (120 ml) bottled
teriyaki sauce

½ cup (115 g) brown sugar, packed

4 cloves garlic, minced

FOR SERVING:

4 cups (632 g) cooked rice

2–3 cups (weight will vary)
steamed vegetables (such as
sugar snap peas, broccoli,
cauliflower, carrots, or a bag
of Asian mixed vegetables)

1. Place the chicken in the slow cooker.
2. In a medium mixing bowl, mix together the chicken broth, teriyaki sauce, brown sugar, and garlic to create a sauce.
3. Pour the sauce over the chicken in the slow cooker.
4. Cover the slow cooker. Cook on LOW for 4 to 6 hours, or until the chicken is cooked through.
5. Using two forks, shred the chicken.

NOTES: *To serve, layer cooked rice, shredded chicken, and vegetables in serving bowls. Drizzle some of the cooking liquid from the slow cooker over the top.*

SAUCY ORANGE SESAME CHICKEN

Serves: 8 | **Cook Time:** 4 to 6 hours on LOW plus 1 hour on HIGH
Slow Cooker Size: 6-quart (5.7-L) or larger

Your family will ADORE this recipe any night of the week. Served over rice with a side of steamed veggies, this chicken dish is full of flavor!

4 pounds (1.8 kg) boneless skinless chicken breasts, cut into bite-size pieces

2 cups (475 ml) chicken broth, store-bought or homemade (page 310)

1 cup (235 ml) freshly squeezed orange juice

1 cup (235 ml) rice vinegar

1 cup (235 ml) low-sodium soy sauce

½ cup (170 g) honey

⅓ cup (75 g) brown sugar, packed

2 tablespoons (12 g) freshly grated orange zest

2 teaspoons (2 g) crushed red pepper flakes

½ teaspoon ground ginger

½ teaspoon freshly ground black pepper

½ cup (65 g) cornstarch

FOR SERVING:

3 cups (474 g) cooked rice (white or brown)

Sesame seeds (for garnish)

Sliced green onions (for garnish)

1. Line the slow cooker with a slow cooker liner, if desired, to make cleanup easier.

2. In a medium mixing bowl, mix together the chicken broth, orange juice, vinegar, soy sauce, honey, brown sugar, orange zest, red pepper flakes, ginger, and pepper to create a sauce.

3. Layer the sauce and chicken in the slow cooker in the following order: ⅓ of the sauce, a layer of chicken, ⅓ of the sauce, a layer of chicken, and then the final ⅓ of the sauce.

4. Cover the slow cooker. Cook on LOW for 4 to 6 hours.

5. When the chicken is fully cooked, carefully remove the chicken from the slow cooker and place in a bowl. Cover with foil to keep it warm.

6. Add the cornstarch to the sauce that is in the slow cooker and whisk until it is mixed in well.

7. Cover and cook on HIGH for 1 hour, or until the sauce thickens.

8. Add the chicken back to the sauce and serve over cooked rice.

9. Sprinkle sesame seeds and green onion over the chicken and rice before serving.

SWEET-AND-SPICY KUNG PAO CHICKEN

Serves: 4 to 6 | **Cook Time:** 3½ to 4 hours on LOW | **Slow Cooker Size:** 5-quart (4.7-L) or larger

This recipe packs some heat and spice from the chile peppers and crushed red pepper flakes. Feel free to tone it down by reducing the amount of chile pepper added. Or, if you like it on the spicy side, go ahead and add more! This chicken is great served over steamed white or brown rice or cooked quinoa.

1½–2 pounds (680 g to about 1 kg) boneless skinless chicken breasts

¼ teaspoon kosher salt

¼ teaspoon freshly ground black pepper

4–6 whole dried red chile peppers (or add an additional teaspoon crushed red pepper flakes)

⅔ cup (90 g) roasted unsalted cashews

1 medium red bell pepper, seeded and diced

1 medium zucchini, diced

3 tablespoons (45 ml) cold water

2 tablespoons (18 g) cornstarch

FOR THE SAUCE:

½ cup (120 ml) low-sodium soy sauce

½ cup (120 ml) water

¼ cup (125 g) hoisin sauce

¼ cup (85 g) honey

3 cloves garlic, minced

1 teaspoon freshly grated ginger

¼ teaspoon crushed red pepper flakes

1. Add the chicken to the slow cooker and season with salt and pepper.
2. In a medium mixing bowl, mix together all the ingredients for the sauce. Pour the sauce over the chicken in the slow cooker.
3. Cover the slow cooker. Cook on LOW for 3 hours.
4. Add chile peppers (if desired), cashews, bell peppers, and zucchini.
5. In a small bowl, mix together the cold water and cornstarch to create a slurry to thicken the sauce.
6. Pour the cornstarch slurry in the slow cooker and stir everything to combine.
7. Cover the slow cooker. Cook for an additional 30 minutes to 1 hour, or until the vegetables are tender and the sauce has thickened.

TANGY BBQ PULLED CHICKEN SANDWICHES

Serves: 8 | **Cook Time:** 6 to 8 hours on LOW plus 15 to 20 miniutes on HIGH
Slow Cooker Size: 6-quart (5.7-L)

Both chicken breasts and thighs are used in this recipe because the combination makes a moist pulled chicken. The sauce is a homemade, barbecue-type sauce that features the tang of apple cider vinegar and the unique flavor of molasses. Serve on your favorite rolls or buns for a dinner that is out of this world!

2 pounds (about 1 kg) boneless skinless chicken breasts and thighs

1 small yellow onion, finely diced

15 ounces (425 g) canned tomato sauce

¾ cup (175 ml) apple cider vinegar

¼ cup (80 g) blackstrap molasses

½ cup (75 g) brown sugar

½ teaspoon salt

¼ teaspoon freshly ground black pepper

2 tablespoons (28 ml) cold water

1 tablespoon (8 g) cornstarch

FOR SERVING:

Buns or rolls

1. Place the chicken breasts and thighs in the slow cooker.

2. In a small mixing bowl, mix together the onion, tomato sauce, vinegar, molasses, brown sugar, salt, and pepper to create your sauce.

3. Pour the sauce over the chicken in the slow cooker.

4. Cover the slow cooker. Cook on LOW for 6 to 8 hours.

5. Using tongs, carefully remove the chicken from the slow cooker and place in a separate bowl.

6. Shred the chicken meat with two forks and set aside.

7. Mix together the cold water and cornstarch to create a slurry to thicken the sauce. Pour the slurry into the sauce that is in the slow cooker and stir to mix.

8. Cover the slow cooker. Cook for 15 to 20 minutes on HIGH, until the sauce has thickened.

9. Add the chicken back to the sauce in the slow cooker and toss to coat in the sauce.

10. Serve pulled chicken on buns or rolls.

NOTES: *You can serve these pulled chicken sandwiches as is or top with cheese, coleslaw, pickles, or whatever you like to top your sandwiches with. In Sarah's house the kids love cheese, and the adults love a little coleslaw–which adds a nice crunch and additional flavor!*

ZESTY BUFFALO CHICKEN TACOS

Serves: 6 | **Cook Time:** 5 to 6 hours on LOW
Slow Cooker Size: 4-quart (3.8-L) or larger

Just three simple ingredients and you have the meat filling for these amazing tacos! If you love buffalo chicken wings, you will ADORE these tacos!

1½ pounds (680 g) boneless skinless chicken breasts or thighs

1 cup (235 ml) hot wing buffalo sauce

3 tablespoons (42 g) butter, melted

1. Add the chicken, buffalo sauce, and butter to the slow cooker.
2. Stir well to coat your chicken with the buffalo sauce.
3. Cover the slow cooker. Cook on LOW for 5 to 6 hours.
4. When the chicken is cooked, remove it and shred the meat with two forks.
5. Mix the shredded chicken with leftover sauce in the slow cooker, coating all pieces.

NOTES: *Add the shredded taco meat to flour or corn tortillas. Top with your favorite taco toppings, such as shredded lettuce, cheese, guacamole, salsa, and sour cream. If you want a more authentic buffalo wing experience, use a little blue cheese or ranch salad dressing instead of sour cream!*

SIMPLY THE BEST CHICKEN BRUSCHETTA BAKE

Serves: 6 | **Cook Time:** 5 to 6 hours on LOW or 3 to 4 hours on HIGH | **Slow Cooker Size:** 3½-quart (3.3-L) casserole or 6-quart (5.7-L) oval

The entire family will love this quick-and-easy recipe for dinner. Tender pieces of chicken breasts are combined with stuffing mix, tomatoes, fresh basil, and some mozzarella cheese for a slow cooker casserole that is simply delicious!

1½ pounds (680 g) boneless skinless chicken breasts, cut into bite-size pieces

14.5 ounces (411 g) canned Italian seasoned diced tomatoes, undrained

6 ounces (168 g) packaged chicken flavor stuffing mix

½ cup (120 ml) water

3 cloves garlic, minced

6–8 whole fresh basil leaves, minced

1 cup (115 g) shredded mozzarella cheese

1. Spray the slow cooker with nonstick cooking spray, if desired, to make cleanup easier.
2. Place the chicken in the bottom of the slow cooker.
3. In a medium mixing bowl, combine the tomatoes, stuffing mix, water, and garlic until all the stuffing mix is moistened.
4. Spoon stuffing mixture over the chicken evenly in the slow cooker.
5. Sprinkle fresh basil and mozzarella cheese over the top of the stuffing mixture.
6. Cover the slow cooker. Cook on LOW for 5 to 6 hours or on HIGH for 3 to 4 hours, until the chicken is cooked through.

FAMILY FAVORITE PESTO PARMESAN CHICKEN

Serves: 6 to 8 | **Cook Time:** 4 to 5 hours on LOW or 2 to 3 hours on HIGH plus 15 minutes on LOW
Slow Cooker Size: 5-quart (4.7-L) or larger

Pesto is one of those ingredients that works great in slow cooker cooking because it blends in well, doesn't burn, adds moisture to meat, and adds a ton of flavor! You can make your own when fresh basil is growing like mad in your summer garden, or you can purchase pesto at your grocery store. This chicken recipe comes out great, and the whole family loves it. Serve it over pasta with additional Parmesan cheese on top and a side of garlic bread. There are never any leftovers with this tasty dish!

3–4 pounds (1.4–1.8 kg) boneless chicken tenderloins

1 packet (17 g) Italian dressing mix, store-bought or homemade (page 316)

1 medium onion, sliced into rings

1 cup (130 g) sliced carrots

1 cup (260 g) basil pesto, store-bought or homemade (page 315)

½ cup (120 ml) low-sodium chicken broth, store-bought or homemade (page 310)

¾ cup (75 g) grated Parmesan cheese

1 cup (230 g) sour cream

1. Season the chicken tenderloins with the Italian dressing mix and add to the slow cooker.
2. Add the onions and carrots to the top of the chicken.
3. Cover the slow cooker. Cook on LOW for 4 to 5 hours or on HIGH for 2 to 3 hours, or until the chicken is cooked through.
4. In a separate bowl, mix together the pesto, chicken broth, ¾ cup of Parmesan cheese, and the sour cream until smooth.
5. Pour over the chicken in the slow cooker and stir to coat.
6. Cover the slow cooker. Cook for an additional 15 minutes on LOW.

EASY BUTTERY PARMESAN CHICKEN

Serves: 6 to 8 | **Cook Time:** 5 to 6 hours on LOW or 3 to 4 hours on HIGH plus 30 minutes on LOW
Slow Cooker Size: 6-quart (5.7-L) or larger

One of the tricks to making chicken and other lean cuts of meat moist and tender in the slow cooker is to add a little bit of butter or oil to the dish. Sarah has used butter before for pot roasts, and it has helped make a tough piece of meat absolutely fabulous. In this recipe, butter adds to the creamy and cheesy sauce, and the butter really helps the chicken stay nice and moist.

6 boneless skinless chicken breasts

1 medium onion, diced

1 cup (130 g) baby carrots

2 small zucchini or yellow squash, sliced

1 cup (225 g) unsalted butter, softened

1 cup (230 g) sour cream

1 cup (80 g) shredded Parmesan cheese

1 packet (17 g) Italian dressing mix, store-bought or homemade (page 316)

1. Place the chicken in the bottom of the slow cooker.
2. Spread the vegetables over the chicken.
3. Cover the slow cooker. Cook on LOW for 5 to 6 hours or on HIGH for 3 to 4 hours plus 30 minutes on LOW.
4. Drain excess cooking liquid out of the slow cooker.
5. In a medium bowl, mix together the softened butter, sour cream, Parmesan cheese, and Italian dressing. Mix until combined.
6. Pour the sauce over the chicken and vegetables in the slow cooker.
7. Cover and cook for an additional 30 minutes on LOW.

SAVORY ITALIAN CHICKEN WITH POTATOES

Serves: 8 | **Cook Time:** 6 to 8 hours on LOW
Slow Cooker Size: 6-quart (5.7-L)

Just five simple ingredients tossed in the slow cooker and you have this amazingly delicious recipe. Bottled salad dressing and Parmesan cheese are the flavor backbones of this easy meal!

8 boneless skinless chicken breasts

16 ounces (455 g) bottled Italian salad dressing

8 ounces (225 g) Parmesan cheese, shredded

2 teaspoons (2 g) Italian seasoning, store-bought or homemade (page 316)

4–6 medium potatoes, scrubbed and cut in half or in wedges

1. Squirt a small amount of Italian dressing in the bottom of the slow cooker.
2. Layer the chicken breasts with Italian dressing and Parmesan cheese in the slow cooker.
3. Add a layer of potatoes on top of the chicken and season with more Italian dressing and Parmesan cheese.
4. Cover the slow cooker. Cook on LOW for 6 to 8 hours, or until the chicken is done.

INDIAN BASIL CHICKEN IN COCONUT CURRY SAUCE

Serves: 4 to 6 | **Cook Time:** 6 to 7 hours on LOW or 4 to 5 hours on HIGH
Slow Cooker Size: 5-quart (4.7-L) or larger

Katie loves a good curry chicken, and this recipe is just simply amazing served over white or brown rice. The canned coconut milk adds creaminess, and the basil and other spices just make this dish perfect.

2–3 pounds (about 1–1.4 kg) boneless skinless chicken breasts

8 cloves garlic, minced

1 large red onion, diced

2 jalapeño peppers, seeded and finely chopped

27 ounces (798 ml) canned coconut milk

2 tablespoons (9 g) dried basil leaves

2 teaspoons (10 g) kosher salt

1½ teaspoons yellow curry powder

1 teaspoon fresh ginger, minced

½ teaspoon freshly ground black pepper

½ teaspoon chili powder

2 tablespoons (30 ml) cold water

1 tablespoon (8 g) cornstarch

½ cup (8 g) fresh cilantro leaves, chopped (for garnish)

1. Place the chicken pieces in the bottom of the slow cooker.
2. In a medium bowl, mix together the garlic, onion, jalapeño peppers, coconut milk, basil, salt, curry powder, ginger, pepper, and chili powder until well combined. Pour over the chicken in the slow cooker.
3. Cover the slow cooker. Cook on LOW for 6 to 7 hours or on HIGH for 4 to 5 hours.
4. Remove the chicken from the slow cooker and set aside.
5. In a small bowl, whisk together the cold water and cornstarch with a fork until there are no lumps.
6. Add the cornstarch slurry to the slow cooker and stir into the liquid in the slow cooker.
7. Shred the chicken meat with two forks and add the shredded chicken back to the slow cooker.
8. Cover the slow cooker. Cook for an additional 30 minutes on HIGH, or until the sauce thickens.
9. Garnish with fresh cilantro right before serving.

PULLED TANDOORI CHICKEN

Serves: 4 to 6 | **Cook Time:** 5½ to 6 hours on LOW | **Slow Cooker Size:** 4-quart (3.8-L) or larger

Garam marsala is a specialty spice that is full of flavor. Serve this over rice, rolled in lettuce leaves, or stuffed in pita bread. This chicken is a winner every time.

2–3 pounds (about 1–1.4 kg) boneless skinless chicken breasts

½ cup full-fat coconut milk

3–4 cloves garlic, minced

Juice of 1 lemon

1 tablespoon (20 g) honey

1 tablespoon (7 g) ground cumin

1 teaspoon garam masala spice mix

1 teaspoon ground ginger

½ teaspoon cayenne pepper

¼ teaspoon ground turmeric

¼ teaspoon ground cloves

¼ teaspoon kosher salt

¼ teaspoon freshly ground black pepper

¼ teaspoon cardamom

1. Place the chicken in the slow cooker.
2. Mix the remaining ingredients in a medium mixing bowl until well combined. Pour over the chicken in the slow cooker.
3. Cover the slow cooker. Cook on LOW for 5 hours.
4. Remove the cooked chicken and shred the meat with two forks.
5. Add the chicken back to the slow cooker and cook for an additional 30 minutes to 1 hour on LOW with the lid off to allow some of the liquid to evaporate.

FREEZER MEAL INSTRUCTIONS: *Add the chicken to a gallon-size freezer bag. Mix together the sauce mixture and add it to the bag. Squish the contents of the bag to mix everything together a little bit. Lay the bag flat, remove as much excess air as possible, and seal the bag. Label the bag with the name of the recipe, ingredients, date, and cooking instructions.*

TO COOK THE FREEZER MEAL: *Place the frozen meal in the refrigerator to thaw. Pour the contents of the bag into the cooker and cook the recipe per the directions beginning at step 3.*

ZESTY CILANTRO LIME CHICKEN

Serves: 6 | **Cook Time:** 5 to 6 hours on LOW or 3 to 4 hours on HIGH | **Slow Cooker Size:** 5-quart (4.7-L)

Fresh lime juice, lime zest, and cilantro take this chicken over the top in flavor. Serve the tender and moist chicken as a taco or burrito filling, or for a healthier option, try it in a rice bowl.

16 ounces (455 g) frozen corn

2 whole limes, zested and juiced

1 cup (16 g) chopped fresh cilantro (plus more for garnish)

1 medium yellow onion, diced

1 cup (260 g) salsa

2 cloves garlic, minced

1 teaspoon ground cumin

⅛ teaspoon kosher salt

⅛ teaspoon freshly ground black pepper

1½ pounds (680 g) boneless skinless chicken breasts or thighs

FOR SERVING:

Tortillas or cooked rice

1. In a medium mixing bowl, combine the frozen corn, lime zest and juice, cilantro, onion, salsa, garlic, cumin, salt, and pepper.
2. Pour half of the mixture into the bottom of the slow cooker.
3. Place the chicken breasts on top of the corn mixture.
4. Pour the remaining corn mixture over the top of the chicken.
5. Cover the slow cooker. Cook on LOW for 5 to 6 hours or on HIGH for 3 to 4 hours.
6. Remove the chicken from the slow cooker, shred the meat with two forks, and add it back to the slow cooker.
7. Serve as a filling in tacos, burritos, or taco bowls over rice.

FREEZER MEAL INSTRUCTIONS: *Add all of the ingredients to a gallon-size freezer bag. Squish the contents of the bag to mix everything together a little bit. Lay the bag flat, remove as much excess air as possible, and seal the bag. Label the bag with the name of the recipe, ingredients, date, and cooking instructions.*

TO COOK THE FREEZER MEAL: *Partially thaw the bag in the refrigerator overnight or in a clean kitchen sink filled with cool water for several hours. Thaw just until the contents of the bag can easily be removed from the bag. Put the freezer meal in the slow cooker and cover. Cook for 6 to 7 hours on LOW or for 4 to 5 hours on HIGH.*

SIMPLE CHICKEN AND BLACK BEANS

Serves: 8 | **Cook Time:** 6 to 8 hours on LOW or 3 to 4 hours on HIGH | **Slow Cooker Size:** 6-quart (5.7-L)

This tasty and delicious recipe is a simple slow cooker dump recipe. You just toss everything in the slow cooker and let it cook away for several hours. Serve in flour tortillas as a burrito filling or just top with your favorite toppings such as sour cream, cheese, avocado, etc. for a filling burrito bowl!

3 pounds (1.4 kg) boneless skinless chicken breasts

30 ounces (850 g) canned black beans, drained

20 ounces (567 g) canned diced tomatoes with green chilies, drained

15 ounces (425 g) canned corn kernels, drained

1 packet (28 g) low-sodium taco seasoning mix, store-bought or homemade (page 317)

FOR SERVING:

Tortillas or cooked rice

1. Pat the chicken dry with paper towels and place in the bottom of the slow cooker.
2. Pour the black beans, tomatoes with green chilies, and corn on top of the chicken.
3. Add the taco seasoning.
4. Cover the slow cooker. Cook on LOW for 6 to 8 hours or on HIGH for 3 to 4 hours.
5. Remove the cooked chicken from the slow cooker and shred the meat with two forks.
6. Add the shredded chicken back to the slow cooker and stir to combine with the other ingredients.
7. Serve in tacos, burritos, or over rice.

FREEZER MEAL INSTRUCTIONS: Add all the ingredients to a gallon-size freezer bag. Squish the contents of the bag to mix everything together a little bit. Lay the bag flat, remove as much excess air as possible, and seal the bag. Label the bag with the name of the recipe, ingredients, date, and cooking instructions.

TO COOK THE FREEZER MEAL: Thaw the freezer meal bag in the refrigerator. Pour the contents of the bag into the cooker and cook the recipe per the directions, after placing the contents in the cooker, beginning with step 4.

SOUTHWESTERN CHICKEN SPAGHETTI SQUASH BOATS

Serves: 2 | **Cook Time:** 5½ to 7 hours on LOW | **Slow Cooker Size:** 6-quart (5.7-L) or larger

Using a spaghetti squash in your meals can be a daunting task. If you cook it in the slow cooker first, that task is a breeze. All you need to do is poke the squash a few times, place it in the slow cooker, add a little bit of water, and let it cook. In this recipe, you sauté the cooked squash flesh on the stove top to remove excess liquid and you make up your squash boats inside the hollowed-out squash rind. Be sure to pick out smaller squashes that will fit inside your slow cooker. This recipe serves two people, each squash makes two boats. If you can fit more than one squash in your slow cooker, feel free to double this recipe.

1 small spaghetti squash, washed

2 cups (475 ml) water

1 tablespoon (14 g) unsalted butter

1 packet (28 g) taco seasoning mix, store-bought or homemade (page 317)

1 small zucchini, thinly sliced

1 teaspoon ground cumin

2 pounds (about 1 kg) cooked shredded chicken, from leftovers or a rotisserie chicken

8 ounces (225 g) shredded Mexican cheese blend

1. Pierce the squash four times with a large knife and place in the bottom of the slow cooker.

2. Add the water and cover the slow cooker. Cook on LOW for 5 to 6 hours.

3. Remove the squash from the slow cooker with tongs and a spatula and place it on a cutting board.

4. Using a large knife cut the squash in half, keeping in mind where you pierced the squash before cooking to get intact boats. Be careful: The squash will be hot!

5. Scoop out the seeds and discard.

6. Use a fork to shred the squash flesh into "spaghetti." Add it to a medium skillet set over medium-high heat along with the butter.

7. Add the taco seasoning.

8. Sauté the squash until much of the excess water has been cooked out of the squash.

9. Spoon the seasoned squash back in the squash boats and top with the shredded chicken.

10. Sprinkle the cumin evenly over the chicken.

11. Add a layer of sliced zucchini over the seasoned chicken.

12. Lastly, add a layer of cheese on top of everything.

13. Bake these again in the slow cooker for 30 minutes to 1 hour on LOW, *or* you can cook them in the oven at 350°F (175°C, or gas mark 4) for 15 to 20 minutes, or until the chicken is warmed up and the cheese is melted.

AMAZING PINEAPPLE VERDE CHICKEN

Serves: 6 | **Cook Time:** 4 to 6 hours on LOW or 2 to 3 hours on HIGH
Slow Cooker Size: 5-quart (4.7-L) or larger

Full of flavor, this recipe combines the flavors of sweet and juicy pineapple with the tang of roasted green chilies for a slow cooker chicken recipe that is out of this world. Serve the cooked chicken over nachos, in burritos or tacos, or over rice and beans!

4 boneless skinless chicken breasts or thighs

16 ounces (455 g) verde green salsa

8 ounces (225 g) canned pineapple chunks, in juice

5 ounces (140 g) canned fire-roasted diced green chilies

2 cloves garlic, minced

1. Place the chicken in the bottom of the slow cooker.
2. Add the salsa, pineapple chunks and juice, fire-roasted green chilies, and garlic on top of the chicken.
3. Cover the slow cooker. Cook on LOW for 4 to 6 hours or on HIGH for 2 to 3 hours, or until the chicken is cooked through and easily falls apart with a fork.
4. Remove the chicken from the slow cooker and place on a plate. Shred the meat with two forks.
5. Add the shredded chicken back to the slow cooker and stir everything together to combine.

SIMPLE CHICKEN MOLE

Serves: 6 | **Cook Time:** 4½ to 5½ hours on LOW | **Slow Cooker Size:** 6-quart (5.7-L)

Mole is a traditional Mexican sauce that packs a ton of flavor in this chicken dish. Cocoa powder and peanut butter are the secret ingredients in this slow-cooked mole chicken. We like to serve the shredded chicken over white or brown rice, but feel free to add it to burritos, tacos, or enchiladas, too.

14.5 ounces (411 g) canned diced tomatoes, undrained

½ cup (120 ml) low-sodium chicken broth, store-bought or homemade (page 310)

⅓ cup (50 g) raisins

3 cloves garlic, minced

2 tablespoons (10 g) cocoa powder

2 tablespoons (32 g) peanut butter

1½ tablespoons (11 g) chili powder

1 teaspoon salt

1 teaspoon freshly ground black pepper

½ teaspoon ground cumin

2 pounds (about 1 kg) boneless skinless chicken breasts or thighs

FOR SERVING:

Cooked rice or tortillas

Fresh lime juice

Queso fresco

Diced onion

Cilantro

Avocado

1. In a blender, combine the tomatoes, chicken broth, raisins, garlic, cocoa powder, peanut butter, chili powder, salt, pepper, and cumin. Blend until creamy.

2. Place the chicken in the slow cooker. Pour ¾ of the mole sauce over the chicken.

3. Cover the slow cooker. Cook on LOW for 4½ to 5½ hours, or until the chicken is cooked through and tender.

4. Shred the chicken meat with two forks.

5. Add the remaining mole sauce over the chicken in the slow cooker. Cover and continue cooking for an additional 30 minutes on LOW.

6. Serve over rice or in tortillas as burritos or tacos with your favorite toppings, such as fresh lime juice, queso fresco, diced onion, cilantro, or avocado.

SO-EASY CHICKEN RANCH TACOS

Serves: 6 | **Cook Time:** 5 to 6 hours on LOW or 3 to 4 hours on HIGH
Slow Cooker Size: 4-quart (3.8 L) or larger

Just toss four simple ingredients in the slow cooker and you have some delicious, flavorful meat in this chicken taco recipe. Top your tacos with your favorite toppings for a quick-and-easy meal the whole family will love!

2 pounds (about 1 kg) boneless skinless chicken breasts or thighs, cut into chunks

14 ounces (414 ml) chicken broth

1 packet (28 g) ranch dressing mix, store-bought or homemade (page 318)

1 packet (28 g) taco seasoning mix, store-bought or homemade (page 317)

FOR SERVING:

Taco shells

Shredded cheese

Sour cream

Lettuce

Salsa

Guacamole

1. Add all the ingredients to the slow cooker.
2. Stir well to combine.
3. Cover the slow cooker. Cook on LOW for 5 to 6 hours or on HIGH for 3 to 4 hours.
4. Drain off excess liquid and then shred the chicken meat with two forks.
5. Serve the chicken in taco shells with your favorite taco toppings.

FREEZER MEAL INSTRUCTIONS: *Add all the ingredients to a gallon-size freezer bag. Squish the contents of the bag to mix everything together a little bit. Lay the bag flat, remove as much excess air as possible, and seal the bag. Label the bag with the name of the recipe, ingredients, date, and cooking instructions.*

TO COOK THE FREEZER MEAL: *Place the frozen meal in the refrigerator to thaw. Pour the contents of the bag into the cooker and cook the recipe per the directions beginning at step 2.*

ROASTED TURKEY BREAST WITH ORANGES AND HERBS

Serves: 6 | **Cook Time:** 5 to 7 hours on LOW | **Slow Cooker Size:** 5-quart (4.7-L) or larger

This roasted turkey breast is great for Thanksgiving or Christmas, but in all honesty it is amazing any time of year if you love roasted turkey. It's great for dinner any day of the week, and it is bursting with fresh citrus and herb flavors. Or refrigerate it after it is cooked and slice the meat thin for awesome turkey sandwiches for lunch.

6–7 pounds (2.7–3.2 kg) skin-on bone-in turkey breast

3 medium navel oranges (2 cut into quarters; 1 zested and juiced)

4–5 sprigs fresh thyme

4–5 sprigs fresh rosemary

4–5 sprigs fresh sage leaves

1 tablespoon (15 ml) olive oil

1 tablespoon (2 g) chopped fresh thyme

1 tablespoon (3 g) chopped fresh rosemary

1 tablespoon (3 g) chopped fresh sage

¼ teaspoon kosher salt

¼ teaspoon freshly ground black pepper

1 cup (235 ml) low-sodium chicken stock, store-bought or homemade (page 310)

1. Rinse the turkey breast under cold water in the sink and pat dry with a couple of paper towels.

2. Place the quartered orange slices and sprigs of thyme, rosemary, and sage in the bottom of the slow cooker.

3. Drizzle the olive oil and orange juice over the turkey breast and sprinkle with the chopped thyme, rosemary, sage, orange zest, salt, and pepper. Rub the oil and herbs into the skin of the turkey.

4. Place the turkey breast in the slow cooker on top of the oranges. Pour the chicken stock around the turkey.

5. Cover the slow cooker. Cook on LOW for 5 to 7 hours, or until the turkey reaches 165°F (74°C) on an instant-read thermometer.

6. Remove the turkey breast and tent with aluminum foil for 30 minutes to rest.

7. To brown the skin on the turkey, place under the broiler for 3 to 5 minutes and then tent with foil.

NOTES: *Tenting the turkey under foil and letting it rest for 30 minutes before slicing ensures the turkey breast will be nice and juicy. Don't skip this part. If you are broiling the breast to get browned skin, brown the turkey first, then tent and rest it.*

DELICIOUS TURKEY POTPIE

Serves: 6 to 8 | **Cook Time:** 6 to 7 hours on LOW plus 1 hour on HIGH
Slow Cooker Size: 3½-quart (3.3-L) casserole or 6-quart (5.7-L) oval

This recipe is perfect for using up leftover turkey from Thanksgiving or Christmas. You can also use leftover chicken for a chicken potpie instead. To make this easy we used a store-bought pie crust, but if you are feeling ambitious, you can make a homemade pie crust and use that instead.

1 medium yellow onion, diced

½ cup (112 g) unsalted butter

⅓ cup (42 g) all-purpose flour

3–4 cups (420–560 g) cooked turkey, diced

29 ounces (858 ml) low-sodium chicken or turkey broth, store-bought or homemade (page 310)

1 cup (130 g) frozen peas

1–2 medium carrots, peeled and diced

1 bay leaf

½ teaspoon kosher salt

½ teaspoon freshly ground black pepper

1 refrigerated pie crust (or homemade)

1. In a small skillet on the stove top, sauté the onion in the butter until the onion turns translucent. Add the flour and stir and cook for 1 to 2 minutes. Add this mixture to the slow cooker.

2. Add the cooked and diced turkey (or chicken), broth, peas, carrots, and bay leaf to the slow cooker. Stir well.

3. Sprinkle the salt and pepper into the mixture.

4. Cover the slow cooker. Cook on LOW for 6 to 7 hours, or until the vegetables are tender and the liquid in the slow cooker has thickened.

5. Add the refrigerated pie crust on top of the potpie mixture in the slow cooker.

6. Place a layer of paper towels or a clean flour sack–type kitchen towel between the lid and the crock liner to prevent condensation from dripping onto your pie crust.

7. Cook for 1 additional hour on HIGH, or until the crust is cooked completely.

HEALTHY TURKEY APPLE MEATLOAF

Serves: 4 | **Cook Time:** 4 to 5 hours on LOW | **Slow Cooker Size:** 6-quart (5.7-L) or larger

Shredded apple adds a little bit of sweetness to this great turkey meatloaf. This lightened-up meatloaf goes great with a nice side salad and a baked sweet potato.

1 medium onion, finely chopped

2 teaspoons (10 ml) olive oil

1 large Granny Smith apple, peeled and shredded

½ cup (60 g) bread crumbs

1 large egg

2 teaspoons (10 g) ketchup

2 teaspoons (10 g) Dijon mustard

½ teaspoon kosher salt

¼ teaspoon freshly ground black pepper

1 pinch ground allspice

1 pound (455 g) lean ground turkey

1. In a small skillet on the stove top, sauté the onion in the oil until tender and translucent.
2. In a large bowl, combine the apple, bread crumbs, egg, ketchup, mustard, salt, pepper, and allspice. Stir in the onion.
3. Crumble the ground turkey over the mixture and then mix well with your hands until everything is evenly incorporated together.
4. Spray the bottom of the slow cooker with nonstick cooking spray.
5. Dump the meatloaf mixture into the slow cooker and shape with your hands into a 6- x 5-inch (15- x 13-cm) loaf shape.
6. Cover the slow cooker. Cook on LOW for 4 to 5 hours, or until no pink remains and a meat thermometer reads 165°F (74°C).

FREEZER MEAL INSTRUCTIONS: *Mix the meatloaf mixture according to the instructions above and add the mixed meatloaf to a gallon-size freezer bag. Squish the contents of the bag to mix everything together a little bit. Lay the bag flat, remove as much excess air as possible, and seal the bag. Label the bag with the name of the recipe, ingredients, date, and cooking instructions.*

TO COOK THE FREEZER MEAL: *Fully thaw the bag in the refrigerator for 24 hours or in a clean kitchen sink filled with cool water for 3 to 4 hours, changing the water halfway with fresh cool water. Thaw until the contents of the bag are fully thawed. Cook the recipe per the instructions beginning at step 3.*

Partially thaw the bag in the refrigerator overnight or in a clean kitchen sink filled with cool water for several hours. Thaw just until the contents of the bag can easily be removed from the bag. Dump the freezer meal in the slow cooker and cover. Cook 7 to 9 hours on LOW or 4 to 5 hours on HIGH.

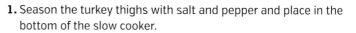

CHIPOTLE ORANGE MARMALADE GLAZED TURKEY THIGHS

Serves: 8 | **Cook Time:** 5 to 6 hours on LOW | **Slow Cooker Size:** 6-quart (5.7-L) or larger

This turkey thigh recipe is big on flavor! Canned chipotle peppers in adobo sauce bring a little bit of heat and smokiness, while orange marmalade brings a touch of sweetness. Each thigh serves two people.

4 bone-in skin-on turkey thighs

½ teaspoon salt

¼ teaspoon freshly ground black pepper

⅔ cup (160 ml) low-sodium chicken stock, store-bought or homemade (page 310)

⅔ cup (200 g) orange marmalade

2 tablespoons balsamic vinegar

2 tablespoons minced chipotle peppers in adobo sauce

2 tablespoons (40 g) honey

1 tablespoon (15 ml) vegetable oil

1 teaspoon chili powder

½ teaspoon garlic powder

4 tablespoons cold water

2 tablespoons (18 g) cornstarch

1. Season the turkey thighs with salt and pepper and place in the bottom of the slow cooker.
2. In a small bowl, combine the chicken stock, marmalade, balsamic vinegar, chipotle peppers, honey, vegetable oil, chili powder, and garlic powder to create a sauce.
3. Pour the sauce over the turkey.
4. Cover the slow cooker. Cook on LOW for 5 to 6 hours, or until the turkey is cooked through and tender.
5. Remove the turkey from the slow cooker and place on a serving platter, cover the platter with foil, and keep warm.
6. Skim fat from the cooking juices in the slow cooker and transfer to a small saucepan on the stove.
7. Bring the liquid to a boil over medium-high heat.
8. While liquid is coming to a boil, mix together the cold water and cornstarch in a small bowl until there are no lumps.
9. Gradually stir the cornstarch slurry into the boiling liquid in the saucepan.
10. Cook while stirring constantly for about 2 or 3 minutes, or until the sauce is thickened.
11. Serve the sauce over the turkey.

HEALTHY MEXICAN TURKEY STUFFED PEPPERS

Serves: 6 | **Cook Time:** 4 to 6 hours on LOW or 2 to 3 hours on HIGH | **Slow Cooker Size:** 6-quart (5.7-L)

Stuffed bell peppers get a healthy twist in this recipe. Ground turkey replaces the traditionally used ground beef, and black beans add in extra texture and fiber. Top each cooked, stuffed pepper with a drizzle of sour cream, fresh cilantro, diced avocado, minced fresh cilantro, and wedges of lime to really brighten up the flavors!

6 medium-size bell peppers (any color), tops cut off, and seeds and ribs removed

1 pound (455 g) lean ground turkey

1 cup (140 g) cooked brown rice

15 ounces (425 g) canned black beans, rinsed and drained

1 cup (162 g) frozen corn kernels

1 cup (235 ml) canned red enchilada sauce

¾ cup (90 g) shredded Cheddar cheese, plus more for topping (optional)

1 teaspoon chili powder

½ teaspoon ground cumin

¼ teaspoon salt

¼ teaspoon freshly ground black pepper

1. Spray the bottom of the slow cooker with nonstick cooking spray. Place the prepared peppers inside.
2. In a large bowl, combine the raw ground turkey, cooked rice, black beans, corn, enchilada sauce, cheese, and seasonings. Mix well.
3. Spoon the turkey filling into the cavity of each bell pepper.
4. Cover the slow cooker. Cook on LOW for 4 to 6 hours or 2 to 3 hours on HIGH, or until the meat is cooked through.
5. Serve with additional cheese and toppings (if desired).

NOTES: *This recipe uses cooked brown rice. It is perfect for when you have a little leftover rice from another meal. But if you don't have leftover brown rice, white rice or Spanish rice will work. You can even find rice you can cook in a matter of minutes in the microwave. That will work great, too.*

CORNISH GAME HENS AND POTATOES

Serves: 4 | **Cook Time:** 6 to 7 hours on LOW or 3 to 4 hours on HIGH
Slow Cooker Size: 5-quart (4.7-L) or larger

If you are looking for a lovely dinner that is made easy in your slow cooker, then look no further than these tasty Cornish game hens. Each person gets half of a hen and some lovely roasted potatoes. Feel free to change up the seasonings on the chicken if you want to try different flavor combinations.

2 tablespoons (10 g) lemon pepper

½ teaspoon salt

2 Cornish game hens (20 to 24 ounces, or 567 to 680 g each)

¼ cup (59 ml) olive oil

1 cup (235 ml) low-sodium chicken broth, store-bought or homemade (page 310)

5–6 medium red potatoes, cut into bite-size pieces

¼ cup (55 g) unsalted butter

1 tablespoon (2 g) ground sage

1. In a small bowl, mix together the lemon pepper and salt.

2. Brush the olive oil over the Cornish hens and then sprinkle the seasoning all over, rubbing it into the skin of the hens.

3. Place the hens in the slow cooker.

4. Add the potatoes around the hens.

5. Pour the chicken stock around the hens onto the potatoes, being careful not to pour directly over the hens as it will wash away the seasoning on the skins.

6. Slice the butter into pats and place them on top of the hens in the slow cooker. Then sprinkle with the sage.

7. Cover the slow cooker. Cook on LOW for 6 to 7 hours or on HIGH for 3 to 4 hours, or until the hens are cooked through and the potatoes are tender.

5

BEEF, BISON, AND VENISON

SIMMERED SLOPPY JOES

Serves: 4 | **Cook Time:** 2 to 4 hours on LOW | **Slow Cooker Size:** 4-quart (3.8-L) or larger

Sloppy Joes are one of those classic dinner recipes that is easy on the budget and easy to make. The hardest part is browning the ground beef on the stove top before you let your slow cooker do the rest of the work simmering the sauce and letting the flavors really meld.

1 pound (455 g) extra-lean ground beef

½ medium onion, chopped

1 medium green bell pepper, seeded and chopped

¾ cup (180 g) ketchup

¼ cup (57 g) barbecue sauce

¼ teaspoon garlic powder

1 teaspoon ground mustard

1 teaspoon Worcestershire sauce

FOR SERVING:

Hamburger buns or rolls

1. In a large skillet on the stove top, cook the ground beef along with the onion and bell pepper until the beef is crumbled and no longer pink. Drain excess fat off and add the beef mixture to your slow cooker.

2. Add the remaining ingredients to the slow cooker and stir to combine.

3. Cover the slow cooker. Cook on LOW for 2 to 4 hours.

4. Serve on your favorite hamburger buns or rolls.

NOTES: *The slow-cooked Sloppy Joe mixture is great to put in freezer bags and freeze for quick dinners or lunches later. All you have to do is thaw and reheat, which can even be done in the microwave.*

CHEESEBURGER SLOPPY JOES

Serves: 8 | **Cook Time:** 2 to 4 hours on LOW | **Slow Cooker Size:** 4-quart (3.8-L) or larger

If you have kids who prefer a cheeseburger over a hamburger, then you are going to love this rendition of traditional Sloppy Joes because they are super cheesy and saucy!

2 pounds (about 1 kg) extra-lean ground beef

1 medium onion, chopped

1 medium red bell pepper, seeded and chopped

14.5 ounces (411 g) canned diced tomatoes, drained

1 teaspoon ground mustard

1 teaspoon dried oregano

1½ teaspoons barbecue seasoning

16 ounces (455 g) processed American cheese, cubed

FOR SERVING:

Hamburger buns or rolls

1. In a large skillet, add the ground beef, onion, and bell pepper. Cook until the meat is browned, crumbed, and no longer pink. Drain the meat to remove fat.
2. Add the cooked meat mixture to the slow cooker.
3. Add the remaining ingredients and stir to combine.
4. Cover the slow cooker. Cook on LOW for to 4 hours, until the cheese is nice and melted.
5. Serve on hamburger buns or rolls.

NOTES: *If you cannot find barbecue seasoning at your local grocery store, just add two squirts of your favorite barbecue sauce instead.*

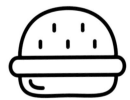

TEX-MEX SLOPPY JOES

Serves: 4 | **Cook Time:** 2 to 4 hours on LOW | **Slow Cooker Size:** 4-quart (3.8-L) or larger

This variation on traditional Sloppy Joes is inspired by the flavors of Tex-Mex food. A little Texas barbecue thing is going on with some Mexican back notes in the form of cumin and jalapeños. The end result is some outstanding flavor! We like to serve the Sloppy Joe meat on hamburger buns and top the meat mixture with a few Fritos corn chips and a little bit of shredded Cheddar cheese. The combination really brings out the flavors!

4–5 slices thick-cut bacon, chopped

1 pound (455 g) extra-lean ground beef

1 medium onion, chopped

1–2 jalapeño peppers, seeded and finely chopped

3–4 cloves garlic, minced

1 tablespoon (8 g) chili powder

1½ teaspoons ground cumin

1½ teaspoons ground coriander

1 cup (235 ml) low-sodium beef stock, store-bought or homemade (page 311)

1 cup (245 g) tomato sauce

2 tablespoons (20 g) brown sugar

2 tablespoons (32 g) Worcestershire sauce

2 tablespoons (28 ml) apple cider vinegar

FOR SERVING:

Hamburger buns or rolls

TOPPINGS (OPTIONAL):

1 cup Fritos corn chips

½ cup (58 g) shredded Cheddar cheese

1. In a large skillet set over medium heat, cook the bacon until crisp. Remove the bacon from the pan and set aside on a paper towel–lined plate to drain.
2. Drain off the excess bacon grease and discard (or save if you save your bacon grease).
3. Add the ground beef, onion, jalapeño peppers, and garlic to the same pan. Cook and crumble the ground beef until it is no longer pink. Drain the excess cooking fat off the meat mixture and add it to the slow cooker.
4. Add the remaining ingredients, including the cooked bacon, to the slow cooker (except the toppings if using). Stir to combine.
5. Cover the slow cooker. Cook on LOW for 2 to 4 hours.
6. Serve on hamburger buns or rolls topped with the Fritos corn chips and cheese (if desired).

ALL-AMERICAN MEATLOAF

Serves: 8 | **Cook Time:** 5¼ to 6¼ hours on LOW | **Slow Cooker Size:** 6-quart (5.7-L)

This meatloaf recipe comes out so tender and is full of flavor. It is best to cook this one in a 6-quart (5.7-L) oval slow cooker so that you can get the traditional shape of the meatloaf. A slow cooker liner helps you lift the meatloaf out of the slow cooker when it is done cooking.

2 pounds (about 1 kg) extra-lean ground beef

2 eggs

¾ cup (175 ml) milk

⅔ cup (77 g) seasoned bread crumbs

¼ cup (40 g) minced onion

3 cloves garlic, minced

1 teaspoon kosher salt

½ teaspoon freshly ground black pepper

TOPPINGS:

½ cup (120 g) ketchup

1 tablespoon (10 g) brown sugar

1 teaspoon prepared mustard

½ teaspoon Worcestershire sauce

1. Line the slow cooker with a slow cooker liner.
2. In a large mixing bowl, add the ground beef and all the remaining ingredients (except for the topping ingredients). Mix together with your hands until everything is well combined but not overmixed.
3. Place the meat mixture in the slow cooker and shape with your hands into a loaf shape, making sure the meatloaf does not touch the sides of the slow cooker.
4. Cover the slow cooker. Cook on LOW for 5 to 6 hours. Check the internal temperature of the meatloaf on an instant-read meat thermometer to make sure it has reached 160°F (71°C).
5. In a small bowl, mix together the ketchup, brown sugar, mustard, and Worcestershire sauce until combined to make the topping.
6. Spoon the topping mixture over the meatloaf in the slow cooker and spread it around with the back of the spoon.
7. Cover and continue to cook for 15 minutes.
8. Carefully remove the meatloaf from the slow cooker by lifting the slow cooker liner. Gently place the meatloaf on a platter using two spatulas under the meatloaf. Cut and serve.

NOTES: *Meatloaf sandwiches the next day for lunch are a perfect way to use up the leftovers—if there are any!*

BBQ RANCH MEATLOAF

Serves: 8 | **Cook Time:** 5 to 6 hours on LOW | **Slow Cooker Size:** 6-quart (5.7-L)

Barbecue sauce and ranch dressing mix make the flavors in this meatloaf something that everyone in the whole family will dig into. Serve it with baked potatoes and a side salad for a great dinner.

3 pounds (1.4 kg) extra-lean ground beef

½ cup (60 g) plain bread crumbs

3 eggs, slightly beaten

1 packet (28 g) ranch dressing mix, store-bought or homemade (page 318)

¼ cup (57 g) barbecue sauce, plus more for topping

1 medium red bell pepper, chopped

½ medium onion, chopped

3 cloves garlic, minced

1 teaspoon freshly ground black pepper

1. Line the slow cooker with a slow cooker liner.

2. In a large mixing bowl, mix together the ground beef, bread crumbs, eggs, ranch dressing mix, barbecue sauce, bell pepper, onion, garlic, and pepper together with your hands until combined.

3. Add the meat mixture and form into a loaf shape with your hands, making sure that the meatloaf does not touch the sides of the slow cooker.

4. Cover the slow cooker. Cook on LOW for 5 to 6 hours, or until a meat thermometer reads 160°F (71°C) and there is no pink inside the meatloaf.

5. Add additional barbecue sauce to the top of the meatloaf and spread it around with the back of a spoon during the last 30 minutes of cooking time.

FREEZER MEAL INSTRUCTIONS: Mix the meatloaf mixture in a large bowl. Transfer the meat to a gallon-size zippered freezer bag and squish out as much air as possible before zipping closed. Label your bag with the name of the dish and cooking instructions. Place in the freezer.

TO COOK THE FREEZER MEAL: Place the frozen meal in the refrigerator for 24 hours to fully thaw OR place the frozen bag in a sink of cold water to thaw for several hours until completely thawed. Shape the meat into a meatloaf shape in the slow cooker and cook according to the directions in the recipe beginning with step 4.

BEEFY FRENCH ONION CASSEROLE

Serves: 6 | **Cook Time:** 6 to 8 hours on LOW plus 15 to 20 minutes on HIGH
Slow Cooker Size: 3½-quart (3.3-L)

If you love French onion soup, then you are going to love the flavors in this yummy beefy casserole. Round steak is simmered with onions and mushrooms in the slow cooker. Then, it's shredded and topped with a package of stuffing mix and shredded Swiss cheese. So good!

1 pound (455 g) beef round steak, cut into 4 to 6 pieces

8 ounces (225 g) white button mushrooms, sliced

1 small onion, sliced

2 cloves garlic, minced

2 teaspoons (10 ml) sherry vinegar

1 teaspoon dried thyme

1 can (10.75 ounces, or 305 g) French onion soup

6.25 ounces (177 g) herb stuffing mix

¼ cup (55 g) butter, melted

8 ounces (225 g) shredded Swiss cheese

Water

1. Place the beef, mushrooms, onion, garlic, vinegar, thyme, and French onion soup in the slow cooker. Stir to combine.

2. Cover the slow cooker. Cook on LOW for 6 to 8 hours.

3. Shred the beef into bite-size pieces with two forks.

4. In a medium mixing bowl, add the dry stuffing mix, melted butter, and ½ cup (120 ml) of liquid from your slow cooker. Toss and add additional water if there is not enough cooking liquid.

5. Sprinkle the stuffing mixture over the beef mixture in the slow cooker. Cover and cook on HIGH for 10 to 15 minutes.

6. Add the shredded Swiss cheese over the top of the stuffing. Cover once more and cook on HIGH for about 5 minutes, or until the cheese is melted.

WESTERN BEEF CASSEROLE

Serves: 4 to 6 | **Cook Time:** 3 to 4 hours on LOW or 1 to 2 hours on HIGH
Slow Cooker Size: 5-quart (4.7-L) or larger

Your family will love this delicious and easy recipe for crock-pot Western beef casserole. Saddle up to a heaping bowl of beautifully seasoned ground beef and veggies. Top with your favorite fresh toppings for a simple dinner.

1½–2 pounds (680 g to about 1 kg) extra-lean ground beef, browned and crumbled

16 ounces (455 g) canned kidney beans, drained and rinsed

16 ounces (455 g) frozen or canned corn kernels, drained if using canned

1 can (10.75 ounces, or 305 g) condensed tomato soup

1 cup (115 g) shredded sharp Cheddar cheese

1 medium yellow onion, chopped

½ teaspoon chili powder

¼ cup (60 ml) water or milk

TOPPINGS (OPTIONAL):

Sour cream

Salsa

Sliced avocado

Tortilla chips

1. Add all the ingredients to the slow cooker and stir to combine.
2. Cover the slow cooker. Cook on LOW for 3 to 4 hours or on HIGH for 1 to 2 hours.
3. Top servings of casserole with your favorite toppings.

FREEZER MEAL INSTRUCTIONS: *Brown the ground beef and drain excess fat off. Add all the ingredients to a gallon-size zippered freezer bag and squish out as much air as possible before zipping closed. Label your bag with the name of the dish and cooking instructions. Place in the freezer.*

TO COOK THE FREEZER MEAL: *Thaw the freezer meal bag in the refrigerator. Pour the contents of the bag into the cooker and cook the recipe per the directions beginning with step 1.*

HEARTY CHEESEBURGER BAKE

Serves: 6 | **Cook Time:** 1 to 2 hours on HIGH | **Slow Cooker Size:** 5-quart (4.7-L)

All-purpose baking mix makes a fluffy crust on this cheeseburger casserole dish. A frugal meal that everyone will love!

1 pound (455 g) extra-lean ground beef

1 medium onion, chopped

1 medium green bell pepper, seeded and chopped

1 can (10.75 ounces, or 305 g) Cheddar cheese soup

¼ cup (60 ml) milk

2 cups (240 g) all-purpose baking mix, store-bought or homemade (page 321)

¾ cup (175 ml) water

1. In a large skillet on the stove top, cook the ground beef with the onion and bell pepper until the meat is crumbled and no longer pink. Drain off excess fat and add the Cheddar cheese soup and milk. Stir to combine. Spoon the mixture into the bottom of the slow cooker and spread evenly.
2. In a medium mixing bowl, mix together the all-purpose baking mix and water until a dough forms.
3. Evenly spoon the dough mixture on top of the meat mixture.
4. Cover the slow cooker. Cook on HIGH for 1 to 2 hours, or until the dough is cooked through and dry to the touch.

COWBOY CASSEROLE

Serves: 8 | **Cook Time:** 7 to 8 hours on LOW or 3 to 4 hours on HIGH plus 1 hour on LOW
Slow Cooker Size: 6-quart (5.7-L)

Feeding a crew on a budget? Check out this warm, hearty, and easy recipe for crock-pot cowboy casserole. It is sure to please even your hungriest cowboys!

1 pound (455 g) extra-lean ground beef, browned, crumbled, and drained to remove excess fat

6 whole potatoes, sliced and unpeeled

1 large onion, chopped

1–2 cloves garlic, minced

16 ounces (455 g) canned low-sodium kidney beans, undrained

15 ounces (425 g) canned diced tomatoes, undrained

10.5 ounces (298 g) canned cream of mushroom soup

½ teaspoon dried oregano

1 teaspoon kosher salt

¼ teaspoon freshly ground black pepper

1 cup (115 g) shredded Cheddar cheese

1. Mix all the ingredients except for the cheese in the slow cooker and stir to combine.
2. Cover the slow cooker. Cook on LOW for 7 to 8 hours or on HIGH for 3 to 4 hours.
3. Remove the lid and sprinkle the shredded cheese on top.
4. Cover and cook for an additional 1 hour on LOW.

NOTES: *Feel free to add a bag of frozen vegetables to the slow cooker with the hamburger and potatoes. Frozen corn, carrots, peas, and green beans all work great in this recipe!*

SAVORY GROUND BEEF OVER RICE

Serves: 4 | **Cook Time:** 6 hours on LOW or 3 hours on HIGH | **Slow Cooker Size:** 4-quart (3.8-L) or larger

This easy dinner recipe tastes fantastic. We love that it can be made ahead of time into a freezer meal for when you need something to make for the family on a busy day.

1½ pounds (680 g) extra-lean ground beef, browned, crumbled, and drained of excess fat

1 medium yellow onion, chopped

2 stalks celery, diced

1 can (10.75 ounces, or 305 g) cream of chicken or cream of celery soup

1 teaspoon low-sodium soy sauce

¼ teaspoon dried oregano

FOR SERVING:

1–2 cups (185–370 g) white or brown rice

1. Place the ground beef, onion, celery, cream of chicken soup, soy sauce, and oregano in the slow cooker. Stir to combine.

2. Cover the slow cooker. Cook on LOW for 6 hours or on HIGH for 3 hours, stirring once or twice during cooking if desired.

3. About 30 minutes before the end of the cooking time, prepare your rice on the stove top or in a rice cooker according to the package directions.

4. When your rice is cooked. Spoon rice onto plates and then spoon the beef mixture over rice.

5. Serve with your favorite side vegetable.

FREEZER MEAL INSTRUCTIONS: Place all ingredients in a gallon-size zippered freezer meal bag (except rice). Squish out as much air as possible before closing. Label the bag with the dish name and cooking instructions. Lay flat in the freezer.

TO COOK THE FREEZER MEAL: Thaw the freezer meal bag in the refrigerator. Pour the contents of the bag into the cooker and cook the recipe per the directions beginning with end of step 1 (stir).

BEEFY AU GRATIN POTATOES

Serves: 4 to 6 | **Cook Time:** 6 to 7 hours on LOW or 3 to 4 hours on HIGH
Slow Cooker Size: 5-quart (4.7-L) or larger

Ground beef, potatoes, and cheese make up the base of this fantastic main dish. Full of great flavors!

1 teaspoon ground paprika

1 teaspoon dried parsley flakes

1 teaspoon kosher salt

½ teaspoon garlic powder

½ teaspoon freshly ground black pepper

3 pounds (1.4 kg) russet potatoes, peeled and thinly sliced

1 large white onion, thinly sliced

1 pound (455 g) extra-lean ground beef, browned, crumbled, and drained of excess fat

3 cups (345 g) shredded sharp Cheddar cheese

½ cup (120 ml) low-sodium beef broth, store-bought or homemade (page 311)

1. In a small bowl, mix together the paprika, parsley flakes, salt, garlic powder, and black pepper.

2. In the slow cooker, layer half of the sliced potatoes, half of the onions, half of the spice mixture, half of the beef, and then half of the cheese. Repeat the layers a second time.

3. Pour the beef broth evenly over the layers.

4. Cover the slow cooker. Cook on LOW for 6 to 7 hours or 3 to 4 hours on HIGH, until the potatoes are cooked fork-tender.

BOLD HAMBURGER GOULASH

Serves: 10 to 12 | **Cook Time:** 4 to 5 hours on LOW or 2 to 3 hours on HIGH plus 30 minutes on LOW
Slow Cooker Size: 6-quart (5.7-L) or larger

Growing up, one of my favorite meals my mother would make was hamburger goulash. We would eat it for days, even cold. This recipe is very similar to my Mother's but spicier. Feel free to replace a can of stewed tomatoes with hot salsa, and you can even add red chili peppers if your family loves the heat!

1 pound (455 g) extra-lean ground beef

1 small onion, chopped

58 ounces (1.6 kg) canned stewed tomatoes, undrained

15 ounces (425 g) canned kidney beans, drained and rinsed

15 ounces (425 g) canned black beans, drained and rinsed

1 small green bell pepper, seeded and chopped

3 cloves garlic, minced

2 tablespoons (16 g) chili powder

1 tablespoon (16 g) Worcestershire sauce

2 teaspoons (5 g) ground paprika

1 teaspoon ground cumin

2 beef bouillon cubes

¼ teaspoon freshly ground black pepper

2 cups (186 g) uncooked elbow macaroni pasta

FOR SERVING:

1–2 cups (115–230 g) shredded Cheddar cheese

1. In a large skillet on the stove top, add the ground beef and onion. Brown and crumble the beef until no longer pink. Drain off excess fat and add to the slow cooker.

2. Add the remaining ingredients, except for the elbow macaroni pasta and shredded Cheddar cheese, to the slow cooker. Stir to combine.

3. Cover the slow cooker. Cook on LOW for 4 to 5 hours or on HIGH for 2 to 3 hours.

4. Add the uncooked macaroni pasta to the slow cooker and stir to combine, making sure all the pasta covered in the sauce. Cover and cook for an additional 30 minutes on LOW (set a timer as you don't want the pasta to overcook). You can also cook the pasta on the stove top according to the package directions, drain, and add the cooked pasta before serving.

5. Serve topped with shredded Cheddar cheese.

FREEZER MEAL INSTRUCTIONS: Follow step 1 above. Add the drained ground beef and onion mixture to a gallon-size zippered freezer bag. Add the remaining ingredients except for the pasta and cheese. Squish out as much air as possible before zipping closed. Label your bag with the name of the dish and cooking instructions.

TO COOK THE FREEZER MEAL: Thaw the freezer meal bag in the refrigerator. Cook the recipe per the directions, starting at step 2. Do not add the macaroni or cheese until 30 minutes before serving. Macaroni noodles can also be cooked on the stove top al dente and added right before serving.

SALISBURY STEAK MEATBALLS

Serves: 6 | **Cook Time:** 4 to 5 hours on LOW or 2 to 3 hours on HIGH | **Slow Cooker Size:** 5-quart (4.7-L) or larger

All the flavors of the classic Salisbury steak are in a family-friendly format with this delicious and easy meatball recipe. We like to serve the meatballs over cooked rice for dinner. You can serve them as is right out of the slow cooker as an appetizer, too.

16 ounces (455 g) frozen homestyle beef meatballs

1 tablespoon (28 g) onion soup mix, store-bought or homemade (page 319)

½ cup (120 ml) milk

⅓ cup (42 g) all-purpose flour

20 ounces (567 g) canned cream of chicken soup

1 package (28 g) au jus mix, store-bought or homemade (page 320)

¾ cup (175 ml) water

FOR SERVING:

5–6 cups (790–948 g) cooked brown or white rice

1. Add the frozen meatballs to the slow cooker.

2. In a bowl, whisk together the remaining ingredients (except for the rice) and pour over the meatballs. Stir to coat.

3. Cover the slow cooker. Cook on LOW for 4 to 5 hours or on HIGH for 2 to 3 hours.

4. Serve meatballs and sauce over cooked rice.

SLOW-COOKED TRADITIONAL COTTAGE PIE

Serves: 6 | **Cook Time:** 5 to 6 hours on LOW
Slow Cooker Size: 3½-quart (3.3-L) casserole OR 4-quart (3.8-L) oval

Cottage pie is the beef equivalent of shepherd's pie, which uses ground lamb. When you make mashed potatoes for dinner one night, be sure to make a little extra. Homemade mashed potatoes are the best, but Heidi has used instant mashed potatoes in a pinch and her family cannot really tell the difference!

I do prefer to make this dish in my casserole slow cooker because it makes it look more like a traditional oven-baked casserole. But a 4-quart (3.8-L) or larger slow cooker will work well, too.

3 cups (720 g) leftover mashed potatoes (or use instant potatoes)

2 pounds (about 1 kg) extra-lean ground beef

1 large yellow onion, chopped

2 cloves garlic, minced

3 tablespoons (48 g) canned tomato paste

8 ounces (225 g) white button mushrooms, sliced

2 medium carrots, peeled and chopped

1 cup (235 ml) low-sodium beef stock, store-bought or homemade (page 311)

¼ cup (60 ml) dry white wine (or beef stock if you don't cook with alcohol)

2 teaspoons (10 g) Worcestershire sauce

½ teaspoon dried thyme

½ cup (65 g) frozen peas

Salt and pepper, to taste

1. Warm leftover mashed potatoes in the microwave or on the stove top, adding a splash of milk if needed to make the potatoes a spreadable consistency. If using instant potatoes, prepare them according to the directions on the package and season with salt and pepper to taste. Set aside.

2. In a large skillet on medium-high heat on the stove top, cook the ground beef along with the onion and garlic until the meat is no longer pink. Drain off any excess fat.

3. Add the tomato paste to the beef mixture in the pan and cook for 2 to 3 minutes.

4. Add the mushrooms, carrots, beef stock, wine (or additional beef stock if using), Worcestershire sauce, and thyme. Bring to a boil.

5. Reduce heat to low and simmer the mixture in the skillet, uncovered, until most of the liquid is evaporated. Stir in the peas.

6. Taste the mixture and season with salt and pepper to taste.

7. Transfer the beef mixture to a slow cooker that has been sprayed with nonstick cooking spray. Spread the mashed potatoes over the top of the beef mixture.

8. Cover the slow cooker. Cook on LOW for 5 to 6 hours, or until you can see the beef mixture bubbling around the edges of the mashed potato topping.

9. Serve immediately straight from the slow cooker.

NOTES: *If you would like the topping of the cottage pie to be browned, you can place the stoneware crock in a 350°F (175°C, or gas mark 4) oven and cook for 20 minutes.*

MEATBALL PARMESAN CASSEROLE

Serves: 6 to 8 | **Cook Time:** 3 to 4 hours on HIGH | **Slow Cooker Size:** 3½-quart (3.3-L)

Sometimes Katie's kids can be picky eaters, and they are not always keen on eating meat. But for whatever reason, when that meat is turned into meatballs, their eyes light up and they are willing to eat dinner. This casserole is easy to make because you can use fully cooked homemade or frozen meatballs, and it makes a great dinner. Serve it with a side salad and some nice crusty bread, and the kids (and adults) will eat it up. Katie likes to cook this in a casserole slow cooker, but it also works great in a large 6-quart (5.7-L) oval slow cooker as well.

48 ounces (1.4 kg) jarred marinara sauce, divided

20–25 large fully cooked meatballs, frozen or homemade

½ teaspoon Italian seasoning, store-bought or homemade (page 316)

2 cups (225 g) shredded mozzarella cheese

¼ cup (20 g) shredded Parmesan cheese

FOR SERVING (OPTIONAL):

Cooked pasta

Hoagie rolls

1. Spread 2 cups (490 g) of the marinara sauce over the bottom of the slow cooker.
2. Layer the meatballs on top of the sauce.
3. Pour the remaining sauce on top of the meatballs.
4. Sprinkle the Italian seasoning over the sauce.
5. Add the mozzarella and Parmesan over the top of everything.
6. Cover the slow cooker. Cook on HIGH for 3 to 4 hours, or until everything is hot and bubbly.
7. Serve as is or over cooked pasta or in hoagie rolls as a sandwich.

FIESTA TAMALE BAKE

Serves: 6 | **Cook Time:** 5¼ to 6¼ hours on LOW or 2 to 3 hours on HIGH | **Slow Cooker Size:** 4-quart (3.8-L)

All the yummy Southwestern flavors Heidi's family loves are in this easy-to-make dish. Ground beef is seasoned just right with tomatoes, onions, garlic, and taco seasoning mix. A cornmeal batter is added, and it is all baked in the slow cooker. If you use ground beef that you have already cooked and stashed away in your freezer, it comes together in a matter of minutes.

1 pound (455 g) extra-lean ground beef

½ cup (80 g) finely chopped onion

1 clove garlic, minced

¾ cup (105 g) yellow cornmeal

1 large egg

1½ cups (355 ml) milk

15.25 ounces (432 g) canned corn kernels, drained

14.5 ounces (411 g) canned diced tomatoes, undrained

2.25 ounces (64 g) canned sliced black olives, drained

1.25 ounces (35 g) taco seasoning mix, store-bought or homemade (page 317)

1 cup (115 g) shredded Cheddar cheese

1–2 whole green onions, sliced thin (optional)

1. In a large skillet on the stove top, brown and crumble your ground beef with the onion and garlic until the meat is no longer pink. Drain off excess fat.

2. In a large mixing bowl, mix together the cornmeal, egg, and milk until smooth and no lumps appear.

3. Add the beef mixture, corn, tomatoes, olives, and taco seasoning to the cornmeal batter. Mix well to combine.

4. Pour the batter in the bottom of the greased slow cooker.

5. Cover the slow cooker. Cook on LOW for 5 to 6 hours or on HIGH for 2 to 3 hours.

6. Sprinkle the top with the cheese. Cover and cook for an additional 15 minutes on LOW, until the cheese is melted.

7. To serve, spoon into bowls or onto plates and garnish with green onions (if desired).

SUPER EASY SLOW-COOKED TACO MEAT

Serves: 8 | **Cook Time:** 5 to 7 hours on LOW | **Slow Cooker Size:** 4-quart (3.8-L) or larger

With this recipe, you can easily make your own beefy taco meat in the slow cooker without precooking the ground beef. We prefer to season the meat with our homemade taco seasoning mix, but if you don't want to bother making your own, just use a packet of low-sodium taco seasoning mix.

2 pounds (about 1 kg) extra-lean ground beef

2–3 cloves of garlic, minced

1 medium onion, diced

1 packet (28 g) low-sodium taco seasoning mix, store-bought or homemade (page 317)

1. Place the raw ground beef, garlic, and onion in the slow cooker.
2. Cover the slow cooker. Cook on LOW for about 4 to 6 hours.
3. Every 2 hours during cooking time, stir the ground beef to get it to cook evenly and to crumble the meat up.
4. When it has fully cooked, carefully drain off any fat that has cooked from the beef.
5. Add the taco seasoning and stir to mix.
6. Cover and cook for an additional 1 hour on LOW.

NOTES: *The key to this recipe is making sure you use extra-lean ground beef. Look for packages that are at least 95% lean 5% fat or lower. This will ensure that you don't have to drain off too much fat and your taco meat is not too greasy. Also, don't add the taco seasoning until after you have drained the ground beef. Otherwise, you will just be pouring off all the taco flavor!*

SAVORY CABBAGE ROLLS

Serves: 8 | **Cook Time:** 4 to 5 hours on LOW | **Slow Cooker Size:** 6-quart (5.7-L)

Cabbage rolls are a fun old-school dinner that Katie likes to make for Sunday dinner. There is a bit of prep work involved. But when you have everything prepped and in the cooker, you can just let it do its thing and cook away while you go on about your day.

This recipe uses cooked rice. You can cook the rice either on the stove top or in a rice cooker, or just wait until you have leftover white or brown rice from a different dinner.

1 head fresh cabbage

1 large onion, diced

2 pounds (about 1 kg) extra-lean ground beef

3 whole eggs

1 teaspoon salt

1 teaspoon freshly ground black pepper

1 cup (158 g) cooked white or brown rice

1 can (10.75 ounces, or 305 g) canned tomato soup

11.5 ounces (340 ml) 100% vegetable juice

2 tablespoons (32 g) Worcestershire sauce

1. Remove the stem from the cabbage and peel back each individual leaf.

2. In a large stockpot fitted with a colander or steaming rack, add 2 inches (5 cm) of water and place pot on the stove top. Put the cabbage head in the colander or on the steaming rack. Cover the pan and steam the cabbage for 1 to 2 minutes.

3. Carefully remove the cabbage from the steaming pot and place in a bowl of ice-cold water. Set aside.

4. In a small skillet on the stove top, cook the onions until translucent and starting to turn brown. Remove from the heat and set aside.

5. In a large mixing bowl, mix together the ground beef, eggs, salt, pepper, cooked onions, and rice.

6. Taking one cabbage leaf at a time, add a heaping tablespoon of the meat mixture to the bottom half of the leaf.

7. Roll the cabbage around the meat mixture.

8. Layer the cabbage rolls in the bottom of the slow cooker.

9. In a small bowl, mix together the tomato soup, vegetable juice, and Worcestershire sauce. Pour over the cabbage rolls in the slow cooker.

10. Cover the slow cooker. Cook on LOW for 4 to 5 hours.

NOTES: *There is no right or wrong way to roll cabbage rolls. Being the frugal person that I am, I like to use as much of the cabbage as I can. I will cut the larger cabbage leaves in two and make two smaller rolls. Any leftovers freeze well, too. So, you could make up a batch and freeze them. Then, you can just reheat for dinner or lunches on a different day.*

SHORTCUT SWEDISH MEATBALLS

Serves: 8 | **Cook Time:** 4 hours on HIGH | **Slow Cooker Size:** 5-quart (4.7-L) or larger

These Swedish meatballs are quick, easy, and full of great flavor. We use frozen meatballs, a can of cream of mushroom soup, plus a few other prepared foods to make this recipe come together quickly. Spoon the meatballs and the creamy sauce over cooked egg noodles for dinner or serve them as an appetizer at your next party!

28 ounces (794 g) frozen fully cooked meatballs

1 can (10.75 ounces, or 305 g) cream of mushroom soup

14.5 ounces (411 g) low-sodium beef broth, store-bought or homemade (page 311)

2 tablespoons (32 g) steak sauce

1 tablespoon (16 g) Worcestershire sauce

1 teaspoon garlic powder

½ teaspoon kosher salt

½ teaspoon ground paprika

½ teaspoon freshly ground black pepper

1 cup (230 g) sour cream

1. Add the frozen meatballs to the slow cooker.
2. In a medium mixing bowl, mix together the remaining ingredients except for the sour cream until well combined to create the sauce.
3. Pour the sauce mixture over the frozen meatballs.
4. Cover the slow cooker. Cook on HIGH for 3½ hours.
5. Add the sour cream and stir to mix it in well.
6. Cover and cook for an additional 30 minutes on HIGH.

MOUTHWATERING BBQ BONELESS BEEF RIBS

Serves: 6 to 8 | **Cook Time:** 8 to 12 hours on LOW or 4 to 6 hours on HIGH
Slow Cooker Size: 5-quart (4.7-L) or larger

You don't have to wait for summer to enjoy great fall-off-the-bone ribs because with this recipe you can have saucy ribs any time of the year. To add an additional layer of flavor, we like to either broil the ribs or toss them on the grill for a few minutes to give the ribs that nice charred flavor. But you can skip that step if you want to and just get them straight from the slow cooker.

3 pounds (1.4 kg) boneless beef ribs

2 cups (455 g) barbecue sauce

1 cup (240 g) ketchup

½ cup (75 g) brown sugar

¼ cup (60 ml) apple cider vinegar

2 teaspoons (10 g) Worcestershire sauce

1 dash hot sauce (optional)

1. Optional: Preheat the oven to the broil setting or heat up your gas barbecue grill. Broil or grill ribs for about 5 to 7 minutes per side, just until you get some nice browning on them.
2. Loosely place the ribs in the slow cooker.
3. In a medium mixing bowl, mix together the remaining ingredients until combined to create the sauce.
4. Pour the sauce mixture over the ribs in the slow cooker and toss to coat.
5. Cover the slow cooker. Cook on LOW for 8 to 12 hours or on HIGH for 4 to 6 hours, until nice and tender.

FREEZER MEAL INSTRUCTIONS: *Follow steps 2 through 4 above. Don't broil or grill the ribs first as the meat will be partially cooked. Place everything in a gallon-size zippered freezer bag and squish out as much air as possible before zipping closed. Label your bag with the name of the dish and cooking instructions.*

TO COOK THE FREEZER MEAL: *Place the frozen meal in the refrigerator to thaw. Pour the contents of the bag into the cooker and cook the recipe per the directions beginning at step 4.*

HONEY CARIBBEAN BBQ BEEF BACK RIBS

Serves: 6 | **Cook Time:** 5 to 6 hours on LOW or 2 to 3 hours on HIGH plus 2 to 3 minutes under the broiler
Slow Cooker Size: 6-quart (5.7-L) or larger

Bottled Caribbean jerk wing sauce is what gives these tasty ribs amazing island flavor. The final touch is brushing the ribs with your favorite barbecue sauce, so you get both smoky traditional barbecue rib flavor with that Caribbean island flavor. Serve these ribs with steamed basmati rice and fresh pineapple.

½ cup (120 ml) Caribbean jerk wing sauce

2 teaspoons (10 ml) olive oil

1 teaspoon salt

¼ teaspoon freshly ground black pepper

4 pounds (1.8 kg) beef back ribs, separated into 2 rib sections

2 cups (455 g) honey barbecue sauce

1. In a small mixing bowl, combine the Caribbean jerk wing sauce, olive oil, salt, and pepper until well mixed.

2. Tear off enough sheets of aluminum foil so that you have one sheet of foil for every 2 rib sections. Stack the sheets up in a pile on your countertop.

3. Place 2 ribs on a sheet of foil and brush the jerk wing sauce mixture on all sides of the ribs. Wrap the foil around the ribs top and bottom first and then each side so that they are easy to unwrap when hot.

4. Place the foil packets of ribs in the slow cooker with the seam side up.

5. Cover the slow cooker. Cook on LOW for 5 to 6 hours or on HIGH for 2 to 3 hours.

6. Line a rimmed baking sheet with foil or parchment paper.

7. Carefully unwrap each packet of ribs with tongs and place on the prepared baking sheet.

8. Baste the honey barbecue sauce on all sides of the ribs.

9. Broil the ribs for 2 to 3 minutes on each side, watching to make sure they do not burn.

LICK-YOUR-FINGERS STICKY HONEY BEEF RIBS

Serves: 6 to 8 | **Cook Time:** 6 to 7 hours on LOW plus 10 minutes under the broiler
Slow Cooker Size: 6-quart (5.7-L) or larger

The key to this recipe is finding the best beef ribs you can find. Scout out your local grocery stores and ask the butcher for their recommendation for the best ribs with a good amount of meat on the bones and easy-to-remove fat. These will typically be short ribs or baby back ribs. Make sure the rack of ribs you purchase will fit inside your slow cooker though. You can always cut them down to make them fit. If your butcher will do it for you, ask them to trim the fat and cut away the membrane. Otherwise you can easily do this at home yourself.

3–4 pounds (1.4–1.8 kg) beef short
or baby back ribs

¼ cup (38 g) brown sugar

1 tablespoon (15 g) kosher salt

2 teaspoons (2 g) dried oregano

2 teaspoons (10 g) Worcestershire sauce

½ cup (170 g) honey

FOR BROILING OR GRILLING:

1 cup (228 g) barbecue sauce

2 teaspoons (4 g) prepared mustard

1 tablespoon (20 g) honey

1. Trim the rack of ribs if you were not able to get your butcher to do it for you. Remove the membrane and excess fat. If your rack of ribs is large, cut it into several pieces to fit inside your slow cooker.
2. In a small mixing bowl, mix together the brown sugar, salt, oregano, and Worcestershire sauce to create a rub.
3. Lay your rack of ribs on a baking sheet and massage the rub into the meat on the ribs.
4. Spray the slow cooker with nonstick cooking spray to make cleanup easier, if desired.
5. Place the ribs in the slow cooker.
6. Drizzle the ½ cup of honey all over the ribs.
7. Cover the slow cooker. Cook on LOW for 6 to 7 hours, or until the ribs are fully cooked and tender.
8. Remove the ribs from the slow cooker and place them on a rimmed baking sheet covered in foil. Turn your oven on to the broil setting or turn your barbecue grill on to high heat.
9. In a small mixing bowl, mix together the barbecue sauce, mustard, and tablespoon of honey to create your sauce.
10. Baste the ribs with the sauce mixture using a basting brush. Broil or grill for about 5 minutes, flip the ribs over and baste them with more sauce. Broil or grill for about 5 minutes on the second side.
11. Cut ribs into manageable serving sizes, either individual ribs or a portion of 3 to 4 ribs.
12. Have wet wipes handy when you serve to keep your fingers from getting too sticky . . . or just lick your fingers!

SAVORY BEEF AND NOODLES

Serves: 6 to 8 | **Cook Time:** 7 to 8 hours on LOW or 3 to 4 hours on HIGH plus 1 to 1½ hours on HIGH
Slow Cooker Size: 6-quart (5.7-L)

Tender chuck beef roast is simmered away in a savory sauce, then the meat is shredded and goes back in the slow cooker. Frozen egg noodles are then added to the slow cooker and allowed to cook for another hour or so until done. Then, the dish is thickened with some heavy cream—or Greek yogurt if you are trying to watch your calories—and your dish is ready to be served to your family. We know they will gobble it up!

4 cups (940 ml) low-sodium beef broth, store-bought or homemade (page 311)

1 medium onion, chopped

1 clove garlic, minced

2 teaspoons (10 g) Worcestershire sauce

1 teaspoon seasoned salt

½ teaspoon freshly ground black pepper

2 pounds (about 1 kg) beef chuck roast, trimmed of excess fat

12 ounces (340 g) frozen egg noodles

½ cup (120 ml) heavy cream or Greek yogurt

1. Add the beef broth, onion, garlic, Worcestershire sauce, seasoned salt, and black pepper to the bottom of the slow cooker.

2. Place the trimmed beef roast in the slow cooker.

3. Cover the slow cooker. Cook on LOW for 7 to 8 hours or on HIGH for 3 to 4 hours.

4. Remove the roast from the slow cooker, leaving the liquid in the slow cooker.

5. Shred the roast into bite-size pieces using two forks and return the meat to the slow cooker.

6. Add the frozen noodles to the slow cooker; stir to cover all the noodles with the liquid.

7. Cover and cook for an additional 1 to 1½ hours on HIGH, or until the noodles are cooked through and tender.

8. Stir in the heavy cream and serve.

PERFECT ROAST BEEF AND GRAVY

Serves: 10 | **Cook Time:** 7 to 8 hours on LOW or 3 to 4 hours on HIGH
Slow Cooker Size: 6½-quart (6.2-L) or larger

Sarah's grandfather preferred a dry, overcooked beef roast. Due to this, her mother rarely made beef roast. When her mother received her first slow cooker and made pot roast, she was amazed how moist and flavorful the roast became. She was hooked!

This recipe cooks up to a large 5-pound (2.3 kg) beef roast, which will serve about 10 people, figuring a half a pound (225 g) of uncooked meat per person.

5 pounds (2.3 kg) chuck beef roast, trimmed of excess visible fat

1 teaspoon garlic salt, divided

1 teaspoon freshly ground black pepper, divided

1 teaspoon minced dried onions

1 packet (24 g) brown gravy mix (prepared) or jar of prepared brown gravy

1½ pounds (680 g) small yellow or red potatoes

1 pound (455 g) baby carrots

2 medium onions, quartered

1. Spread out a large sheet of aluminum foil on the countertop and place the beef roast on top of the foil.
2. Tenderize the meat with a fork by piercing it about 20 to 30 times.
3. Season the roast with ½ teaspoon of garlic salt, ½ teaspoon pepper, and all of the dried onion.
4. Bring the sides of the foil up and over the sides of the roast and pour the prepared brown gravy over the roast. Carefully fold the foil toward the top of the roast, completely wrapping it in the foil.
5. Lay the foil-wrapped roast in the slow cooker with the seam side up.
6. In the open spaces around the roast in the slow cooker, add the potatoes and carrots and season them with the remaining garlic salt and pepper.
7. Cover the slow cooker. Cook on LOW for 7 to 8 hours or on HIGH for 4 to 5 hours, or until the internal temperature of the roast reaches 180°F (82°C) on an instant-read thermometer.
8. Carefully remove the roast from the slow cooker, unwrap the foil, and place the roast on a serving platter. Scoop potatoes and carrots out and place them around the roast.
9. Tent the serving platter with foil and let it rest for 5 minutes.
10. Add the gravy and drippings from the roast to a gravy boat to serve with the roast.

NOTES: *When the pot roast is cooked in the slow cooker, it often becomes so moist and tender that it basically falls apart as it cooks down. If you want to be able to slice the meat versus having it be shredded beef, the trick is to wrap the roast in aluminum foil as it cooks in the slow cooker. This helps the pot roast hold its shape.*

TANGY PINEAPPLE PULLED BEEF

Serves: 8 | **Cook Time:** 6 hours on LOW or 4 hours on HIGH | **Slow Cooker Size:** 6-quart (5.7-L)

This recipe is an easy way to add a sweet and tangy flavor to beef that tastes amazing. Shred the beef and serve on your favorite buns or rolls, with or without the pineapple in your sandwich.

3 pounds (1.4 kg) beef chuck roast, trimmed of excess fat

20 ounces (567 g) canned pineapple tidbits, drained

8 ounces (225 g) bottled French salad dressing

1 cup (150 g) brown sugar

Salt and pepper, to taste

FOR SERVING:

Buns or rolls

1. Cut the roast into 2 to 3 large pieces.
2. Spray the slow cooker with nonstick cooking spray or line with a slow cooker liner, if desired, to make clean up easier.
3. Place the beef in the slow cooker.
4. In a small mixing bowl, mix together the pineapple, French dressing, and brown sugar. Pour over the beef in the slow cooker.
5. Cover the slow cooker. Cook on LOW for 6 hours or on HIGH for 4 hours, or until beef is tender and easily shredded.
6. Remove the beef from the slow cooker and shred the meat with two forks.
7. Add the shredded beef to a large bowl, and spoon in as much or as little as you like of the cooking liquid and pineapple from the slow cooker, and toss to coat in the sauce.
8. Season to taste with salt and pepper.
9. Serve on your favorite buns or rolls.

FREEZER MEAL INSTRUCTIONS: Cut up the beef roast and create the sauce mixture. Place the beef inside a gallon-size zippered freezer bag and pour the sauce over it. Squish out as much air as possible before zipping closed. Label your bag with the name of the dish and cooking instructions.

TO COOK THE FREEZER MEAL: Thaw the freezer meal bag in the refrigerator. Pour the contents of the bag into the cooker and cook the recipe per the directions beginning at number 4.

NO-EFFORT KOREAN BEEF

Serves: 6 | **Cook Time:** 7 to 8 hours on LOW or 3 to 4 hours on HIGH plus 30 miniutes on HIGH
Slow Cooker Size: 6-quart (5.7-L)

This recipe really hits the spot when you are in the mood for some yummy Asian food. Tender beef chuck roast is cut into cubes and simmered in the slow cooker in a delicious Korean-inspired sauce. Serve over white or brown rice for a great dinner the whole family will love.

3 pounds (1.4 kg) boneless beef chuck roast, cut into 1-inch (2.5-cm) cubes

1 cup (235 ml) low-sodium beef broth, store-bought or homemade (page 311)

½ cup (120 ml) low-sodium soy sauce

½ cup (120 g) light brown sugar, packed

5 cloves garlic, minced

1 tablespoon (15 ml) toasted sesame oil

1 tablespoon (15 ml) rice wine vinegar

2 tablespoons (12 g) freshly grated ginger

1–2 teaspoons Asian hot sauce

½ teaspoon onion powder

½ teaspoon freshly ground black pepper

¼ cup (60 ml) cold water

2 tablespoons (18 g) cornstarch

FOR SERVING:

Cooked rice

1 teaspoon sesame seeds

2–3 green onions, thinly sliced

1. Place the cubed chuck roast in the slow cooker.
2. In a large mixing bowl, whisk together the beef broth, soy sauce, brown sugar, garlic, sesame oil, vinegar, ginger, hot sauce (as much or as little as you like), onion powder, and pepper. Pour over the beef in the slow cooker and stir to combine.
3. Cover the slow cooker. Cook on LOW for 7 to 8 hours or on HIGH for 3 to 4 hours.
4. In a small bowl, mix together the cold water and cornstarch to create a slurry to thicken the sauce.
5. Stir the slurry into the slow cooker. Cover the slow cooker. Cook for an additional 30 minutes on HIGH, or until the sauce has thickened.
6. Serve immediately over rice, garnishing with sesame seeds and green onion.

EASY FRENCH DIP SANDWICHES

Serves: 6 | **Cook Time:** 8 to 10 hours on LOW or 5 to 7 hours on HIGH
Slow Cooker Size: 6-quart (5.7-L)

Some days you really just need something that is super easy to throw in the slow cooker. Let it cook away all day, and you can come home to something tasty for dinner to feed your family. This recipe has just three ingredients (plus rolls or buns for serving), and it could not be any easier to make. Best of all, it really can be cooked all day in the slow cooker.

3 pounds (1.4 kg) beef chuck roast

29 ounces (858 ml) canned beef consommé

1 medium onion, chopped

FOR SERVING:

Hoagie buns or rolls

1. Trim the beef roast and remove the membrane and any visible fat. Cut it into large 2-inch (5-cm) chunks.
2. Place the beef, consommé, and onions in the slow cooker.
3. Cover the slow cooker. Cook on LOW for 8 to 10 hours or on HIGH for 5 to 7 hours.
4. Remove the chunks of beef from the slow cooker and shred them. Place the shredded beef on rolls or buns.
5. Strain the liquid from the slow cooker and pour it into bowls for dipping your sandwiches in.

NOTES: *Top your sandwiches with sliced mozzarella, provolone, or Swiss cheese for extra flavor!*

HOT BALSAMIC ROAST BEEF SANDWICHES

Serves: 6 to 8 | **Cook Time:** 6 to 8 hours on LOW or 3 to 4 hours on HIGH
Slow Cooker Size: 6-quart (5.7-L)

If you are looking for a super easy recipe for a weekday meal, this is it! This easy-to-prepare recipe really hits the spot. The sweet and tangy balsamic vinegar glaze adds the right touch to these delicious sandwiches!

3–4 pounds (1.4–1.8 kg) boneless round of chuck beef roast

14.5 ounces (411 g) low-sodium beef broth, store-bought or homemade (page 311)

½ cup (120 ml) balsamic vinegar glaze

1 tablespoon (16 g) Worcestershire sauce

1 tablespoon (15 ml) low-sodium soy sauce

¼ cup (85 g) honey

1 teaspoon dried rosemary

5 cloves garlic, minced

FOR SERVING:

Hoagie buns or rolls

1. Trim the beef roast to remove the membrane and any visible fat. Place in the slow cooker.
2. In a small bowl, mix together the remaining ingredients and pour over the beef in the slow cooker.
3. Cover the slow cooker. Cook on LOW for 6 to 8 hours or on HIGH for 3 to 4 hours.
4. Remove the roast from the slow cooker and shred the beef with two forks. Place the shredded beef on rolls.
5. Strain the liquid from the slow cooker and pour it into bowls for dipping your sandwiches.

BEEF AND SPINACH OVER ORZO

Serves: 8 to 10 | **Cook Time:** 6 to 7 hours on LOW or 5 hours on HIGH | **Slow Cooker Size:** 6-quart (5.7-L)

Orzo pasta is a fun way to change up a meal. It looks a bit like rice pilaf and it pairs very well with this nutritious beef and spinach dish. Sarah loves adding fresh spinach to meals because it sneaks in so many added vitamins and yet the family doesn't mind because it doesn't have an overwhelming flavor that overpowers the dish.

1 tablespoon (15 ml) olive oil

2 pounds (about 1 kg) beef roast, trimmed and cut into cubes or small chunks

28 ounces (794 g) canned diced tomatoes

4 cups (220 g) fresh baby spinach

1 cup (235 ml) low-sodium beef broth, store-bought or homemade (page 311)

1 cup (100 g) grated Parmesan cheese

3 stalks celery, chopped

3 cloves garlic, minced

2 bay leaves

1 small yellow onion, chopped

1 teaspoon Italian seasoning, store-bought or homemade (page 319)

Salt and pepper, to taste

FOR SERVING:
½ pound (225 g) orzo pasta

Parmesan cheese (optional)

1. Heat a large skillet on the stove top until hot and add the olive oil. Place the beef chunks in the hot pan and sear until browned on all sides.

2. Add the seared beef to the slow cooker and add the remaining ingredients except for the orzo pasta.

3. Cover the slow cooker. Cook on LOW for 6 to 7 hours or on HIGH for 5 hours.

4. About 20 minutes before serving, prepare the orzo pasta on the stove top according to the directions on the package until al dente. Drain.

5. Serve beef and spinach over the cooked pasta. Top with additional shredded Parmesan cheese (if desired) and season with salt and pepper to taste.

CHUNKY BEEF POTPIE

Serves: 6 to 8 | **Cook Time:** 4 to 6 hours on LOW plus 45 minutes in oven
Slow Cooker Size: 4-quart (3.8-L)

This hearty steak pie is a little bit more involved than most recipes, but it isn't all that complicated. The filling for the pie is cooked in the slow cooker so that you end up with very tender beef. Then it is poured into a refrigerated pie crust (or homemade crust if you are feeling ambitious) and baked in the oven. Sarah's oldest daughter absolutely raved about this recipe, and Sarah gets pretty excited if she can impress her!

2 pounds (about 1 kg) beef stew meat (or chuck roast cut into cubes)

10.5 ounces (298 g) canned cream of chicken soup

2 cups (260 g) sliced carrots (can also use frozen)

1 packet (28 g) onion soup mix, store-bought or homemade (page 319)

3 tablespoons (24 g) brown gravy mix

2 cloves garlic, minced

1 tablespoon (16 g) Worcestershire sauce

1 tablespoon (15 g) ketchup

1 package of refrigerated pie crusts (2 crusts per package)

¼ cup (20 g) shredded Parmesan cheese

1. Place all the ingredients except the pie crust and Parmesan cheese in the slow cooker and stir to combine.
2. Cover the slow cooker. Cook on LOW for 4 to 6 hours.
3. Give everything a good stir after done cooking.
4. Preheat the oven to 425°F (220°C, or gas mark 7).
5. Lay one of the pie crusts in the bottom of a 9-inch (23-cm) pie plate.
6. Scoop the meat mixture from the slow cooker into the pie crust.
7. Sprinkle the Parmesan cheese over the meat mixture.
8. Lay the second pie crust over the meat mixture, seal the edge, and flute. Cut slits in several spots of the top crust so that steam can escape.
9. Place the pie on a rimmed baking sheet and bake for 15 minutes.
10. Pull the pie out of the oven and cover the edges of the pie with strips of foil to prevent the edges of the crust from burning.
11. Bake for an additional 30 minutes, until the crust is golden-brown and the filling is bubbling.

CHIPOTLE BARBACOA SHREDDED BEEF

Serves: 8 | **Cook Time:** 8 to 10 hours on LOW or 6 to 7 hours on HIGH | **Slow Cooker Size:** 6-quart (5.7-L)

Chipotle peppers in adobo sauce are a wonderful way to add a ton of flavor to shredded beef made in the slow cooker. They are simply smoked jalapeño peppers, so there is a little bit of heat, but not too much. And the smokiness they add is just out of this world. Make a batch of this beef in the slow cooker, shred it up, and freeze it in freezer bags. All you have to do is pull out a bag, thaw it, and heat it up. You can use the meat in all sorts of Mexican-type dishes, such as burritos, tacos, taquitos, and burrito bowls. A personal favorite way is to include some of the shredded beef in cheese quesadillas.

4 pounds (1.8 kg) boneless beef chuck roast

1 teaspoon kosher salt

1 teaspoon freshly ground black pepper

2 tablespoons (30 ml) vegetable oil

½ cup (120 ml) apple cider vinegar

¼ cup (38 g) brown sugar, packed

5–6 cloves garlic, minced

1 tablespoon (3 g) dried oregano

4 teaspoons (10 g) ground cumin

¼ teaspoon ground cloves

¾ cup (175 ml) low-sodium beef stock, store-bought or homemade (page 311)

¼ cup (60 ml) freshly squeezed lime juice

3 to 4 chipotle peppers in adobo sauce (add more if you like it spicy)

2 bay leaves

1. Trim as much fat off the chuck roast as possible and cut the roast into 6 to 8 large pieces. Pat the pieces dry with paper towels and season with the salt and pepper on all sides.

2. Heat a large skillet over medium-high heat on the stove top. Add the oil to the pan and sear the meat on all sides until a nice crust forms. Transfer the seared meat to the slow cooker.

3. In a blender, add the remaining ingredients except for the bay leaves. Blend until smooth.

4. Pour the sauce over the beef in the slow cooker and add the bay leaves.

5. Cover the slow cooker. Cook on LOW for 8 to 10 hours or on HIGH for 6 to 7 hours.

6. Remove the beef from the slow cooker and shred the meat with two forks. Return the shredded beef to the sauce in the slow cooker. Stir to coat and serve.

MOROCCAN BEEF

Serves: 8 to 10 | **Cook Time:** 4 hours on LOW | **Slow Cooker Size:** 6-quart (5.7-L)

This aromatic beef dish is full of wonderful and exotic flavors. Honey and ginger give it great flavor, while turmeric and paprika give it a wonderful color. You can use precut beef stew meat or, if you are trying to save a little money, cut your own beef chuck roast into cubes.

This is a very large dish designed to feed a large family or to have leftovers for lunches the next day. You can easily cut the recipe in half and retain the same 4-hour cooking time.

5 pounds (2.3 kg) beef stew meat or chuck roast, cut into cubes

1 tablespoon (15 ml) olive oil, divided

1 large yellow onion, chopped

3 cloves garlic, minced

2 tablespoons (14 g) ground paprika

1 tablespoon (7 g) ground cumin

2 teaspoons (3 g) ground ginger

1 teaspoon kosher salt

½ teaspoon freshly ground black pepper

2 cups (260 g) sliced carrots (about 5 medium carrots)

½ cup (65 g) chopped dried apricots

½ cup (75 g) golden raisins

1 tablespoon (20 g) honey

2 cups (475 ml) low-sodium beef broth, store-bought or homemade (page 311)

FOR SERVING:

2 cups (185 g) uncooked brown or white rice

1. Heat a large skillet over high heat until hot. Add half of the olive oil to the hot pan.
2. Sear the cubes of beef in two batches in the hot oil, until browned on all sides.
3. Add the onion and garlic to the second batch of the beef to brown as well.
4. Add the meat, onion, and garlic to a slow cooker that has been sprayed with nonstick cooking spray.
5. Measure all the dried spices into a small bowl and mix well.
6. Add the carrots, apricots, and raisins to the slow cooker.
7. Coat the meat, carrots, and dried fruit with the spice mixture, mixing well to coat everything in the spices.
8. Drizzle the honey over the meat and toss to coat.
9. Add the beef broth.
10. Cover the slow cooker. Cook on LOW for 4 hours.
11. Serve over brown or white rice that has been cooked on the stove top or in a rice cooker according to the package directions.

SAUCY MONGOLIAN BEEF

Serves: 6 | **Cook Time:** 4 to 5 hours on LOW or 2 to 3 hours on HIGH | **Slow Cooker Size:** 6-quart (5.7-L)

Skip ordering take-out and make this delicious Mongolian-inspired beef dish at home instead. Tender flank steak strips and grated carrots are simmered in yummy Asian-inspired sauce for several hours. Then, serve over rice or noodles and garnish with fresh green onion slices—which adds a nice pop of color and flavor, too!

2 pounds (about 1 kg) beef flank steak, cut into strips

¼ cup (32 g) cornstarch

1 tablespoon (15 ml) vegetable oil

2 cloves garlic, minced

¾ cup (175 ml) low-sodium soy sauce

¾ cup (175 ml) water

¾ cup (113 g) brown sugar

1 cup (110 g) grated carrots

FOR SERVING:

Cooked rice or noodles

2–3 green onions, sliced thin

1. Add the strips of flank steak to a gallon-size zippered plastic bag and add the cornstarch. Seal the bag and shake to coat.

2. Add the oil, garlic, soy sauce, water, brown sugar, and carrots to the slow cooker. Stir to combine.

3. Add the cornstarch-coated steak strips and stir again until coated in the sauce.

4. Cover the slow cooker. Cook on LOW for 4 to 5 hours or on HIGH for 2 to 3 hours, until the beef is cooked through and tender.

5. Serve beef and sauce over rice or noodles and garnish with sliced green onions.

NOTES: *If you are short on time, you can purchase already-cut beef strips. Look for packages that say "stir-fry strips" in the butcher department of most major grocery stores. Also look for bags of preshredded carrots in the produce section!*

FRENCH DIJON BEEF

Serves: 4 | **Cook Time:** 7 to 8 hours on LOW plus 30 minutes on HIGH
Slow Cooker Size: 5-quart (4.7-L) or larger

Dijon mustard gives this beef dish a great tangy flavor, and the onion, garlic, and mushrooms add depth. The sauce is thickened up at the end of the cooking time in the slow cooker for a rich gravy that is full of flavor.

4 beef round steaks

½ teaspoon kosher salt

½ teaspoon freshly ground black pepper

2 tablespoons (30 ml) olive oil

8 ounces (225 g) white button mushrooms, sliced

1 large onion, sliced into strips

3 cloves garlic, minced

¾ cup (175 ml) low-sodium beef broth

½ cup (120 ml) dry white wine (or substitute beef broth)

¼ cup (60 g) Dijon mustard

1 teaspoon dried thyme

1 tablespoon (14 g) unsalted butter, melted

2 tablespoons (16 g) all-purpose flour

1. Season the steak with salt and pepper.
2. Heat the olive oil in a skillet on the stove top and sear the steak on both sides until golden-brown.
3. Remove the steak from the skillet and transfer to the slow cooker.
4. Add the mushrooms, onion, and garlic to the slow cooker.
5. In a medium mixing bowl, whisk together the beef broth, white wine, Dijon mustard, and thyme. Pour over the steak and vegetables in the slow cooker.
6. Cover the slow cooker. Cook on LOW for 7 to 8 hours.
7. In a small mixing bowl, add the melted butter and 1 cup (235 ml) of the liquid from the slow cooker. Whisk in the flour until no lumps appear.
8. Add this liquid back to the slow cooker. Leave the lid off and cook for an additional 30 minutes on HIGH, or until the liquid thickens.

ITALIAN MARSALA BEEF

Serves: 6 | **Cook Time:** 6 to 8 hours on HIGH | **Slow Cooker Size:** 5-quart (4.7-L) or larger

This super simple recipe requires no prebrowning of the meat. The only prep work really needed is to slice an onion and dump everything else in the slow cooker. You can serve the beef and delightful Marsala sauce over cooked rice or egg noodles for a dinner everyone loves.

2 pounds (about 1 kg) beef stew meat

1 medium onion, sliced thin

8 ounces (225 g) canned mushrooms (or fresh mushrooms)

2 teaspoons beef bouillon granules

½ cup (120 ml) Marsala wine

½ teaspoon dried parsley

1 tablespoon (15 ml) steak sauce

10.5 ounces (298 g) canned cream of mushroom soup

FOR SERVING:
Cooked egg noodles or rice

1. Add beef, onions, and mushrooms in the slow cooker.
2. In a medium mixing bowl, mix the remaining ingredients (except the cooked noodles or rice) and pour over the meat.
3. Cover the slow cooker. Cook on HIGH for 6 to 8 hours, or until the meat is very tender.
4. Spoon the meat-and-sauce mixture over cooked egg noodles.

SUPER SIMPLE BEEF TIPS

Serves: 6 | **Cook Time:** 6 to 8 hours on LOW | **Slow Cooker Size:** 6-quart (5.7-L)

Tender beef tips slow-cooked for hours—this is the perfect meal to make on busy days. The prep time is only a few minutes, which is great for busy mornings when you barely have time to make breakfast, let alone prep dinner, too. Best of all, this dish can be made into a freezer meal so that you have it ready to go: All you have to do is thaw it in the refrigerator overnight or in the sink in cool water for a few hours.

1½ pounds (680 g) beef stew meat

16 ounces (455 g) baby carrots

3 cloves garlic, minced

1 medium yellow onion, sliced into strips

1 package (28 g) onion soup mix, store-bought or homemade (page 319)

1 beef bouillon cube

1 teaspoon dried oregano

1 teaspoon ground paprika

12 ounces (340 g) canned evaporated milk

FOR SERVING:

1½ cups (285 g) long-grain rice, cooked

Pepper, to taste

1. Add all the ingredients to the slow cooker except for the cooked rice.
2. Stir to combine.
3. Cover the slow cooker. Cook on LOW for 6 to 8 hours, until the beef is cooked through and almost falling apart.
4. Thirty minutes before the end of the cooking time, prepare the rice on the stove top or in a rice cooker according to the package directions.
5. Serve the beef tips, carrots, and gravy over rice.
6. Season with pepper to taste.

FREEZER MEAL INSTRUCTIONS: Add all the ingredients except for the rice and evaporated milk (it may curdle) to a gallon-size zippered freezer bag and squish out as much air as possible before zipping closed. Label your bag with the name of the dish and cooking instructions.

TO COOK THE FREEZER MEAL: Thaw the freezer meal bag in the refrigerator. Pour the contents of the bag into the cooker and cook the recipe per the directions beginning at step 1. Be sure to add the can of evaporated milk, which was not frozen, and stir in well. The rice should be cooked separately 30 minutes before serving.

BEEF SIRLOIN TIPS WITH MUSHROOMS

Serves: 6 | **Cook Time:** 6 to 8 hours on LOW | **Slow Cooker Size:** 6-quart (5.7-L)

About half of Heidi's family LOVES mushrooms and the other half hates them. Heidi is in the love camp. She could eat mushrooms every single day. She makes this recipe whenever she wants something "grown-up" and tells the folks who hate mushrooms to just pick them out or to make themselves a bowl of cereal. Sometimes Mommy needs a meal that isn't macaroni and cheese and chicken nuggets!

2 pounds (about 1 kg) beef sirloin, cut into 1-inch (2.5-cm) cubes

¼ cup (32 g) all-purpose flour

2 tablespoons (30 ml) olive oil

1 large yellow onion, diced

5 cloves garlic, minced

8 ounces (225 g) fresh white button mushrooms, sliced

1 cup (245 g) tomato sauce

¾ cup (175 ml) dry red wine (or use beef stock if you don't cook with alcohol)

½ cup (120 ml) beef stock

2 bay leaves

6–8 sprigs fresh thyme

Salt and pepper, to taste

1. Place the cubed beef in a gallon-size zippered plastic bag and add flour. Shake to coat the meat lightly in the flour.
2. Heat a large skillet over medium-high heat. Add the olive oil and all the beef and brown the meat on all sides until golden-brown.
3. Add the browned beef, onion, garlic, and mushrooms to the slow cooker.
4. In a medium mixing bowl, whisk together the tomato sauce, red wine, and beef stock. Pour over the meat and vegetables in the slow cooker and stir to combine.
5. Add the bay leaves and sprigs of fresh thyme to the slow cooker.
6. Cover the slow cooker. Cook on LOW for 6 to 8 hours, until the beef is cooked and tender.
7. Remove the bay leaves and thyme sprigs and discard.
8. Season with salt and pepper to taste before serving.

NOTES: If you would like to thicken the sauce, whisk together 1 tablespoon (9 g) of cornstarch with 2 tablespoons (28 ml) of cold water to create a thickening slurry. Mix the slurry into the slow cooker during the last 60 minutes of cooking time.

DAD'S CHILI COLORADO

Serves: 12 | **Cook Time:** 8 to 10 hours on LOW or 4 to 5 hours on HIGH
Slow Cooker Size: 6-quart (5.7-L)

Heidi's dad was not much of a cook. In fact, she can only really recall three things he cooked for them as a family growing up: spaghetti and meatballs, navy beans and Indian fry bread, and this recipe for Chili Colorado. The recipe is easy and is one of her favorites. She makes it every couple of months, and her family is always excited to see and smell this recipe simmering away in the slow cooker.

They wrap the stewed beef up in tortillas with cheese and sour cream, and then ladle a little bit of the cooking liquid over the top of the burritos and eat them wet. If there are any leftovers (this recipe makes a lot!), she will package it up in freezer bags and freeze it for another dinner or Sunday lunch. Or she will add a few cans of whatever beans she has on hand (pinto, navy, kidney, black…they all work) and serve the leftovers up as a more traditional bean chili. So good!

2–3 pounds (about 1–1.4 kg) beef stew meat (or pork)

1 medium onion, chopped

3 cloves garlic, minced

43.5 ounces (1.2 kg) canned diced tomatoes, undrained

27 ounces (765 g) canned diced fire-roasted green chilies, undrained

1 teaspoon ground cumin

1 teaspoon kosher salt

1 teaspoon freshly ground black pepper

½ teaspoon chili powder (optional)

FOR SERVING:

Burrito-size flour tortillas

Shredded Cheddar or Monterey Jack cheese (optional)

Sour cream (optional)

1. Throw everything in the slow cooker except for the tortillas, cheese, and sour cream. Stir to combine.

2. Cover the slow cooker. Cook on LOW for 8 to 10 hours or on HIGH for 4 to 5 hours, until the meat is very tender and falling apart.

3. With a slotted spoon, scoop out the meat, tomatoes, onions, and green chilies onto flour tortillas. Add cheese and sour cream and roll up into burritos.

4. Place the burritos on plates and ladle some of the liquid from the slow cooker over the top of the burritos. Garnish with extra cheese and sour cream (if desired).

NOTES: *After it is cooked, this dish freezes well. Just let it cool and put in labeled freezer bags. You can also add three to four cans of drained beans to the leftovers and serve it as a traditional beef and bean chili.*

BEEFY BLACK BEAN ENCHILADAS

Serves: 8 | **Cook Time:** 2 to 3 hours on HIGH
Slow Cooker Size: 3½-quart (3.3-L) casserole or 6-quart (5.7-L) oval

Enchiladas are always a tasty option for dinner, and this recipe cooks perfectly in a casserole slow cooker. If you don't have one yet, you can also make it in a 6-quart (5.7-L) oval slow cooker, too. It just won't be quite as pretty, but it will still taste great!

There is a bit of prep work involved in this recipe because you need to cook up the beefy filling before you make your enchiladas. Make the filling the night before so that getting everything ready for dinner the next day is super easy.

1 pound (455 g) beef stew meat (or extra-lean ground beef)

1 small onion, chopped

16 ounces (455 g) canned black beans, drained and rinsed

16 ounces (455 g) canned corn kernels, drained

8 ounces (225 g) shredded Cheddar cheese, divided

2 teaspoons (5 g) chili powder

1 teaspoon ground cumin

1 teaspoon kosher salt

16 ounces (455 g) jarred salsa, divided

8 ounces (225 g) cream cheese, divided

8 medium-size flour tortillas

Nonstick cooking spray

1. Heat a large skillet on the stove top. Cook the beef and onion until the beef is no longer pink inside. Drain off any excess fat.

2. In a mixing bowl, mix together the beef, onion, beans, corn, 1 cup (115 g) of the shredded cheese, all the spices and ½ cup (130 g) of the salsa and stir to combine.

3. Spray the slow cooker with nonstick cooking spray.

4. Pour a thin layer of salsa on the bottom of the slow cooker.

5. Cut the cream cheese into 8 pieces.

6. Scoop out ⅛th of the meat mixture onto a flour tortilla, add a piece of cream cheese to the top of the beef, and roll the tortilla up around the filling.

7. Lay the rolled tortilla seam side down in the bottom of the slow cooker.

8. Continue with the remaining meat mixture, cream cheese, and tortillas.

9. Add the remaining salsa to the top of the enchiladas and then the remaining shredded Cheddar cheese.

10. Cover the slow cooker. Cook on HIGH for 2 to 3 hours, until everything is warm and bubbly and the cheese is melted. Do not overcook.

NOTES: *You can also use corn tortillas if you don't like or can't eat flour tortillas. You may be able to get more enchiladas using corn tortillas.*

SPICY BBQ BISON BRISKET

Serves: 8 | **Cook Time:** 8 to 9 hours on LOW plus 10 to 15 minutes on HIGH
Slow Cooker Size: 6-quart (5.7-L)

Bison brisket is a nice lean cut of meat that comes out nice and tender when cooked all day in the slow cooker. This dish has everything Heidi loves in slow-cooked dinners: potatoes, carrots, meat, and a sweet barbecue sauce with added heat from crushed red pepper flakes. Feel free to add more (or less) red pepper flakes to suit your spice level tolerance. Heidi personally likes it with a little more heat, so she goes a little wild with them!

¾ cup (171 g) of your favorite brand of brown sugar barbecue sauce

¼ cup (32 g) all-purpose flour

2 teaspoons (10 g) Worcestershire sauce

¼–1 teaspoon crushed red pepper flakes

8–10 small Yukon gold potatoes

3–4 medium carrots, peeled and cut into 2-inch (5-cm) chunks

3 pounds (1.4 kg) bison brisket

1. In a small bowl, whisk together the barbecue sauce, flour, Worcestershire sauce, and crushed red pepper flakes until there are no lumps of flour remaining.

2. Place the potatoes and carrots in the bottom of the slow cooker and place the brisket on top of the vegetables. Refrigerate the remaining sauce for use later in the recipe.

3. Top with ½ cup (about 120 ml) of the sauce mixture.

4. Cover the slow cooker. Cook on LOW for 8 to 9 hours.

5. Remove the meat from the slow cooker and place it on a cutting board. Tent the meat with foil and let the meat rest for 10 minutes.

6. While the meat is resting, remove the potatoes and carrots from the slow cooker with a slotted spoon. Place them on a platter.

7. Whisk the remaining sauce mixture into the juices in the slow cooker. Cook uncovered on HIGH for 10 to 15 minutes, or until thickened.

8. Slice the meat across the grain into thin slices and add it to the platter with the vegetables. Drizzle with the sauce from the slow cooker before serving.

HEARTY BISON POT ROAST WITH POTATOES AND CARROTS

Serves: 6 to 8 | **Cook Time:** 7 to 8 hours on LOW or 3 to 4 hours on HIGH
Slow Cooker Size: 5-quart (4.7-L) or larger

Bison is a healthy and lean meat that easily replaces beef in most dishes. However, because the meat is so lean, it tends to dry out. That is why we love cooking a nice bison roast in the slow cooker because the low, moist cooking environment gives the connective tissue in the roast time to really break down slowly and the meat becomes nice and tender. If you have access to bison, give this recipe a try!

2 tablespoons (30 ml) olive oil

3½–4 pounds (1.6–1.8 kg) bison roast

4–5 medium carrots, peeled and cut into 1 to 1½-inch (2.5- to 3-cm) chunks

3–4 large red potatoes, cut into chunks

1 medium yellow onion, sliced

2 cups (475 ml) low-sodium beef broth, store-bought or homemade (page 311)

2 cloves garlic, minced

2 tablespoons (32 g) Worcestershire sauce

1 teaspoon dried thyme

½ teaspoon kosher salt

½ teaspoon freshly ground black pepper

1. Heat the olive oil in a large skillet on the stove top. Add the bison roast. Sear the meat 3 to 4 minutes per side. Add the roast to the bottom of the slow cooker.

2. Arrange the carrots, potatoes, and onions around the roast in the slow cooker.

3. Add the remaining ingredients to the slow cooker.

4. Cover the slow cooker. Cook on LOW for 6 to 8 hours, or until the roast is very tender.

NOTES: *You can turn the liquid in the slow cooker into delicious gravy to pour over the roast and vegetables. Simply pour out the cooking liquid in a saucepan. Bring to a simmer over medium heat. Measure out ¼ cup (32 g) of flour and ½ cup (120 ml) of cold water and whisk together with a fork until no lumps appear. Pour the flour-and-water mixture into the simmering cooking liquid. Stir continuously while simmering until the gravy thickens, about 2 to 3 minutes.*

MELT-IN-YOUR MOUTH VENISON TENDERLOIN

Serves: 6 | **Cook Time:** 5 to 6 hours on LOW
Slow Cooker Size: 6-quart (5.7-L)

If you have hunters in your family and a freezer full of deer meat, then you are going to love this simple four-ingredient recipe. The venison tenderloin is already a nice and tender piece of meat (hence the "tender" in the word). And when you cook it in the slow cooker, you get a melt-in-your-mouth piece of meat. In this dish, you get a nice gravy to serve over the meat, too.

2 pounds (about 1 kg) venison tenderloin, sliced into 1-inch (2.5-cm)-thick slices

10.5 ounces (298 g) canned low-sodium cream of mushroom soup

10.5 ounces (298 g) canned low-sodium cream of chicken soup

1 packet (28 g) ranch dressing mix, store-bought or homemade (page 318)

FOR SERVING:

Cooked rice or egg noodles, cooked on the stove top (optional)

1. Add all the ingredients to the slow cooker.
2. Cover the slow cooker. Cook on LOW for 5 to 6 hours, stirring at least once during the cooking process.
3. Pour some of the gravy that is made in the slow cooker over the tenderloin slices and serve over rice or noodles (if desired).

SWEET BACON AND GARLIC VENISON LOIN

Serves: 6 | **Cook Time:** 6 to 7 hours on LOW
Slow Cooker Size: 5-quart (4.7-L) or larger

Bacon, brown sugar, and garlic combine to make a moist, tender, and full-of-flavor venison loin roast. The combination really is amazing! The bacon is wrapped around the loin in the slow cooker and cooked, which gives the meat a great bacon flavor. Then it is crisped up in the oven at the end of the slow cooking time.

2½–3 pounds (1.1–1.4 kg) venison loin

1 tablespoon (15 ml) olive oil

4 cloves garlic, minced

½ cup (115 g) brown sugar, packed

½ teaspoon kosher salt

½ teaspoon freshly ground black pepper

10–12 slices bacon

1. Rub the olive oil over the venison loin.
2. In a bowl, mix together the garlic, brown sugar, salt, and pepper.
3. Rub the brown sugar mixture over all surfaces of the loin, making sure to use all the mixture.
4. Wrap the loin with the bacon slices, tucking the ends of the bacon underneath the loin in the slow cooker.
5. Cover the slow cooker. Cook on LOW for 6 to 7 hours.
6. Remove the loin and place on a rimmed baking sheet.
7. Preheat the oven to 350°F (175°C, or gas mark 4).
8. Place the baking sheet with the bacon-wrapped loin in the oven. Cook for 15 minutes, or until the bacon is crispy.

SO-EASY VENISON BOURGUIGNON

Serves: 6 | **Cook Time:** 8 to 10 hours on LOW or 4 to 5 hours on HIGH | **Slow Cooker Size:** 6-quart (5.7-L)

Katie's family eats a lot of venison meat, and this recipe is a hearty and delicious way to prepare the meat. One of the tips she has learned along the way to mask the "gamey" taste that venison has is to rinse the meat first before cooking and then add a little cinnamon to the recipe. It really does work!

5 slices thick-cut bacon, chopped

3 pounds (1.4 kg) venison, cut into 1-inch cubes

1 teaspoon kosher salt

1 teaspoon freshly ground black pepper

1 cup (235 ml) red cooking wine

2 cups (475 ml) low-sodium beef broth, store-bought or homemade (page 311)

8 ounces (225 g) canned tomato sauce

¼ cup (60 ml) low-sodium soy sauce

¼ cup (32 g) all-purpose flour

5 medium carrots, peeled and sliced

1 pound (455 g) potatoes, peeled and cut into bite-size chunks

8 ounces (225 g) fresh mushrooms, sliced

3 cloves garlic, minced

2 tablespoons (4 g) dried thyme

1 teaspoon ground cinnamon (optional, but lessens the gamey taste)

1. In a large skillet on the stove top, cook the chopped bacon until crisp. Spoon the cooked bacon onto a paper towel–lined plate and let drain. Add the drained bacon to the slow cooker.

2. Season the venison meat with salt and pepper and sear the meat on all sides in the same skillet with a couple of tablespoons (about 30 ml) of the bacon fat. Add the meat to the slow cooker.

3. Add the red wine to the skillet and let the wine reduce by half while scraping the browned bits from the pan. Slowly add the beef broth, tomato sauce, and soy sauce. Whisk in the flour until there are no lumps. Add the sauce to the slow cooker.

4. Add the remaining ingredients to the slow cooker.

5. Cover the slow cooker. Cook on LOW for 8 to 10 hours or on HIGH for 4 to 5 hours.

VENISON GYROS WITH TZATZIKI SAUCE

Serves: 6 to 8 | **Cook Time:** 6 to 7 hours on LOW | **Slow Cooker Size:** 5-quart (4.7-L) or larger

We're not sure if the Greeks eat venison, but this recipe is one of Katie's family's favorites. It is a nice and lighter way to eat deer meat for either dinner or lunch. Katie often will slow-cook the meat ahead of time and then just heat it up and make pita sandwiches for lunches throughout the week.

2 pounds (about 1 kg) venison roast

¼ cup (59 ml) olive oil

3 cloves garlic, minced

2 tablespoons (30 ml) fresh lemon juice

1 teaspoon dried oregano
(Greek oregano, if you can find it)

½ teaspoon ground cinnamon

½ teaspoon kosher salt

½ teaspoon freshly ground black pepper

TZATZIKI SAUCE:

1 cup (200 g) plain Greek yogurt

1 medium cucumber, peeled,
seeded, and grated

1 tablespoon (4 g) fresh or dried dill

1 clove garlic, minced

¼ teaspoon kosher salt

FOR SERVING:

Pita bread

Sliced tomatoes

Sliced onion

1. Rinse the venison roast under cool tap water. Slice the meat into thin strips. Add the meat to the slow cooker.

2. In a small mixing bowl, mix together the olive oil, garlic, lemon juice, oregano, cinnamon, salt, and pepper. Pour over the meat in the slow cooker and toss to coat.

3. Cover the slow cooker. Cook on LOW for 6 to 7 hours, or until the meat is tender.

4. While the meat is cooking, prepare the tzatziki sauce. Mix all the ingredients in a small bowl and refrigerate while the meat is cooking to let the flavors meld together.

5. Serve the cooked meat in the pita bread with the tzatziki sauce and topped with onions and tomatoes.

MEXICAN-FLAVORED SHREDDED VENISON

Serves: 4 to 6 | **Cook Time:** 8 to 10 hours on LOW | **Slow Cooker Size:** 5-quart (4.7-L) or larger

If you need a venison recipe that can be cooked all day long in the slow cooker while you are at work, then this is the recipe for you. The venison is slow-cooked with great Mexican flavor, and it can be used in whatever dishes your family likes. Use it for burritos, tacos, nachos, enchiladas, tostadas, quesadillas, and more. Make up a batch and freeze it after it is cooked so that all you have to do is decide what's for dinner, then thaw and heat up the meat and just go about making dinner. It is nice to know that you have something in the freezer to help make meals just a little bit easier.

2 tablespoons (30 ml) olive oil

2–3 pounds (about 1–1.4 kg) venison roast

2 cups (475 ml) low-sodium beef broth, store-bought or homemade (page 311)

1 cup (260 g) chunky mild salsa

2 tablespoons (30 ml) apple cider vinegar

1 teaspoon ground cumin

1 teaspoon garlic salt

1 teaspoon chili powder

1 teaspoon onion powder

½ teaspoon ground cinnamon

½ teaspoon freshly ground black pepper

1. Heat the olive oil in a large skillet on the stove top. Sear the venison on both sides until golden-brown. Place the seared meat in the bottom of the slow cooker.

2. In a medium mixing bowl, mix together the salsa, vinegar, and all the spices and then pour over the top of the venison roast.

3. Cover the slow cooker. Cook on LOW for 8 to 10 hours, or until the meat is cooked and tender.

4. Shred the meat with two forks.

5. Serve the shredded meat in your favorite Mexican dish.

NOTES: *After it is cooked, the shredded meat and the liquid from the slow cooker can be frozen in labeled freezer bags for up to 6 months.*

VENISON SHAWARMA BOWLS

Serves: 6 | **Cook Time:** 5 to 6 hours on LOW | **Slow Cooker Size:** 5-quart (4.7-L) or larger

This recipe is very versatile. The meat can be added to rice, a soft-shell taco, or even a salad!

8 ounces (225 g) plain Greek yogurt

½ cup (120 ml) apple cider vinegar

5 tablespoons (25 g) shawarma seasoning, store-bought or homemade (page 316)

1 tablespoon (7 g) garlic powder

¼ teaspoon kosher salt

2 pounds (about 1 kg) venison, sliced thinly

FOR SERVING:

2 cups (316 g) cooked rice

2 cups (110 g) chopped mixed greens

3 Roma tomatoes, diced

1 small cucumber, peeled and diced

1. In a large mixing bowl, mix together the yogurt, vinegar, and all the seasonings until well combined.
2. Place the venison in the sauce and coat the meat with the sauce.
3. Cover the bowl and marinate overnight in the refrigerator.
4. In the morning, remove the meat from the marinade. Place the roast in the slow cooker and discard the marinade.
5. Cover the slow cooker. Cook on LOW for 5 to 6 hours, or until the meat is cooked all the way through.
6. Serve meat over a bowl of cooked rice topped with your favorite toppings.

FREEZER MEAL INSTRUCTIONS: Mix the marinade and pour over the venison inside a gallon-size zippered freezer bag. Squish out as much air as possible before zipping closed. Label your bag with the name of the dish and cooking instructions.

TO COOK THE FREEZER MEAL: Place the frozen meal in the refrigerator to thaw. Place the venison in the cooker and discard the marinade. Cook the recipe per the directions beginning at step 5.

6

PORK AND LAMB

SWEET APRICOT AND HONEY PORK CHOPS

Serves: 4 | **Cook Time:** 4 to 5 hours on LOW | **Slow Cooker Size:** 4-quart (3.8-L) or larger

Apricot preserves, dried apricots, and honey are combined in this sweet-yet-savory pork chop recipe. The pork chops come out super tender and tasty. Serve these pork chops with a side of mashed potatoes and steamed vegetables.

4 boneless medium-thick pork chops

¾ teaspoon kosher salt

¼ teaspoon freshly ground black pepper

¼ teaspoon dried rosemary, crushed

1 tablespoon (15 ml) olive oil

¼ cup (60 ml) apple cider vinegar

2 tablespoons (40 g) honey

¼ cup (80 g) apricot preserves

⅓ cup (43 g) chopped dried apricots

¼ teaspoon crushed red pepper flakes

1. Season the pork chops on both sides with salt, pepper, and rosemary.
2. In a large skillet set over medium-high heat on the stove top, heat the olive oil until hot and add the seasoned pork chops to the pan. Sear and brown the chops on both sides for 3 to 4 minutes per side until golden-brown.
3. Transfer the pork chops to the bottom of the slow cooker.
4. In the same pan, add the remaining ingredients. Cook while stirring, until the preserves have melted and the mixture comes to a simmer.
5. Reduce heat to low and simmer the sauce for 2 to 3 minutes, until the sauce is reduced slightly.
6. Pour the sauce over the pork chops in the slow cooker.
7. Cover the slow cooker. Cook on LOW for 4 to 5 hours.
8. Serve the pork chops with the sauce from the slow cooker spooned over the top.

DRUNKEN PEACH WHISKEY PORK CHOPS

Serves: 6 | **Cook Time:** 4 hours on LOW | **Slow Cooker Size:** 6-quart (5.7-L)

Moist and juicy pork chops are slow-cooked in a simple peach sauce laced with whiskey. This recipe has only five ingredients and is a snap to prepare—so you can have dinner on the table with little effort! Serve these juicy pork chops with a side of rice pilaf and some sort of vegetable such as broccoli or Brussel sprouts.

12 ounces (340 g) peach preserves

⅓ cup (80 ml) whiskey

1 clove garlic, minced

2 tablespoons (30 ml) vegetable oil

6 boneless thick-cut pork chops (about 6 ounces or 170 g each)

1. In a small mixing bowl, stir together the peach preserves, whiskey, and garlic. Set aside.

2. In a large frying pan set over medium-high, heat the oil until very hot but not smoking. Add the pork chops in a single layer and brown quickly on both sides until golden, about 2 to 3 minutes per side. You may need to do this in two batches to avoid overcrowding the pan if your pan is not large enough to hold all 6 pork chops.

3. Place the browned pork chops in the bottom of the slow cooker and pour the peach whiskey sauce over the pork chops.

4. Cover the slow cooker. Cook on LOW for 4 hours.

5. Serve the pork chops with peach sauce spooned over them and enjoy!

NOTES: *If you are watching your sugar intake, you can use sugar-free peach preserves or an all-fruit peach spread. Both work great in this recipe!*

BOURBON AND APPLE PORK CHOPS

Serves: 6 | **Cook Time:** 4 hours on HIGH | **Slow Cooker Size:** 6-quart (5.7-L)

This recipe is to die for! Savory chops are cooked in a great sauce filled with fresh apples and spiked with bourbon. The bourbon cooks off nicely in the slow cooker and just leaves the great flavor behind. Serve this with mashed potatoes and a nice vegetable side—and your meal is complete!

6 medium-thick boneless pork chops

Salt and pepper, to season the meat

1 tablespoon (2 g) fresh thyme leaves

4 medium apples, cored and thinly sliced

⅓ cup (75 g) light brown sugar, packed

¼ teaspoon ground cinnamon

½ cup (120 ml) bourbon

¼ cup (60 ml) cold water

1 tablespoon (8 g) cornstarch

1. Season both sides of each pork chop with a little salt and pepper and the fresh thyme. Place in the bottom of the slow cooker.

2. In a medium mixing bowl, combine the sliced apples, brown sugar, cinnamon, and bourbon. Stir to coat the apples.

3. Pour the apple mixture over the pork chops in the slow cooker.

4. Cover the slow cooker. Cook on HIGH for 4 hours, or until the chops are cooked and tender.

5. Pour juices from the slow cooker in a small saucepan and bring to a simmer on the stove top.

6. In a small cup, whisk the cold water and cornstarch with a fork until there are no lumps to create a thickening slurry.

7. Add the slurry to the simmering juices in the saucepan and cook while stirring constantly until the sauce has thickened.

8. Serve the sauce over the apples and pork chops.

NOTES: *You can substitute apple juice for the bourbon if you do not cook with alcohol. The flavor will be different, but it will still taste delicious.*

PINEAPPLE BBQ PORK CHOPS

Serves: 6 | **Cook Time:** 5 to 6 hours on LOW | **Slow Cooker Size:** 5-quart (4.7-L) or larger

You will want to prepare these pork chops the night before so that they have time to marinate. The pineapple barbecue sauce tenderizes the pork chops and adds a ton of flavor. The next day just pop them in your slow cooker and let them cook. I like to plate the pork chops on top of a bed of steamed white or brown rice, and then spoon a little of the sauce from the slow cooker over everything.

6 bone-in medium-thick pork chops

¼ teaspoon kosher salt

¼ teaspoon freshly ground black pepper

20 ounces (567 g) canned pineapple chunks in 100% pineapple juice, undrained

1 medium yellow onion, chopped

1 cup (228 g) barbecue sauce

2 tablespoons (40 g) honey

1. Season the pork chops with salt and pepper on both sides.
2. In large mixing bowl, add the can of pineapple with the juice, the onion, barbecue sauce, and honey. Stir to combine.
3. Add the pork chops to the liquid in the bowl and push the chops into the liquid so that they are covered completely.
4. Cover the bowl with plastic wrap and place in the refrigerator to marinate overnight.
5. In the morning, add the entire contents of the bowl to the slow cooker.
6. Cover the slow cooker. Cook on LOW for 5 to 6 hours.

FREEZER MEAL INSTRUCTIONS: *Follow steps 1 through 3 above except use a gallon-size freezer bag instead of a large bowl. Squish out as much air as possible before zipping closed. Label your bag with the name of the dish and cooking instructions.*

TO COOK THE FREEZER MEAL: *Place the frozen meal in the refrigerator to thaw. Cook the recipe per the directions beginning at step 5.*

HONEY PORK CHOPS WITH APPLES

Serves: 6 | **Cook Time:** 6 to 7 hours on LOW
Slow Cooker Size: 5-quart (4.7-L) or larger

This simple four-ingredient recipe is the perfect dinner for a cool autumn day, but Katie has been known to make it year-round because her family loves it so much. Tart Granny Smith apples are placed on the bottom of the slow cooker, pork chops go on top of the apples, a sprinkle of cinnamon and drizzle of honey is added, and then it is slow-cooked until tender.

4 medium Granny Smith apples, cored and sliced into ¼-inch (6-mm) slices

6 thick-cut pork chops

½ cup (170 g) honey

2 tablespoons (14 g) ground cinnamon

1. Place half of the sliced apples in the bottom of the slow cooker.
2. Layer the pork chops on top of the apples and then add the remaining sliced apples on top of the pork chops.
3. Drizzle the honey and sprinkle the cinnamon over the top of everything.
4. Cover the slow cooker. Cook on LOW for 6 to 7 hours.

SAVORY RANCH PORK CHOPS

Serves: 6 | **Cook Time:** 4 to 6 hours on LOW or 2 to 3 hours on HIGH | **Slow Cooker Size:** 6-quart (5.7-L)

If you are looking for a quick-and-easy way to prepare pork chops for dinner, this recipe cannot be beat. Canned cream of chicken soup and a packet of ranch dressing mix (or homemade) provide a creamy flavorful sauce that the pork chops are simmered in while they slow-cook.

6 medium-thick pork chops (bone-in or boneless)

1 cup (235 ml) water

1 can (10.75 ounces, or 305 g) cream of chicken soup

2 ounces (55 g) ranch dressing mix, store-bought or homemade (page 318)

FOR SERVING (OPTIONAL):

Cooked rice, potatoes, or noodles

1. Add the pork chops to the bottom of the slow cooker.
2. In a medium mixing bowl, mix together the water, cream of chicken soup, and ranch dressing until combined.
3. Pour the sauce over the pork chops.
4. Cover the slow cooker. Cook on LOW for 4 to 6 hours or on HIGH for 2 to 3 hours.
5. Serve the pork chops over cooked rice, potatoes, or noodles (if desired), spooning the sauce from the slow cooker over the chops.

NOTES: *If you are watching your sodium intake, look for low-sodium cream of chicken soup and make your own ranch dressing mix.*

JUST PEACHY PORK CHOPS

Serves: 6 | **Cook Time:** 5 to 6 hours on LOW or 2 to 3 hours on HIGH
Slow Cooker Size: 6-quart (5.7-L)

Turn fresh summer peaches into a delicious sauce that glazes delicious, tender pork chops. Summer is the perfect time of year to make these pork chops because that is when peaches are in season. In a pinch, you can use thawed frozen peaches so that you can make this any time of the year!

4–6 medium peaches

1 small yellow onion, chopped

¼ cup (60 g) ketchup

¼ cup (85 g) honey barbecue sauce

2 tablespoons (20 g) brown sugar

1 tablespoon (15 ml) low-sodium soy sauce

½ teaspoon garlic salt

½ teaspoon ground ginger

2–3 tablespoons (30–45 ml) olive oil

6 medium-thick boneless pork chops

1. Peel and pit the fresh peaches and place in a blender or food processor. Blend until smooth, adding a little bit of water, if needed, to help the peaches blend until perfectly smooth.

2. Add the onion, ketchup, barbecue sauce, brown sugar, soy sauce, garlic salt, and ground ginger to the blender or food processor. Blend until the onion is finely minced into the sauce.

3. Working in two batches so as to not overcrowd the pan, add 1 table-spoon (15 ml) of olive oil to a large skillet that has been heated over medium-low heat. Place 2 to 3 pork chops in the hot oil and brown the pork chops for 3 to 5 minutes per side.

4. Remove the pork chops with tongs as they finish browning and place them in the slow cooker. Brown the remaining pork chops and transfer them to the slow cooker when they are browned.

5. Pour the peach sauce over the pork chops.

6. Cover the slow cooker. Cook on LOW for 5 to 6 hours or on HIGH for 2 to 3 hours, or until the chops are cooked through.

TENDER APPLESAUCE PORK CHOPS

Serves: 6 to 8 | **Cook Time:** 7 to 8 hours on LOW | **Slow Cooker Size:** 6-quart (5.7-L) or larger

Just five simple ingredients tossed in the slow cooker and you have this delicious recipe for tender pork chops that practically fall off the bone. You can use anywhere from 6 to 8 pork chops in this recipe, so it is perfect if you are feeding a larger family or if you just want to have a few extra chops to eat for lunches during the week as leftovers.

6–8 medium-thick pork chops

2 tablespoons (14 g) dried minced onion

1½ teaspoons ground ginger

¼ teaspoon kosher salt

¼ teaspoon freshly ground black pepper

2–3 cups (490–735 g) cinnamon applesauce

FOR SERVING (OPTIONAL):

Cooked rice or pasta

1. Season the pork chops with the dried onion, ginger, salt, and pepper on all sides. Place half of the pork chops in the bottom of the slow cooker.

2. Spread half of the applesauce over the top of the seasoned pork chops.

3. Add the remaining pork chops on top and cover in the remaining applesauce.

4. Cover the slow cooker. Cook on LOW for 7 to 8 hours.

5. Serve the pork chops over rice or pasta (if desired).

NOTES: If you don't have cinnamon applesauce, you can use plain unsweetened applesauce and add a ¼ teaspoon of ground cinnamon per cup of applesauce used.

ITALIAN PARMESAN BREADED PORK CHOPS

Serves: 6 | **Cook Time:** 6 to 8 hours on LOW or 3 to 4 hours on HIGH
Slow Cooker Size: 3½-quart (3.3-L) casserole or 6-quart (5.7-L) or larger oval

Sarah made this recipe for a wonderful Sunday evening meal with her family. She was able to put it together after church in her casserole slow cooker and even with her father-in-law unexpectedly visiting from out of town, they still had plenty for everyone. Sarah's family really enjoyed this recipe, and she really loved how easy it was to put together. She served the pork chops with mashed potatoes and some California-blend frozen vegetables (cauliflower, broccoli, and carrots) that she just heated up quickly in the microwave.

Nonstick cooking spray

1 cup (130 g) sliced carrots

1 small yellow onion, sliced

2 cups (200 g) grated
Parmesan cheese

1½ cups (168 g) Italian seasoned
bread crumbs

2 tablespoons (14 g)
ground paprika

1 tablespoon (15 g) kosher salt

1 tablespoon (1 g) dried parsley

2 teaspoons (5 g) garlic powder

1 teaspoon freshly ground
black pepper

6 medium-thick pork chops

1. Spray the bottom and sides of the slow cooker with nonstick cooking spray.

2. Spread the sliced carrots and onion in the bottom of the slow cooker.

3. In a pie plate or shallow bowl, mix together the Parmesan cheese, bread crumbs, and spices.

4. Place each pork chop in the Parmesan cheese mixture and coat the pork chops on both sides. Place the coated chops in the slow cooker, squishing them as needed so that they will fit in the slow cooker without too much overlapping.

5. Take the remaining Parmesan cheese mixture and sprinkle over the pork chops in any areas that need more coating.

6. Cover the slow cooker. Cook on LOW for 6 to 8 hours or on HIGH for 3 to 4 hours, or until the pork chops are cooked through.

HONEY DIJON PORK CHOPS AND POTATOES

Serves: 4 | **Cook Time:** 4 to 6 hours on LOW or 3 to 5 hours on HIGH
Slow Cooker Size: 4-quart (3.8-L) or larger

Pork chops and red potatoes are slow-cooked for hours with tangy Dijon mustard and just a touch of honey for sweetness. We love this elegant recipe because it can also be made into a slow cooker freezer meal for days when you are just too busy to put something together for dinner.

1 cup (240 g) grainy Dijon mustard

¼ cup (59 ml) olive oil

½ cup (120 ml) chicken broth, store-bought or homemade (page 310)

2 tablespoons (40 g) honey

½ teaspoon freshly ground black pepper

½ teaspoon onion powder

6 medium red potatoes, cut into ¼-inch (6-mm) slices

4 thick-cut pork chops

1. In a medium mixing bowl, mix together the Dijon mustard, olive oil, chicken broth, honey, pepper, and onion powder until combined.

2. Add the pork chops and sliced potatoes to the bottom of the slow cooker.

3. Pour the sauce mixture over the chops and potatoes.

4. Cover the slow cooker. Cook on LOW for 4 to 6 hours or on HIGH for 3 to 5 hours, or until the potatoes are fork-tender and the pork chops are cooked through.

FREEZER MEAL INSTRUCTIONS: Mix together all the ingredients for the Dijon sauce in a bowl. Place the pork chops and potatoes in a gallon-size zippered freezer bag. Dump the sauce mixture into the bag and massage the bag to coat the pork chops and potatoes in the sauce. Squish out as much air as possible before zipping closed. Label your bag with the name of the dish and cooking instructions.

TO COOK THE FREEZER MEAL: Place the frozen meal in the refrigerator to thaw. Cook the recipe per the directions beginning at step 2.

SIMPLE ITALIAN PORK CHOPS

Serves: 6 | **Cook Time:** 6 to 8 hours on LOW
Slow Cooker Size: 6-quart (5.7-L)

With just four simple ingredients this recipe is quick and easy and full of great flavor. Use your favorite brand of bottled Italian salad dressing (even fat-free work) to bring great zesty flavor to this dish!

3 medium yellow onions, sliced

2 cups (230 g) Italian seasoned bread crumbs

16 ounces (455 g) bottled Italian salad dressing

6 medium-thick bone-in pork chops

1. Place a layer of sliced onion in the bottom of the slow cooker.

2. Add the bread crumbs and half of the Italian salad dressing to a large shallow bowl. Mix together until all the bread crumbs are moistened. Let sit for about 5 minutes to allow the bread crumbs to absorb the salad dressing.

3. Pour in the remaining half of the salad dressing, mix to combine, and let it sit again for 5 minutes to absorb.

4. Place a pork chop in the bowl and pat the pork chop firmly into the bread crumb mixture coating on each side.

5. Place a layer of coated pork chops on top of the onions, and add a layer of onions on top of the pork chops. Continue layering with pork chops and onions.

6. Cover the slow cooker. Cook on LOW for 6 to 8 hours.

7. Carefully remove the pork chops and onions from the slow cooker and serve.

HOMESTYLE PORK CHOPS AND STUFFING

Serves: 4 | **Cook Time:** 4 to 6 hours on LOW
Slow Cooker Size: 6-quart (5.7-L)

Sarah's family loves stuffing as a side dish or as part of the main dish even. This simple recipe comes together in literally 5 minutes, and everyone in the family loves it. Serve these pork chops with the stuffing with a side of sautéed green beans or corn to complete the meal!

6 ounces (168 g) boxed stuffing mix
(chicken or pork flavored)

1½ cups (355 ml) low-sodium chicken broth, store-bought or homemade (page 310)

4 medium-thick pork chops

1 can (10.75 ounces, or 305 g) cream of mushroom soup

1. In a medium mixing bowl, mix together the stuffing mix and the broth. Set aside.

2. Place the pork chops in the bottom of the slow cooker.

3. Pour the soup over the pork chops and spread evenly over the top.

4. Add the moistened stuffing to the top of the pork chops and spread it around evenly.

5. Cover the slow cooker. Cook on LOW for 4 to 6 hours.

SLOW-COOKED CHEESY POTATOES AND HAM

Serves: 8 | **Cook Time:** 6¼ to 8¼ hours on LOW or 3 to 4 hours on HIGH
Slow Cooker Size: 6-quart (5.7-L)

My family loves casserole, and this recipe is a big hit with everyone. Ham, green beans, and cheesy potatoes baked in the slow cooker create a delicious, creamy, cheesy flavor! This is a great recipe to use up leftover ham from the holidays!

28 ounces (794 g) frozen cubed hash brown potatoes

2 cups (460 g) sour cream

2½ cups (287 g) shredded three-cheese blend, divided

1 can (10.75 ounces, or 305 g) canned cream of chicken soup

1 medium yellow onion, chopped

4 ounces (115 g) cream cheese, softened

2 tablespoons (28 g) unsalted butter, melted

2 teaspoons (4 g) freshly ground black pepper

2 teaspoons (5 g) ground paprika

1½ pounds (680 g) sliced ham

14.5 ounces (411 g) canned green beans, drained

1. In a large mixing bowl, mix together the potatoes, sour cream, 2 cups (230 g) of the cheese, cream of chicken soup, onion, cream cheese, butter, pepper, and paprika.

2. Take 4 slices of the ham and place them in the bottom of the slow cooker so that they cover the bottom.

3. Chop the remaining ham into bite-size pieces and stir into the creamy mixture in the bowl.

4. Carefully fold in the drained green beans.

5. Pour the mixture into the slow cooker and spread it evenly over the ham slices.

6. Cover the slow cooker. Cook on LOW for 6 to 8 hours or on HIGH for 3 to 4 hours.

7. Remove the lid and sprinkle the remaining ½ cup (57 g) of shredded cheese evenly over the top of the casserole. Cover and cook for an additional 10 to 15 minutes to allow the cheese to melt.

SIMPLY THE BEST BAKED PINEAPPLE HAM

Serves: 8 to 10 | **Cook Time:** 30 minutes on HIGH plus 6 to 7 hours on LOW plus 35 to 45 minutes on HIGH
Slow Cooker Size: 6-quart (5.7-L) or larger

This whole ham recipe really is the best, and it is perfect for Christmas, Thanksgiving, or Easter. A whole ham is decorated with pineapple slices and whole cloves and then glazed with a sweet yet tangy glaze. The ham comes out tender, moist, and full of great sweet and salty flavor!

3–4 pounds (1.4–1.8 kg) whole boneless ham, unsliced

14 ounces (397 g) canned sliced pineapple rings, drained (reserve juice from the can)

Whole cloves

1⅓ cups (300 g) brown sugar

2 teaspoons (4 g) prepared mustard

2 tablespoons (30 ml) apple cider vinegar

1 cup (235 ml) pineapple juice (from the canned pineapple)

GLAZE:

2 tablespoons (28 ml) pineapple juice (from the canned pineapple)

2 tablespoons (18 g) cornstarch

1. Place the ham on a rimmed baking sheet and secure slices of canned pineapple to the surface of the ham with toothpicks.

2. Stud the ham and pineapple slices with whole cloves. Use as many or as little as you like.

3. Line the slow cooker with aluminum foil.

4. Add 1 cup (235 ml) of the reserved pineapple juice from the can of pineapple to the bottom of the slow cooker.

5. Place the ham in the slow cooker.

6. In a small mixing bowl, mix together the brown sugar, mustard, and apple cider vinegar. Spoon the mixture evenly over ham.

7. Cover the slow cooker. Cook on HIGH for 30 minutes, reduce heat to LOW and cook for an additional 6 hours, until the ham is heated through and has reached an internal temperature of 140°F (60°C) on an instant-read thermometer.

8. Remove the ham from the slow cooker using two large forks and place on a baking sheet while you prepare the glaze.

9. Combine the ham drippings from the slow cooker, 2 tablespoons (28 ml) of pineapple juice, and the cornstarch in a saucepan on the stove top set on high heat. Whisk constantly until thickened and coats the back of a spoon. The glaze should be quite thick.

10. Place the ham back in the slow cooker and spoon the glaze over the entire ham.

11. Cover and cook on HIGH for 35 to 45 minutes, until the glaze is slightly caramelized and shiny.

12. Remove the ham from the slow cooker and let it rest for 15 minutes before slicing.

SWEET HONEY MAPLE BBQ PORK RIBS

Serves: 4 to 6 | **Cook Time:** 6 to 8 hours on LOW plus 2 to 3 minutes under the broiler
Slow Cooker Size: 6-quart (5.7-L) or larger

Sarah's favorite types of ribs to cook and eat are St. Louis–style or baby back ribs, and this recipe works great for either kind. The tricky part of this recipe is just finding a rack of ribs that are small enough to fit in your slow cooker. When you have procured the right size rack of ribs, the rest of the recipe is rather straightforward. To make sure the ribs come out fall-off-the-bone tender, you will want to have the time to baste the ribs while they cook. And the trick to getting that nice caramelization that makes ribs so finger-licking is to throw the ribs under the broiler on your oven when they are done slow-cooking. These ribs are worth the effort!

3½ pounds (1.6 kg) St. Louis–style or baby back pork ribs

1 cup (228 g) honey barbecue sauce

⅓ cup (115 g) honey

¼ cup (80 g) real maple syrup

¼ cup (85 g) honey mustard

1 teaspoon kosher salt

1 teaspoon ground paprika

½ teaspoon freshly ground black pepper

½ teaspoon ground cinnamon

FOR BROILING:

1 cup (228 g) honey barbecue sauce

1 tablespoon (20 g) honey

1. In a small mixing bowl, combine together the barbecue sauce, honey, maple syrup, honey mustard, salt, paprika, black pepper, and cinnamon.

2. Place the ribs in the slow cooker so that they are standing up on their sides, curved around the slow cooker with the meaty part of the ribs facing outside next to the stoneware liner. If you are doing two racks of ribs, the ends of the racks can overlap each other.

3. Pour the sauce mixture across the tops of the ribs and spread the sauce over the ribs with a basting brush.

4. Cover the slow cooker. Cook on LOW for 6 to 8 hours, basting the ribs with the sauce in the slow cooker every 2 hours or so.

5. Preheat the oven at the broil setting.

6. Cover a rimmed baking sheet with aluminum foil. Remove the ribs from the slow cooker and place them on the baking sheet.

7. In a small bowl, mix together the other cup of barbecue sauce and tablespoon of honey. Baste the ribs with this mixture and place under the broiler on your oven for 2 to 3 minutes per side so that the sauce can caramelize. Be careful not to burn.

8. Cut the ribs using a knife or kitchen sheets into 2 to 3 rib sections for serving.

AUTUMN CRANBERRY AND ORANGE PORK ROAST

Serves: 8 to 10 | **Cook Time:** 6 to 8 hours on LOW or 3 to 4 hours on HIGH
Slow Cooker Size: 6-quart (5.7-L) or larger

Your mouth will water as this pork roast simmers away all day in your slow cooker! With only five simple ingredients, this recipe is easy to prepare and will impress your family or guests! This pork roast is great to make in the fall when canned cranberry sauce goes on sale at the grocery stores—but you really can make it any time of year.

3 pounds (1.4 kg) boneless rolled pork roast

14 ounces (397 g) canned whole-berry cranberry sauce

1 large orange

2 teaspoons (5 g) dried minced onion

1 teaspoon dried ground sage

1. Rinse the pork roast under cold running water in the sink and pat dry with paper towels.

2. Place the roast in the bottom of the slow cooker.

3. In a small bowl, combine the cranberry sauce, the zest and juice from the orange, dried onion, and sage.

4. Pour over the pork roast in the slow cooker.

5. Cover the slow cooker. Cook on LOW for 6 to 8 hours or on HIGH for 3 to 4 hours, until cooked through and tender.

6. Remove the roast from the slow cooker and place on a platter, tent with aluminum foil, and let rest for 5 to 10 minutes before slicing to allow the juices to redistribute throughout the meat.

SLOW-COOKED PORK LOIN AND STUFFING

Serves: 8 | **Cook Time:** 6 to 8 hours on LOW or 3 to 4 hours on HIGH
Slow Cooker Size: 6-quart (5.7-L)

Tender pork loin is cooked in a creamy sauce while the stuffing cooks right in there with the flavorful pork!

3–5 pounds (1.4–2.3 kg) pork loin roast

¼ teaspoon kosher salt

¼ teaspoon freshly ground black pepper

6 ounces (168 g) boxed stuffing mix

1 large yellow onion, chopped

1 can (10.75 ounces, or 305 g) cream of celery soup

¼ cup (60 ml) water

¼ teaspoon ground paprika

1. Coat the slow cooker insert with nonstick cooking spray.

2. Place the pork loin in the bottom of the slow cooker. Season with salt and pepper.

3. Sprinkle the dry stuffing mix over the pork loin.

4. Layer the onions on top of the stuffing mix.

5. In a small mixing bowl, mix together the can of cream of celery soup and ¼ cup of water and carefully pour over everything in the slow cooker.

6. Sprinkle ground paprika over the top.

7. Cover the slow cooker. Cook on LOW for 6 to 8 hours or on HIGH for 3 to 4 hours.

NOTES: *You can use any other flavor of cream soup that you like, such as cream of mushroom, cream of chicken, etc.*

ASIAN PORK LO MEIN

Serves: 6 to 8 | **Cook Time:** 6 to 7 hours on LOW or 3 to 4 hours on HIGH plus 30 minutes on HIGH
Slow Cooker Size: 5-quart (4.7-L) or larger

Pork roast is cooked in a flavorful Asian-inspired sauce for several hours, cubed or shredded, and tossed with fresh vegetables and cooked noodles for a complete dinner that is full of great flavor!

1½–2 pounds (680 g to about 1 kg) boneless pork shoulder or pork butt roast

½ cup (120 ml) low-sodium soy sauce

3 cloves garlic, minced

¼ cup (38 g) brown sugar, packed

1 tablespoon (15 ml) oyster sauce

1 tablespoon (16 g) ground fresh chili paste

1 tablespoon (6 g) fresh grated ginger

1 teaspoon toasted sesame oil

3 cups (213 g) fresh broccoli florets

5 ounces (140 g) canned sliced water chestnuts, drained

2 cups (260 g) thinly sliced carrots

1 cup (63 g) fresh snow peas

16 ounces (455 g) lo mein noodles (or spaghetti noodles), cooked according to the instructions on the package

1. Add the pork roast to the slow cooker.
2. In a small bowl, mix together the soy sauce, garlic, brown sugar, oyster sauce, chili paste, ginger, and sesame oil until combined. Pour over the pork.
3. Cover the slow cooker. Cook on LOW for 6 to 7 hours or on HIGH for 3 to 4 hours.
4. Remove the pork from the slow cooker and cut into bite-size pieces or use two forks to shred the meat.
5. Return the pork to the slow cooker with the cooking liquid.
6. Add the broccoli, water chestnuts, carrots, and snow peas, and stir to combine the vegetables with the meat.
7. Cover and cook for an additional 30 minutes on HIGH, until the vegetables are tender.
8. While the vegetables are cooking, prepare the noodles on the stove top according to the directions on the package.
9. Turn off the slow cooker and add the cooked noodles to the slow cooker and toss to combine.

BROWN SUGAR TERIYAKI PORK TENDERLOIN

Serves: 6 to 8 | **Cook Time:** 7 to 8 hours on LOW or 4 to 5 hours on HIGH
Slow Cooker Size: 5-quart (4.7-L) or larger

Tender pork tenderloin is cooked in the slow cooker with a sweet-yet-savory brown sugar teriyaki sauce. When it is done cooking, serve the sliced pork with a little bit of the sauce spooned over each serving.

2 tablespoons (30 ml) vegetable oil

2 pounds (about 1 kg) pork tenderloin

1 cup (235 ml) low-sodium chicken broth, store-bought or homemade (page 310)

½ cup (114 g) bottled teriyaki sauce

¼ cup (38 g) brown sugar, packed

4 cloves garlic, minced

2–3 medium red chile peppers, minced

1 medium yellow onion, sliced

½ teaspoon kosher salt

¼ teaspoon freshly ground black pepper

1. In a large skillet heated over medium-high heat on the stove top, heat the vegetable oil until hot.
2. Place the pork tenderloin in the skillet and sear the meat on all sides for 2 to 3 minutes until it becomes golden-brown.
3. Place the meat in the bottom of the slow cooker.
4. In a medium mixing bowl, combine the remaining ingredients until well mixed.
5. Pour over the pork in the slow cooker.
6. Cover the slow cooker. Cook on LOW for 7 to 8 hours or on HIGH for 4 to 5 hours.
7. Remove the tenderloin from the slow cooker and tent with foil. Allow the meat to rest for 5 to 10 minutes to allow the juices to redistribute throughout the meat.
8. Slice the pork into thick slices and spoon some of the liquid from the slow cooker over each slice of meat.

NOTES: *The red chile peppers add a little bit of heat and flavor to this dish but feel free to use more or less depending on your preferences.*

LEMONY DIJON PORK LOIN WITH CHERRY SAUCE

Serves: 4 | **Cook Time:** 6 to 8 hours on LOW | **Slow Cooker Size:** 6-quart (5.7-L)

Lemon juice and zest and Dijon mustard give this pork great tang and flavor, which is served with an easy-to-make sauce made out of frozen cherries. This dish will really impress your family or guests!

4 cloves garlic, minced

1 lemon, zested and juiced

1 tablespoon (15 ml) olive oil

1 tablespoon (15 g) coarse ground Dijon mustard

1 teaspoon dried rosemary

½ teaspoon kosher salt

⅛ teaspoon freshly ground black pepper

1 pound (455 g) boneless top loin pork roast

CHERRY SAUCE:

½ cup (120 ml) apple juice

¼ cup (80 g) red currant jelly

2 teaspoons (6 g) cornstarch

1 teaspoon coarse ground Dijon mustard

1 cup (155 g) frozen unsweetened pitted dark sweet cherries, thawed.

1. In a small bowl, combine the garlic, lemon zest, lemon juice, olive oil, mustard, rosemary, salt, and pepper.

2. Spread the mustard mixture over the entire pork roast and place the roast in the slow cooker.

3. Cover the slow cooker. Cook on LOW for 6 to 8 hours, or until an instant-read thermometer reads 145°F (63°C) when inserted into the thickest part of the roast.

4. While the roast is cooking in the slow cooker, prepare the sauce. In a small saucepan, combined the apple juice, currant jelly, cornstarch, and mustard. Cook while stirring constantly over medium heat until thickened and bubbly. Cook and stir for 1 more minute.

5. Reduce heat to low. Add the thawed frozen cherries and stir until mixture is heated through.

6. When the pork is done cooking, remove from the slow cooker and tent with foil. Allow roast to rest for 5 to 10 minutes to let the juices redistribute throughout the meat.

7. Slice the meat and serve with the warm cherry sauce.

DELICIOUS SLOW-COOKED PORK MARSALA

Serves: 4 to 6 | **Cook Time:** 6½ to 7½ hours on LOW | **Slow Cooker Size:** 5-quart (4.7-L) or larger

Thick slices of pork loin are cooked in the slow cooker with fresh mushrooms, onions, and a lovely sweet Marsala wine sauce. Serve the pork and the sauce over egg noodles for a perfect dinner.

1½–2 pounds (680 g to about 1 kg) boneless pork loin

1 teaspoon kosher salt

1 teaspoon freshly ground black pepper

3 tablespoons (45 ml) olive oil, divided

16 ounces (455 g) fresh white button mushrooms, sliced

1 medium yellow onion, diced

¾ cup (175 ml) sweet Marsala wine

½ cup plus 2 tablespoons (148 ml) water, divided

2 tablespoons (18 g) cornstarch

FOR SERVING:
Cooked noodles

1. Slice the pork loin into thick slices. Season with salt and pepper.
2. Working in 2 batches, heat 1 tablespoon (15 ml) of the olive oil in a large skillet over medium-high heat. Sear the pork slices until golden-brown on each side. Place the pork in the bottom of the slow cooker.
3. Heat an additional 1 tablespoon (15 ml) of oil in the skillet and sauté the mushrooms and sliced onion until both are starting to turn brown. Add to the slow cooker.
4. In the same skillet, add the sweet Marsala wine and ½ cup water (120 ml), and simmer while scraping the browned bit from the pan. Reduce the liquid by half and add to the slow cooker.
5. Cover the slow cooker. Cook on LOW for 6 to 7 hours.
6. In a small bowl, mix together the 2 remaining (28 ml) tablespoons of water and the cornstarch to create a thickening slurry. Stir the slurry into the slow cooker.
7. Cover and cook for an additional 30 minutes on LOW, until the sauce has thickened.
8. Serve the pork over egg noodles with the sauce spooned over top.

DELIGHTFUL MAPLE BALSAMIC PORK TENDERLOIN

Serves: 4 to 6 | **Cook Time:** 5 to 6 hours on LOW | **Slow Cooker Size:** 6-quart (5.7-L)

Two pork tenderloins are marinated overnight in a yummy marinade based on real maple syrup and balsamic vinegar for a sweet and tangy flavor, then seared quickly in a pan and slow-roasted in the slow cooker for a few hours until cooked and tender. Serve with your favorite vegetable side and mashed potatoes or rice pilaf for a flavorful dinner the whole family will love.

2 tablespoons (30 ml) olive oil

**2 pork tenderloins, about
16 ounces (455 g) each**

MARINADE/SAUCE:

2 shallots, minced

2 cloves garlic, minced

2 teaspoons (1 g) dried thyme

½ cup (161 g) real maple syrup

¼ cup (60 ml) balsamic vinegar

¼ cup (60 g) Dijon mustard

2 tablespoons (30 ml) olive oil

1 teaspoon kosher salt

**½ teaspoon freshly ground
black pepper**

¼ teaspoon cayenne pepper

1. In a large mixing bowl, combine all the ingredients for the marinade and whisk until well combined.

2. Place the pork tenderloins in a gallon-size zippered food storage bag and pour the marinade over the pork. Zip the bag closed and massage the pork gently to coat in the marinade. Place the bag on a plate in the refrigerator for at least 6 hours or overnight.

3. When the meat has marinated, heat the 2 tablespoons (30 ml) of olive oil in a large skillet over medium-high heat until hot but not smoking.

4. With tongs, carefully remove the pork tenderloins from the plastic bag and pat off any excess marinade and sear the pork for 2 to 3 minutes per side until nice and golden-brown.

5. Add the seared meat to the bottom of the slow cooker.

6. Add the marinade from the bag to the same pan you seared the pork and bring it to a simmer. Let the marinade simmer for about 5 minutes, or until reduced slightly. Pour over the pork in the slow cooker.

7. Cover the slow cooker. Cook on LOW for 5 to 6 hours.

8. Remove the pork from the slow cooker and place on a cutting board. Tent with aluminum foil and let rest for 5 to 10 minutes to allow the juices from the meat to redistribute.

9. Slice the pork into medallions and serve with some of the sauce from the slow cooker over the top.

HOMESTYLE POTATOES, SAUSAGE, AND GREEN BEANS

Serves: 6 | **Cook Time:** 6 to 8 hours on LOW | **Slow Cooker Size:** 4-quart (3.8-L) or larger

This recipe is reminiscent of a Depression-era recipe my grandma used to make. Very easy and frugal too! Potatoes, smoked kielbasa sausage, and green beans are cooked in the slow cooker for a complete dinner that doesn't break the bank!

6 medium potatoes, peeled and diced

1 pound (455 g) fresh green beans, cut into 1- to 2-inch (2.5- to 3.5-cm) pieces

1 pound (455 g) kielbasa sausage, sliced ½-inch (1-cm) thick

1 tablespoon (15 g) seasoned salt

13.5 ounces (400 ml) low-sodium chicken broth, store-bought or homemade (page 310)

1. Add all the ingredients to the slow cooker and stir to combine.
2. Cover the slow cooker. Cook on LOW for 6 to 8 hours.

PERFECT SAUSAGE AND BACON BAKE

Serves: 10 | **Cook Time:** 6 to 8 hours on LOW or 4 hours on HIGH
Slow Cooker Size: 3½-quart (3.3-L) casserole or 6-quart (5.7-L) oval

My family likes to have breakfast for dinner whenever they can, and this casserole is really a breakfast-type dish, but because it requires some precooking of the sausage and bacon, I like to make it for dinner instead. I like to use my casserole slow cooker because it makes for a really beautiful dish when it is all done. You can of course use a 6-quart (5.7-L) or larger oval slow cooker, too.

10 slices bacon

1 pound (455 g) ground pork breakfast sausage

2½ cups (570 ml) evaporated milk or heavy cream

2 teaspoons dried parsley

1 teaspoon kosher salt

½ teaspoon freshly ground black pepper

¼ cup (40 g) chopped yellow onion

3 cups (160 g) unseasoned dried stuffing cubes (or dried French bread cubes)

¼ cup (55 g) butter, melted

10 large eggs

1. Cook the bacon in a frying pan or bake in the oven at 350°F (175°C, or gas mark 4) until cooked but not crispy.

2. Cook and crumble the sausage and drain off the excess fat. Put the sausage in a large mixing bowl.

3. In a small saucepan, heat the evaporated milk (or heavy cream) with the spices for 5 minutes, stirring the whole time so it doesn't scald. After 5 minutes, add to the mixing bowl with the sausage. Add the onion and stir.

4. In another bowl mix together the dry stuffing mix and the butter to moisten the dry stuffing cubes.

5. Place the buttered stuffing mixture in the slow cooker.

6. Take each slice of bacon and roll it up and wedge it into the stuffing standing on its edge, distributing the rolls around the slow cooker so that none of the bacon rolls are touching each other.

7. Pour the sausage and cream mixture evenly over the stuffing and bacon in the slow cooker. Do not stir.

8. Carefully break each egg in various spots over the top of the casserole so that none of the eggs are touching another. Do not stir.

9. Cover the slow cooker. Cook on LOW for 6 to 8 hours or on HIGH for 4 hours, or until the eggs and stuffing are cooked.

NOTES: *If you would like to serve this casserole for breakfast, make it the evening before, refrigerate it overnight, and heat it in the oven in the morning.*

TANGY BBQ KIELBASA SAUSAGE

Serves: 6 | **Cook Time:** 2 to 3 hours on LOW | **Slow Cooker Size:** 4-quart (3.8-L) or larger

If you need a really simple recipe to make for dinner, this is the recipe for you. With just five ingredients it comes together super quickly and can be served either as a main dish (with a side of mashed potatoes, pasta, or rice and a veggie) or as an appetizer. This is a favorite of my kids because anything that is covered in barbecue sauce is a hit with them!

28 ounces (794 g) pork kielbasa sausage, cut into ½-inch (1-cm) chunks on the diagonal)

2 teaspoons (10 ml) olive oil

14 ounces (397 g) barbecue sauce

2 tablespoons (30 ml) hot wing sauce

1 tablespoon (6 g) prepared mustard

1. Heat a large skillet on the stove top and add the olive oil. Add the sausage and brown the sausage on all sides.

2. Add the browed sausage slices, barbecue sauce, hot wing sauce, and mustard to the slow cooker. Stir to coat.

3. Cover the slow cooker. Cook on LOW for 2 to 3 hours, or until hot, stirring at least once during the cooking time.

EASY ITALIAN SAUSAGE AND PEPPER SANDWICHES

Serves: 6 | **Cook Time:** 6 to 8 hours on LOW | **Slow Cooker Size:** 5-quart (4.7-L) or larger

Heidi makes this recipe at least once a month because it is a favorite of everyone in her family. The little kids usually pick off the peppers, but the older kids will leave them on and have gotten to really love the combination of the peppers and Italian sausage together. Heidi loves this recipe because it comes together quickly, and they can easily have it for dinner or lunch. Leftovers heat up well in the microwave for additional sandwiches, or you can slice up the sausages and serve them, the peppers, and the sauce over pasta. And if you need a recipe that serves a crowd, this one is easily doubled or even tripled. She has brought these tasty sausages to many a church potluck.

6 Italian sausage links, mild or hot depending on preference

2 medium bell peppers, seeded and sliced into strips

1 medium yellow onion, halved and sliced into strips

24 ounces (680 g) jarred marinara sauce

FOR SERVING:

6 submarine style rolls

Provolone or mozzarella cheese, shredded or sliced

1. Place the Italian sausages in the slow cooker.
2. Add the sliced peppers, onion, and marinara sauce over the sausages.
3. Cover the slow cooker. Cook on LOW for 6 to 8 hours.
4. Serve the sausages with peppers and sauce on submarine rolls (gluten-free if you are on a gluten-free diet) and top with cheese.

FREEZER MEAL INSTRUCTIONS: Place everything in a gallon-size zippered freezer bag and squish out as much air as possible before zipping closed. Label your bag with the name of the dish and cooking instructions.

TO COOK THE FREEZER MEAL: Place the frozen meal in the refrigerator overnight to partially thaw ingredients OR place the frozen bag in a sink of cold water to thaw just enough to be able to easily dump the contents of the bag into your slow cooker. Cook on LOW for 7 to 9 hours from a partially frozen state.

SPICY SAUSAGE AND ROTINI

Serves: 7 to 8 | **Cook Time:** 4 to 6 hours on LOW | **Slow Cooker Size:** 6-quart (5.7-L) or larger

Sarah's kids just love pasta recipes with meat and beans, and this recipe is one of their favorites. You can make this in your slow cooker for dinner any day of the week, or you can prep it ahead of time and stash it away in the freezer to have on a day when you are just too busy to fuss with dinner.

1 pound (455 g) hot pork Italian sausage, browned, crumbled and drained of excess fat

29 ounces (822 g) canned spicy diced tomatoes

29 ounces (858 ml) low-sodium chicken broth, store-bought or homemade (page 310)

15 ounces (425 g) canned black beans, drained and rinsed

1 cup (55 g) fresh baby spinach

1 medium yellow onion, diced

3 cloves garlic, minced

1 tablespoon (8 g) chili powder

1 teaspoon ground cumin

1 teaspoon dried oregano

½ cup (120 ml) evaporated milk

16 ounces (455 g) dried rotini pasta

FOR SERVING:

Grated Parmesan cheese

1. Add the sausage, tomatoes, chicken broth, beans, spinach, onion, garlic, chili powder, cumin, and oregano to the slow cooker. Stir to combine.

2. Cover the slow cooker. Cook on LOW for 4 to 6 hours.

3. During the last 30 minutes of cooking time, add the evaporated milk to the slow cooker.

4. Prepare the rotini pasta according to the package directions on the stove top until just al dente.

5. Drain the pasta and add it to the slow cooker. Turn off the slow cooker and let rest for 10 to 15 minutes for the pasta to absorb some of the sauce.

6. Top individual servings with Parmesan cheese before serving.

FREEZER MEAL INSTRUCTIONS: Brown and crumble sausage on the stove top, drain off the excess fat, and add to a gallon-size zippered freezer bag. Add the tomatoes, chicken broth, beans, spinach, onion, garlic, chili powder, cumin, and oregano to the bag. Squish out as much air as possible before zipping closed. Label your bag with the name of the dish and the cooking instructions.

TO COOK THE FREEZER MEAL: Thaw the frozen meal in refrigerator. Begin at step 2 of the recipe. Be sure to add evaporated milk during the last 30 minutes of cooking. Cook pasta al dente and then drain and add it to the sauce right before serving. Serve with Parmesan cheese.

SIMPLY THE BEST BARBECUED PULLED PORK

Serves: 8 to 10 | **Cook Time:** 8 to 10 hours on LOW or 4 to 5 hours on HIGH plus 3 to 4 hours on LOW
Slow Cooker Size: 6-quart (5.7-L)

The secret ingredient in this pulled pork recipe is the addition of pineapple juice. It lends sweetness to the dish, and there is an enzyme in pineapple that acts as a tenderizer and makes this pork so moist and tender.

2 medium yellow onions, divided

3–5 pounds (1.4–2.3 kg) pork butt or shoulder roast

2 cups (475 ml) canned pineapple juice

16 ounces (455 g) bottled barbecue sauce

FOR SERVING:

Buns or rolls

1. Optional, but highly recommended: Line the slow cooker with a slow cooker liner.
2. Slice one of the onions into strips and place ½ of the strips on the bottom of the slow cooker.
3. Add the pork roast on top of the onions and add the remaining ½ of the onion on top.
4. Pour the pineapple juice over the top of the roast.
5. Cover the slow cooker. Cook on LOW for 8 to 10 hours or on HIGH for 4 to 5 hours.
6. Remove the pork from the slow cooker and place in a large bowl or rimmed baking dish. Shred the meat with two forks, discarding any fatty bits from the meat.
7. Carefully drain off all liquid from the slow cooker (if you used a slow cooker liner, you can just remove the liquid and the liner at the same time and discard it).
8. Add the shredded pork back to the slow cooker.
9. Finely mince the remaining onion and add it to the pork along with the bottled barbecue sauce.
10. Cover and cook on LOW for 3 to 4 hours, stirring halfway during the cooking time.
11. Serve the pulled pork on buns or rolls.

ZESTY CITRUS-CHIPOTLE PULLED PORK

Serves: 20 | **Cook Time:** 10 to 12 hours on LOW or 5 to 6 hours on HIGH
Slow Cooker Size: 6-quart (5.7-L) or larger

This twist on the classic pulled pork sandwich is made interesting with the addition of some fresh orange juice and zest and some chipotle peppers in adobo sauce. With just four ingredients, it is super simple to make and the flavor is out of this world. Heidi's husband could eat this every day of the week and be a happy man.

This recipe makes a good 20 servings, so it is perfect for a party or potluck type get-together. Or just freeze up the leftovers and you will have easy dinners or lunches for another day. I love having stuff in the freezer that is already fully cooked, and all I have to do is heat it up and serve it.

3–5 pounds (1.4–2.3 kg) pork shoulder roast

24 ounces (680 g) bottled barbecue sauce

7 ounces (196 g) canned chipotle peppers in adobo sauce

2 large oranges, zested and juiced

FOR SERVING:

Buns or rolls

1. Place the pork in the bottom of the slow cooker.
2. In a blender, blend together the barbecue sauce, entire can of chipotle peppers in adobo sauce, and the zest and juice from the two oranges until everything is smooth and the peppers are fully blended into the sauce.
3. Pour the sauce over the meat in the slow cooker.
4. Cover the slow cooker. Cook on LOW for 10 to 12 hours or on HIGH for 5 to 6 hours.
5. Remove the meat from the slow cooker and place on a rimmed baking sheet and allow to rest for about 20 minutes. Shred the meat with two forks, discarding any fatty bits.
6. While the meat is resting, pour the sauce from the slow cooker into a bowl and skim off as much fat as you can. Set the sauce aside.
7. After the meat has rested and has been shredded, add it back to the slow cooker and add as much or as little of the sauce from the bowl back into the meat. Toss to coat.
8. Serve the cooked meat on buns or rolls, spooning additional sauce on sandwiches as desired.

NOTES: *The spiciness level on this recipe leans toward mild spice. Heidi's four children ate this just fine without complaint. The spice from the peppers does not hit you right away. Instead, it is more of a lingering tingle after you eat. You can easily adjust the heat level by using less (½ of a can). And, of course, if you like it hot, add more!*

SWEET-AND-SPICY BBQ PULLED PORK

Serves: 6 to 8 | **Cook Time:** 7½ to 8½ hours on LOW | **Slow Cooker Size:** 6-quart (5.7-L)

Pork loin is rubbed down with a homemade spicy rub and seared quickly in a pan on the stove top to seal in the juices. Then it's cooked for hours in the slow cooker until super tender. Shred the meat and toss it with whatever brand of bottled barbecue sauce you like for delicious pulled pork sandwiches that pack a ton of flavor!

3–4 pounds (1.4–1.8 kg) pork loin

1 cup (225 g) brown sugar, packed

1 tablespoon (7 g) ground paprika

1 tablespoon (7 g) garlic powder

1 tablespoon (7 g) onion powder

1 tablespoon (5 g) ground cayenne pepper

1 tablespoon (15 g) kosher salt

1 tablespoon (6 g) freshly ground black pepper

1 teaspoon chili powder

1 teaspoon ground cumin

1 teaspoon celery salt

2 tablespoons (30 ml) olive oil

16 ounces (455 g) bottled barbecue sauce

FOR SERVING:

Buns or rolls

1. Pat the pork loin with paper towels to dry.

2. In a medium mixing bowl, mix together the brown sugar and all the spices and seasonings to create a rub.

3. Brush the pork with the olive oil and rub the seasoning mixture liberally over the meat on all sides.

4. Heat a large skillet over medium heat. Sear both sides of the meat for 2 to 3 minutes per side until lightly golden-brown.

5. Place the meat in the slow cooker and cover. Cook on LOW for 7 to 8 hours, or until the meat is tender.

6. Remove the meat from the slow cooker and place on a rimmed baking sheet. Allow the meat to rest for 10 to 15 minutes before shredding with two forks.

7. Place the shredded meat back in the slow cooker and toss in your favorite bottled barbecue sauce.

8. Cover and cook for an additional 30 minutes on low, or until the sauce is hot.

9. Serve the shredded pork on rolls or buns.

AUTUMN APPLE CIDER PULLED PORK

Serves: 6 to 8 | **Cook Time:** 7 to 8 hours on LOW | **Slow Cooker Size:** 6-quart (5.7-L)

One of the nice things about pulled pork is if there are any leftovers, you can serve them over nachos with a little melted cheese!

3–4 pounds (1.4–1.8 kg) pork shoulder roast

2 tablespoons (20 g) brown sugar, packed

2 tablespoons (14 g) ground smoked paprika

1 teaspoon kosher salt

1 teaspoon freshly ground black pepper

1 teaspoon cayenne pepper

1 teaspoon garlic pepper

1 teaspoon onion powder

2 tablespoons (30 ml) olive oil

1 cup (235 ml) apple cider vinegar

½ cup (120 ml) water

FOR SERVING:

Buns or rolls

1. Pat the pork shoulder with paper towels to dry.
2. In a bowl, mix together the brown sugar with the spices and seasonings to create a rub.
3. Brush the pork with the olive oil and rub the seasoning mixture into the meat.
4. Heat a large skillet over medium heat. Sear the pork on all sides for 2 to 3 minutes, until the meat has a light golden-brown coloring.
5. Place the pork in the slow cooker and pour the apple cider vinegar and water over the pork.
6. Cover the slow cooker. Cook on LOW for 7 to 8 hours, or until the meat is tender and falling apart.
7. Remove the meat from the slow cooker, place on a rimmed baking sheet, and allow it to rest for 10 to 15 minutes before shredding with two forks. Discard any bone and fatty bits.
8. Serve the pulled pork on buns or rolls.

OUR FAVORITE ROOT BEER PULLED PORK

Serves: 8 to 10 | **Cook Time:** 8 to 10 hours on LOW | **Slow Cooker Size:** 6-quart (5.7-L) or larger

This recipe is one of the most popular pulled pork recipes on our blog. Pork shoulder butt roast is the perfect cut of pork for this pulled pork recipe because it requires a nice, long cooking time and the meat comes out super tender. A can of root beer adds flavor and tenderizes the meat while it cooks. Use your favorite brand of barbecue sauce to make it super good!

2 tablespoons (30 ml) vegetable oil

4–5 pounds (1.8–2.3 kg) pork shoulder butt roast

1 cup sliced onion (about 1 medium onion)

12 ounces (355 ml) root beer

16 ounces (455 g) bottled barbecue sauce

FOR SERVING:

Buns or rolls

1. Heat the oil in a large skillet over medium heat. Sear the pork on all sides until golden-brown. About 2 to 3 minutes per side.

2. Place the pork roast in the slow cooker and poke holes in the top of the roast with a sharp knife.

3. Add the onions to the slow cooker.

4. Pour the root beer over the roast.

5. Cover the slow cooker. Cook on LOW for 8 to 10 hours, until the meat is tender and falling off the bone.

6. Remove the pork from the slow cooker, place on a rimmed baking sheet, and let rest for 10 to 15 minutes. Shred pork with two forks, discarding bones and any fatty bits.

7. Strain the cooking liquid from the slow cooker into a bowl and set aside.

8. Add the shredded pork back to the slow cooker. Add the barbecue sauce and as much or as little of the cooking liquid back into the slow cooker as you like. Toss the meat to coat in the sauce.

9. Serve the pulled pork over buns or rolls.

SAUCY BBQ BEER PULLED PORK

Serves: 8 to 10 | **Cook Time:** 6½ to 8½ hours on LOW | **Slow Cooker Size:** 6-quart (5.7-L) or larger

This wonderful recipe uses your favorite brand of beer, either imported or domestic, to add just the right amount of tang to the meat. Don't worry though; the alcohol will burn off as it simmers away in the slow cooker. With only four ingredients this recipe, could not get any easier, and you can have dinner on the table in no time flat!

4–5 pounds (1.8–2.3 kg) pork butt roast

12 ounces (340 g) beer

1 large onion, chopped

16 ounces (455 g) bottled barbecue sauce

FOR SERVING:

Buns or rolls

1. Add the roast, beer, and onion to the slow cooker.
2. Cover the slow cooker. Cook on LOW for 6 to 8 hours.
3. Remove the roast from the slow cooker and place on a rimmed baking sheet. Let the meat rest for 10 to 15 minutes.
4. Shred the pork meat with two forks, discarding bone and any fatty bits.
5. Add the shredded pork back to the slow cooker and add the barbecue sauce. Toss to coat the meat in the sauce.
6. Cover the slow cooker. Cook for an additional 30 minutes on LOW, or until the sauce is hot.
7. Serve the shredded pork on buns or rolls.

CREAMY PARMESAN RANCH PULLED PORK

Serves: 6 to 8 | **Cook Time:** 6 to 8 hours on LOW or 3 to 4 hours on HIGH plus 15 minutes on LOW
Slow Cooker Size: 5-quart (4.7-L) or larger

You know you've created a hit when your kids serve themselves multiple second and third helpings of the meal you've made. Sarah really didn't anticipate how it would turn out, but was so pleased that the dish had an almost Alfredo taste that her family absolutely loves. They ate this on flour tortillas, but you could serve this on buns, or pasta, or just by itself. Adding freshly grated Parmesan gives it a great kick as well.

3 pounds (1.4 kg) boneless pork loin roast

1 packet (28 g) dry ranch dressing mix, store-bought or homemade (page 318)

14 ounces (397 g) canned black beans, drained and rinsed

16 ounces (455 g) cream cheese

2 tablespoons (30 ml) lemon juice

½ cup (40 g) shredded Parmesan cheese

FOR SERVING:

Buns, rolls, tortillas, or cooked pasta

1. Trim excess fat from the pork and cut into large chunks. Place in the bottom of the slow cooker.
2. Sprinkle half of the ranch dressing mix over the top of the pork.
3. Add the beans.
4. Cut the cream cheese into cubes and place over the top of the pork.
5. Sprinkle the remaining ranch dressing mix over the top of the cream cheese.
6. Drizzle the lemon juice over the ranch dressing mix.
7. Cover the slow cooker. Cook on LOW for 6 to 8 hours or on HIGH for 3 to 4 hours.
8. Remove the pork from the slow cooker and place on a rimmed baking sheet. Let the pork rest for 10 to 15 minutes and then shred the meat with two forks. Add the shredded pork back to the slow cooker.
9. Toss to coat the pork in the sauce that is in the slow cooker.
10. Add the shredded Parmesan cheese. Cover and cook for an additional 15 minutes on LOW.
11. Serve the pork on a bun or roll, in a tortilla, over pasta, or by itself.

ASIAN PULLED PORK SLIDERS WITH BROCCOLI SLAW

Serves: 30 to 40 sliders | **Cook Time:** 8 to 10 hours on LOW or 5 to 6 hours on HIGH plus 30 minutes on HIGH
Slow Cooker Size: 6-quart (5.7-L) or larger

Serve these beautifully seasoned Asian pork sliders at your next party or even just for dinner. Asian seasonings are used while cooking a pork roast, and then slider rolls are topped with the juicy tender meat and a crunchy Asian slaw. We dare you to just eat one!

⅔ cup (150 g) brown sugar, packed

1–2 cloves garlic, minced

1 tablespoon (15 ml) low-sodium soy sauce

1 tablespoon (15 ml) toasted sesame oil

1 teaspoon Chinese five-spice powder

1 teaspoon freshly ground black pepper

3 pounds (1.4 kg) pork rib eye roast

1¼ cups (295 ml) water, divided

2 teaspoons (6 g) cornstarch

2 tablespoons (16 g) toasted sesame seeds (optional)

1. In a small bowl, combine the brown sugar, garlic, soy sauce, sesame oil, Chinese five-spice powder, and ground pepper. Mix with a fork until you have a wet paste.

2. Place the pork roast in the bottom of the slow cooker. Spread the paste all over the roast, flipping it over, and rubbing it on the other side as well.

3. Pour 1 cup (235 ml) of water around the sides of the pork roast.

4. Cover the slow cooker. Cook on LOW for 8 to 10 hours or on HIGH for 5 to 6 hours.

5. Remove the pork from the slow cooker, place on a rimmed baking sheet, and allow it to rest for 10 to 15 minutes. Shred the pork with two forks, discarding any bone or fatty bits.

6. While the pork is resting, make a slurry of 2 teaspoons of cornstarch and ¼ cup (60 ml) of cold water. Add the slurry to the cooking juices in the slow cooker. Cover the slow cooker. Cook on HIGH for 30 minutes to thicken juices.

7. Add the shredded pork back to the slow cooker, add the sesame seeds (if desired), and toss to coat in the sauce.

ASIAN SLAW:

12 ounces (340 g) broccoli slaw (found in the produce section of most grocery stores)

1 tablespoon (15 ml) toasted sesame oil

¼ cup (60 ml) seasoned rice vinegar

1 clove garlic, minced

FOR SERVING:

2–3 packages of dinner rolls, slider rolls, or Hawaiian sweet rolls

TO MAKE THE SLAW

1. While the pork is cooking in the slow cooker, prepare the slaw.

2. In a large mixing bowl, toss the bagged broccoli slaw with the toasted sesame oil, seasoned rice vinegar, and garlic.

3. Cover the bowl with a lid or plastic wrap and refrigerate while your pork is cooking to allow the flavors in the slaw to meld together.

TO MAKE THE SLIDERS:

1. Split each roll open in half and place a bit of the pulled pork on the bottom roll.

2. Add a little bit of the slaw on top of the meat.

3. Place the top of the bun on the slider and enjoy!

NOTES: *If you cannot find broccoli slaw in your grocery store's produce section, feel free to use a bag of shredded cabbage coleslaw mix or a couple of cups of finely shredded cabbage.*

CUBAN MOJO PORK

Serves: 6 to 8 | **Cook Time:** 7 to 8 hours on LOW or 5 to 6 hours on HIGH plus 30 minutes in the oven
Slow Cooker Size: 5-quart (4.7-L) or larger

Cuban-style pork is packed with flavor. Marinate the meat overnight and dump-and-go in the morning. The meat will fall apart under your fork. Serve with plantains, black beans, and a side of white or yellow rice.

3–4 pounds (1.4–1.8 kg) bone-in pork roast

¾ cup (175 ml) orange juice

½ cup (120 ml) lime juice

½ cup (120 ml) olive oil

8 cloves garlic, minced

2 teaspoons (2 g) dried oregano

2 teaspoons (5 g) ground cumin

1 teaspoon kosher salt

1 teaspoon freshly ground black pepper

Zest of 1 orange

Zest of 1 lime

¼ cup (4 g) fresh chopped cilantro

FOR SERVING:

Cooked rice

Black beans

Plantains

1. In a large mixing bowl, combine the orange juice, lime juice, olive oil, garlic, oregano, cumin, salt, pepper, orange zest, and lime zest to create the marinade.

2. Place the pork roast in a gallon-size zippered food storage bag and pour the marinade in the bag. Zip close and let the meat marinate for 6 hours or overnight in the refrigerator.

3. When ready to cook, place the entire contents of the bag in the slow cooker.

4. Cover the slow cooker. Cook on LOW for 7 to 8 hours or on HIGH for 5 to 6 hours.

5. Preheat the oven to 400°F (200°C, or gas mark 6).

6. Remove the pork from the slow cooker and place on a rimmed baking sheet. Bake in the oven for 30 minutes until browned.

7. Remove from the oven and let the meat rest for 10 to 15 minutes before shredding with two forks. Discard the bones and any fatty bits.

8. Add the shredded pork back to the slow cooker with the liquid.

9. Serve the pulled pork with rice, black beans, and plantains.

FREEZER MEAL INSTRUCTIONS: Follow steps 1 and 2 above. Squish out as much air as possible from the bag before zipping closed. Label your bag with the name of the dish and cooking instructions.

TO COOK THE FREEZER MEAL: Thaw the frozen meal in refrigerator. Begin at step 3 of the recipe and cook in the slow cooker as usual. Brown the pork in oven as directed, shred, and return to the cooker to mix back with the juices.

PORK CARNITAS WITH ZESTY LIME SLAW

Serves: 10 to 12 | **Cook Time:** 10 to 12 hours on LOW or 5 to 7 hours on HIGH
Slow Cooker Size: 6-quart (5.7-L)

A whole pork loin roast is slow-cooked to perfection with just the right amount of spices and seasonings. Once cooked in the slow cooker, the meat is shredded and crisped up slightly in the oven. Serve the pork carnitas with the zesty lime slaw in tortillas for a dinner everyone will rave about!

2–3 pounds (about 1–1.4 kg) pork loin roast

12 ounces (355 ml) beer or chicken stock

1 teaspoon kosher salt

2 teaspoons (5 g) chili powder

2 teaspoons (5 g) ground cumin

1 teaspoon garlic powder

1 teaspoon freshly ground black pepper

½ teaspoon ground cayenne pepper

FOR THE SLAW:

½ cup orange juice

2 tablespoons (30 g) sour cream

1 lime, zested and juiced

¼ cup (4 g) chopped cilantro

1 teaspoon ground cumin

3 cups (270 g) shredded cabbage coleslaw mix (found in the produce section of most grocery stores)

Salt and pepper, to taste

FOR SERVING:

12 flour or corn tortillas

1. Place the pork in the bottom of the slow cooker.
2. In a medium mixing bowl, combine the beer, salt, chili powder, cumin, garlic powder, black pepper, and cayenne pepper. Pour over the pork in the slow cooker.
3. Cover the slow cooker. Cook on LOW for 10 to 12 hours or on HIGH for 5 to 7 hours.
4. Remove the pork from the slow cooker and place on a rimmed baking sheet. Let the pork rest for 10 to 15 minutes before shredding the meat with two forks.
5. Add the shredded pork back to the slow cooker and toss to coat the meat with the juices left in the crock.

TO MAKE THE SLAW:

1. Prepare the slaw while the pork is cooking.
2. In a large bowl, mix together the orange juice, sour cream, lime zest and juice, cilantro, and cumin to create the slaw dressing.
3. Add the shredded cabbage and toss to coat in the slaw dressing.
4. Taste and season with salt and pepper if needed.
5. Cover the bowl and refrigerate until ready to serve pulled pork.

TO SERVE:

1. Heat the tortillas in a dry cast-iron skillet on the stove top.
2. Place the shredded pork in each tortilla.
3. Top with the slaw and enjoy!

SWEET-N-SPICY PINEAPPLE JALAPEÑO PORK TACOS

Serves: 4 to 6 | **Cook Time:** 7 to 8 hours on LOW | **Slow Cooker Size:** 5-quart (4.7-L) or larger

Jalapeño peppers add a nice bit of spice while pineapple adds just a touch of sweetness to the pulled pork. Want more kick? Add more jalapeño peppers. While Katie likes to serve the shredded pork to tortillas and eat them as tacos, you can also serve it over tortilla chips and make some mighty tasty nachos.

2–3 pounds (about 1–1.4 kg) pork shoulder roast

½ teaspoon kosher salt

½ teaspoon freshly ground black pepper

20 ounces (567 g) canned pineapple chunks, undrained

2–4 fresh jalapeño peppers, sliced

1 small yellow onion, diced

1 small lime, juiced

½ cup (8 g) chopped fresh cilantro

FOR SERVING:

Flour or corn tortillas

2 cups (230 g) shredded extra-sharp Cheddar cheese

2 cups (110 g) shredded lettuce

Salsa

Sour cream

1. Add the pork to the bottom of the slow cooker. Season with the salt and pepper.

2. Add the can of pineapple with juice, jalapeño peppers, onion, lime juice, and cilantro to the pork.

3. Cover the slow cooker. Cook on LOW for 7 to 8 hours, or until the pork is very tender.

4. Remove the pork from the slow cooker and place on a rimmed baking sheet. Let rest for 10 to 15 minutes before shredding the meat with two forks. Discard any fatty bits.

5. Serve the shredded pork in tortillas topped with cheese, lettuce, salsa, and sour cream.

EASY SHREDDED PORK TACOS

Serves: 10 to 12 | **Cook Time:** 6 to 8 hours on LOW | **Slow Cooker Size:** 6-quart (5.7-L) or larger

Tacos is a meal Sarah's family has quite often at home because everyone will happily eat it. They enjoy it so much that they eat it for days when they get home from school. Make a large batch and keep plenty of tortillas on hand so the kids can devour them. We love this recipe: It has a tiny bit of bite to it. But it's not too spicy, and the flavor is wonderful. You can, of course, add more heat if you wish!

3½–5 pounds (1.6–2.3 kg) pork tenderloin

2 teaspoons (5 g) ground paprika

1½ teaspoons ground cumin

1 teaspoon chili sauce

1 teaspoon garlic powder

½ teaspoon onion powder

½ teaspoon dried onion flakes

½ teaspoon crushed red pepper flakes

½ teaspoon dried oregano

½ teaspoon kosher salt

¼ teaspoon freshly ground black pepper

2 pinches ground cinnamon

15 ounces (425 g) canned tomato sauce

4 ounces (115 g) canned diced green chilies (mild or hot)

FOR SERVING:

Corn tortillas

Cooking oil

Sour cream

Lettuce

Tomatoes

Guacamole

1. Place the pork in the bottom of the slow cooker.
2. In a small mixing bowl, mix together all the spices and seasonings. Pour the spices onto the pork in the slow cooker.
3. Pour the tomato sauce and green chiles over the pork.
4. Cover the slow cooker. Cook on LOW for 6 to 8 hours, or until the pork is tender.
5. Remove the pork from the slow cooker and place on a rimmed baking sheet. Let the meat rest for 10 to 15 minutes before shredding the pork with two forks.
6. Add the shredded pork back to the slow cooker and toss to coat with the cooking liquids.

TO MAKE TACOS:

1. Fry the tortillas in cooking oil, if desired, to make taco shells.
2. Stuff tortillas with pulled pork and top with your favorite taco toppings.

SWEET CITRUS PULLED PORK BURRITOS

Serves: 6 | **Cook Time:** 6 to 8 hours on LOW or 4 to 5 hours on HIGH
Slow Cooker Size: 4½-quart (4.3-L) or larger

Orange marmalade gives the pork a little bit of sweetness and fruity flavor while hot salsa brings just a touch of heat. Sarah loves preparing this pork dish as a freezer meal so that she can have something prepped and ready to go in the slow cooker. It's great for days when she is running kids to their after-school activities and doesn't have a whole lot of time to think about and make dinner.

Serve this yummy pulled pork in flour tortillas as a burrito, or try it on buns or rolls as a variation of pulled pork sandwiches. And if you are watching your carbs, serving the pork as a lettuce wrap is delicious, too!

3 pounds (1.4 kg) pork shoulder
or butt roast

2 tablespoons (28 g) taco seasoning,
store-bought or homemade (page 317)

½ teaspoon kosher salt

½ teaspoon freshly ground black pepper

1 cup (260 g) jarred hot salsa

1 cup (235 ml) low-sodium chicken broth,
store-bought or homemade (page 310)

½ cup (160 g) orange marmalade

½ cup (115 g) brown sugar, packed

FOR SERVING:

Burrito-size flour tortillas

Lettuce

Tomatoes

Beans

Avocado

Shredded cheese

Sour cream

1. Trim away any excess fat from the pork and cut the roast into 3 or 4 large chunks. Place the pork in the bottom of the slow cooker. Season the pork with taco seasoning, salt, and pepper.

2. In a small bowl, mix together the salsa, chicken broth, marmalade, and brown sugar until combined.

3. Add the salsa mixture to the pork in the slow cooker and toss to coat the meat.

4. Cover the slow cooker. Cook on LOW for 6 to 8 hours or on HIGH for 4 to 5 hours.

5. Remove the meat onto a rimmed baking sheet and let the pork rest for 10 to 15 minutes before shredding it with two forks.

6. Strain the liquid from the slow cooker into a bowl to remove the solids.

7. Add the shredded pork back to the slow cooker and add as much or as little of the strained cooking liquids back into the pork. Toss to coat.

8. Serve the shredded pork in the warmed flour tortillas with your favorite burrito fillings.

FREEZER MEAL INSTRUCTIONS: *Use a fresh pork roast, not frozen or previously frozen. Follow steps 1 through 3 above. Place everything in a gallon-size zippered freezer bag and squish out as much air as possible before zipping closed. Label your bag with the name of the dish and cooking instructions.*

TO COOK THE FREEZER MEAL: *Thaw the freezer meal bag in the refrigerator. Pour the contents of the bag into the cooker and cook the recipe per the directions beginning at step 4.*

SLOW-ROASTED HONEY ORANGE LAMB CHOPS

Serves: 6 | **Cook Time:** 7 to 8 hours on LOW or 3 to 4 hours on HIGH | **Slow Cooker Size:** 6-quart (5.7-L)

Orange juice and zest, honey, and thyme make a great sauce that gives these tender lamb chops just the right flavor. Watch your chops carefully so that you don't overcook them, and they will come out perfectly. The orange honey sauce will thicken a little bit while the lamb cooks, and you can spoon it over the meat when serving.

2 tablespoons (30 ml) vegetable oil

6 medium thickness bone-in lamb chops

½ cup (120 ml) orange juice

2 tablespoons (40 g) honey

2 tablespoons (18 g) cornstarch

1 teaspoon orange zest

1 teaspoon kosher salt

¼ teaspoon dried thyme

1. Heat the oil in a large skillet on the stove top over medium heat until hot. Sear the lamb chops for 2 to 3 minutes per side until golden-brown. Add the browned chops to the bottom of the slow cooker.

2. In a medium mixing bowl, combine the orange juice, honey, cornstarch, orange zest, salt, and thyme until well mixed. Pour over the chops in the slow cooker.

3. Cover the slow cooker. Cook on LOW for 7 to 8 hours or on HIGH for 3 to 4 hours.

GRANDMA PAT'S IRISH SHEPHERD'S PIE

Serves: 6 | **Cook Time:** 5 to 6 hours on LOW
Slow Cooker Size: 3½-quart (3.3-L) casserole OR 4-quart (3.8-L) round or oval

Heidi's grandma Patricia was of Irish descent, and she was born on Saint Patrick's Day. They would often have this recipe on her birthday. Heidi's grandma came from a farming family up in New Hampshire and Vermont, and she always had various farm animals that she raised for sale or slaughter even when she moved to California where she raised her family. So, eating lamb was not all that uncommon.

Use leftover mashed potatoes for the topping on this recipe. If you are in a pinch, instant mashed potatoes will work. I prefer to cook this dish in my rectangular casserole slow cooker because it looks more like a traditional oven-baked casserole. But a 4-quart (3.8-L) or larger round or oval slow cooker will work, too!

3 cups leftover prepared mashed potatoes (or use instant potatoes)

2 pounds (about 1 kg) ground lamb meat

1 large yellow onion, chopped

2 cloves garlic, minced

¼ cup (64 g) canned tomato paste

2 medium carrots, peeled and chopped

½ cup (65 g) frozen peas

2 ribs celery, diced

1 cup (235 ml) low-sodium beef stock, store-bought or homemade (page 311)

¼ cup (60 ml) dry white wine (or beef stock if you don't cook with alcohol)

2 teaspoons (10 g) Worcestershire sauce

½ teaspoon dried thyme

Salt and pepper, to taste

1. Warm leftover mashed potatoes in the microwave or on the stove top, adding a splash of milk if needed to make them spreadable. If using instant potatoes, prepare them according to the directions on the package and season with salt and pepper to taste. Set aside.

2. In a large skillet on medium-high heat on the stove top, cook the ground lamb along with the onion and garlic until the meat is no longer pink. Drain off any excess fat.

3. Add the tomato paste to the lamb mixture in the pan and cook for 2 to 3 minutes.

4. Add the carrots, peas, celery, beef stock, wine (or additional beef stock if using), Worcestershire sauce, and dried thyme. Bring to a boil.

5. Reduce heat to low and simmer the mixture in the skillet, uncovered, until most of the liquid is evaporated. Stir in the peas. Taste the mixture and season with salt and pepper to taste.

6. Transfer the lamb mixture to a slow cooker that has been sprayed with nonstick cooking spray.

7. Spread mashed potatoes over the top of the lamb mixture.

8. Cover the slow cooker. Cook on LOW for 5 to 6 hours, or until you can see the lamb mixture bubbling around the edges of the mashed potato topping.

9. Serve immediately straight from the slow cooker.

NOTES: *If you would like the topping of the shephers's pie to be browned, place the stoneware crock in a 350°F (175°C, or gas mark 4) oven and cook for 20 minutes.*

HOMESTYLE LAMB ROAST WITH ROOT VEGETABLES

Serves: 6 to 8 | **Cook Time:** 8 hours on LOW | **Slow Cooker Size:** 6-quart (5.7-L)

Each year our family purchases a whole lamb butchered from friends whose kids raise them as their 4-H project. We get a great deal and fill our freezer with various cuts of lamb. One of my favorite cuts is a boneless leg lamb roast, and cooking it in the slow cooker is great because it has a long cooking time and allows me to go on about my day without worrying about it.

6 medium potatoes, peeled and diced into ¾-inch (2-cm) cubes

8 medium carrots, peeled and sliced into ¼ in (6-mm) slices

1 large yellow onion, diced

3 to 4 pounds (1.4–1.8 kg) boneless leg of lamb roast

¼ teaspoon kosher salt

¼ teaspoon freshly ground black pepper

2 tablespoons (30 ml) olive oil

¼ cup (60 ml) balsamic vinegar

¼ cup (60 ml) water

2 tablespoons (4 g) fresh rosemary, minced

2 tablespoons (4 g) fresh thyme, minced

6 cloves garlic, minced

¼ cup (60 g) stone-ground mustard

1. Add the potatoes, carrots, and onions to the bottom of the slow cooker.
2. Generously season the lamb roast with salt and pepper on all sides.
3. Heat a large skillet (cast-iron preferred) on the stove top until very hot. Add the olive oil to the hot pan. Add the lamb roast and sear for 2 to 3 minutes per side to develop a golden crust.
4. Remove the roast from the pan and place on top of the vegetables in the slow cooker.
5. Add the balsamic vinegar and water to the hot skillet and deglaze the pan, scraping the browned bits off the pan. Pour this liquid over everything in the slow cooker.
6. In a small bowl, mix together the rosemary, thyme, garlic, and mustard. Spread this mixture all over the lamb coating all sides.
7. Cover the slow cooker. Cook on LOW for 8 hours.

NOTES: *Don't skip the browning of the lamb in the skillet part. This step seals the meat preventing the roast from drying out while cooking as well as adding a ton of flavor. Deglazing the pan you seared the meat in adds one more flavor dimension to the dish. It is worth the extra steps!*

GREEK-STYLE SLOW-COOKED LAMB ROAST

Serves: 4 to 6 | **Cook Time:** 8 to 10 hours on LOW plus 30 minutes in the oven
Slow Cooker Size: 6-quart (5.7-L)

A juicy leg of lamb is cooked all day in the slow cooker with great Greek flavors until it is moist and tender. Then it is popped into a hot oven to crisp it up before it is sliced and ready to serve. This is the perfect slow cooker dish to serve for company because it will surely impress your guests!

2 tablespoons (30 ml) olive oil

3–3½ pounds (1.4–1.6 kg) leg of lamb

1 large yellow onion, quartered

6 cloves garlic, peeled

1 cup (235 ml) low-sodium chicken stock, store-bought or homemade (page 310)

2 lemons, juiced

2 bay leaves

1 tablespoon (2 g) dried thyme

2 teaspoons (5 g) ground paprika

2 teaspoons (5 g) garlic powder

2 teaspoons (2 g) dried oregano

2 teaspoons (1 g) dried rosemary

½ teaspoon kosher salt

½ teaspoon freshly ground black pepper

1. Heat a large skillet over medium-high heat on the stove top and add the leg of lamb, searing the meat on all sides until golden-brown. Remove the lamb from the skillet and add to the bottom of the slow cooker.

2. In the same pan, sauté the onion quarters and whole garlic cloves until just lightly toasted, being careful not to burn the garlic. Add to the slow cooker with the lamb.

3. Add the chicken stock, lemon juice, bay leaves, thyme, paprika, garlic powder, oregano, rosemary, salt, and pepper to the slow cooker.

4. Cover the slow cooker. Cook on HIGH for 8 to 10 hours.

5. Remove the lamb from the slow cooker and place on a rimmed baking sheet. Use a spoon to scrape off any large fatty bits from the top and bottom of the meat.

6. Strain the liquid from the slow cooker and spoon off any excess fat from the top of the liquid. Use a standard blender or immersion blender to puree the liquid into a sauce to serve with the lamb.

7. Preheat the oven to 350°F (175°C, or gas mark 4).

8. Bake the lamb in the oven for 30 minutes to crisp up the outside of the leg of lamb.

9. Remove the lamb from the oven, tent with foil, and allow the meat to rest for 10 to 15 minutes before slicing the meat against the grain into ½-inch (1-cm) slices.

10. Serve the sliced lamb with the sauce.

BALSAMIC BROWN SUGAR SHREDDED LAMB

Serves: 6 | **Cook Time:** 5 to 6 hours on LOW | **Slow Cooker Size:** 6-quart (5.7-L)

Sweet and tangy, this yummy pulled lamb makes a rather easy dish for dinner or lunch. I prefer to tuck some of this delicious meat into pockets of pita bread, but it is also great on your favorite buns or rolls, too.

3 pounds (1.4 kg) lamb shoulder roast

¼ teaspoon kosher salt

¼ teaspoon freshly ground black pepper

2 tablespoons (30 ml) olive oil

3 cloves garlic, minced

1 cup (225 g) brown sugar, packed

⅓ cup (80 ml) balsamic vinegar

¼ teaspoon cayenne pepper

FOR SERVING:

Buns, rolls, pita bread, or wraps

1. Trim the lamb to remove excess fat and season with salt and pepper on all sides.

2. Add the olive oil to a large skillet and heat over medium-high heat. When the oil is hot, sear the meat on all sides for 2 to 3 minutes until golden-brown. Add the lamb to the slow cooker.

3. Turn the heat down to medium-low, add the garlic to the same pan, and sauté for 1 minute, being careful not to burn it.

4. Add the brown sugar, balsamic vinegar, and cayenne pepper to the same pan. Whisk while cooking until the sauce has thickened slightly. Pour the sauce over the lamb in the slow cooker.

5. Cover the slow cooker. Cook on LOW for 5 to 6 hours.

6. Remove the lamb from the slow cooker and place on a rimmed baking sheet. Allow the meat to rest for 10 to 15 minutes before shredding with two forks.

7. Add the shredded meat back to the cooking liquids in the slow cooker and toss to coat.

8. Place the shredded lamb on buns, rolls, or tucked inside a pita bread or wrap.

MOROCCAN LAMB TAGINE

Serves: 6 to 8 | **Cook Time:** 5 to 6 hours on LOW | **Slow Cooker Size:** 5-quart (4.7-L) or larger

A tagine is a Moroccan or North African pottery dish, and the meal cooked in the pottery dish is also called a tagine. Instead of the earthenware pottery vessel, this lamb tagine is cooked in the slow cooker with the same luscious slow-cooked flavor. Serve the lamb stew over cooked couscous topped with pine nuts for a great dinner that is sure to impress!

2 teaspoons (5 g) ground cinnamon

1 teaspoon ground coriander

1 teaspoon ground cumin

1 teaspoon ground turmeric

1 teaspoon ground ginger

¼ teaspoon kosher salt

¼ teaspoon freshly ground black pepper

1 pound (455 g) lamb roast, trimmed and cut into small bite-size pieces

1 medium yellow onion, chopped

1 tablespoon (20 g) honey

1 cup (235 ml) low-sodium chicken stock, store-bought or homemade (page 310)

13.5 ounces (383 g) canned garbanzo beans, drained and rinsed

FOR SERVING:

3 cups (471 g) couscous, cooked

¼ cup (35 g) toasted pine nuts

1. In a small mixing bowl, mix together the cinnamon, coriander, cumin, turmeric, ginger, salt, and pepper.

2. Toss the cubed lamb meat in the spice mixture to coat. Add the lamb to the slow cooker.

3. Add the onion, honey, chicken stock, and garbanzo beans to the slow cooker.

4. Cover the slow cooker. Cook on LOW for 5 to 6 hours.

5. Before serving, cook the couscous according to the package directions and toast the pine nuts.

6. Serve the lamb over the cooked couscous and garnish with toasted pine nuts.

RUBY PORT WINE BRAISED LAMB SHANKS

Serves: 4 | **Cook Time:** 4 to 5 hours on LOW | **Slow Cooker Size:** 5-quart (4.7-L) or larger

Juicy lamb shanks are slow-cooked in a lovely port wine sauce for a dish that is elegant yet simple. Serve the shanks over mashed potatoes with some of the luscious sauce spooned over the top. You don't have to use expensive port wine in this recipe either (leave that for drinking!). Instead, look for whatever is inexpensive at your local liquor store.

4 medium-thick lamb shanks

⅛ teaspoon kosher salt

⅛ teaspoon freshly ground black pepper

2 tablespoons (30 ml) olive oil, divided

3 cloves garlic, minced

1 medium yellow onion, finely chopped

1 medium carrot, finely chopped

1 rib celery, finely chopped

¼ cup (32 g) all-purpose flour

2 cups (475 ml) low-sodium beef stock, store-bought or homemade (page 311)

4 cups (940 ml) ruby port wine

¼ cup (64 g) tomato paste

2 teaspoons (1 g) dried thyme

3 bay leaves

FOR SERVING:

Prepared mashed potatoes

1. Season the lamb shanks with salt and pepper on both sides.

2. Heat half of the oil in a large skillet over high heat. Add 2 lamb shanks and brown on both sides until golden, approximately 2 to 3 minutes per side. Remove from the pan and place in the bottom of the slow cooker. Repeat with the remaining 2 lamb shanks.

3. Turn the heat down to medium and add the remaining 1 tablespoon (15 ml) of oil, garlic, onion, carrot, and celery. Sauté for 4 to 5 minutes, until the onion is softened and starting to turn translucent.

4. Add the flour into the onion mixture and cook for 1 minute. Add the remaining ingredients and stir to combine.

5. Pour the sauce mixture over the lamb shanks in the slow cooker.

6. Cover the slow cooker. Cook on LOW for 4 to 5 hours.

7. Remove the lamb from the slow cooker and place on a rimmed baking sheet, tent with foil, and allow the meat to rest for 10 to 15 minutes.

8. While the meat is resting, strain the liquid from the slow cooker into a large saucepan, pressing the vegetables with the back of a spoon to squeeze out as much liquid as possible.

9. Skim excess fat off the sauce. Cook over medium-high heat on the stove top, until the liquid reduces by half and is syrupy.

10. Add the meat to the saucepan and reheat in the sauce.

11. Serve the lamb shanks over mashed potatoes and spoon the sauce over before serving.

CURRIED LAMB SHANKS

Serves: 4 | **Cook Time:** 4 to 5 hours on LOW | **Slow Cooker Size:** 5-quart (4.7-L) or larger

This curry dish has a ton of great flavors and will really make your mouth sing. The lamb shanks are cooked in the curry sauce until they are falling-off-the-bone tender, then the sauce is reduced until thickened to really concentrate the flavors. Serve the lamb over rice or with naan bread.

4 medium-thick lamb shanks

4 tablespoons (59 ml) coconut oil

4 cloves garlic, minced

1 medium yellow onion, chopped

1 tablespoon (6 g) ground ginger

2 tablespoons (12 g) garam masala

1 tablespoon (6 g) ground coriander

2 teaspoons (5 g) ground turmeric

1 teaspoon ground cumin

1 teaspoon chili powder

1 teaspoon kosher salt

½ teaspoon ground cinnamon

4 bay leaves

4–6 cups (940 ml to 1.4 L) low-sodium beef broth, store-bought or homemade (page 311)

FOR SERVING:

Cooked rice

Naan bread

1. Heat a large skillet over medium-high heat and add oil to the pan. Add the lamb shanks to the pan and sear the meat until golden-brown, about 2 to 3 minutes per side. Transfer the lamb to the bottom of the slow cooker.

2. Add the garlic, onion, and all the spices and seasonings to the pan. Cook while stirring constantly until you begin to smell the spices and the onion cooks down a little bit.

3. Add the spice mixture on top of the lamb shanks in the slow cooker.

4. Add enough beef broth to the slow cooker so that the shanks are submerged only halfway. Depending on the size of your slow cooker, this could be anywhere from 4 to 6 cups (940 ml to 1.4 L) of broth.

5. Cover the slow cooker. Cook on LOW for 4 to 5 hours, flipping the lamb shanks over halfway through the cooking time.

6. Remove the lamb from the slow cooker and place on a rimmed baking sheet, tent with foil, and allow the meat to rest for 10 to 15 minutes.

7. While the meat is resting, strain the liquid from the slow cooker into a large saucepan.

8. Skim excess fat off the sauce. Cook over medium-high heat on the stove top, until the liquid reduces by half and thickens.

9. Add the lamb to saucepan and reheat in the sauce.

10. Serve the lamb hot over rice or with naan bread with some of the curry sauce spooned over top.

7

VEGETABLE MAIN COURSES

CHEESY CHILI CORN BREAD CASSEROLE

Serves: 8 | **Cook Time:** 4 to 5 hours on LOW
Slow Cooker Size: 3½-quart (3.3-L) casserole or 6-quart (5.7-L) oval

This quick chili is made up, put in the bottom of the slow cooker, and topped with corn bread laced with cheese. Then it's baked in the slow cooker for a dinner that is comforting and full of flavor! It's great to bake this in a 3½-quart (3.3-L) casserole slow cooker because it ends up looking more like a traditional oven-baked casserole. A 6-quart (5.7-L) or larger oval slow cooker will work, too!

1 medium onion, chopped

1 jalapeño pepper, seeded and finely chopped

15.5 ounces (439 g) canned kidney beans, drained and rinsed

15.5 ounces (439 g) canned black beans, drained and rinsed

15 ounces (425 g) canned red enchilada sauce

2 cloves garlic, minced

1 cup (162 g) frozen corn kernels

1 teaspoon ground cumin

8.5 ounces (241 g) boxed corn muffin mix

8 ounces (225 g) shredded Cheddar cheese

1. Heat a large skillet over medium-high heat. Spray with nonstick cooking spray and add the onions and pepper. Cook while stirring occasionally, until the onions are translucent and start to turn golden-brown.

2. Add the kidney beans, black beans, enchilada sauce, garlic, corn, and cumin to the pan. Cook and stir until heated through and beginning to simmer, about 5 minutes. Spoon the mixture into the bottom of the slow cooker.

3. Prepare the corn muffin mix according to package directions; stir in the cheese. Spread the batter over the chili mixture.

4. Cover the slow cooker. Cook on HIGH for 4 to 5 hours, or until a toothpick inserted in the middle of the corn bread topping comes out clean.

NOTES: *Feel free to top your chili and corn bread casserole with your favorite toppings, such as sour cream, additional cheese, sliced jalapeños, etc.*

CRUSTLESS VEGGIE PIE

Serves: 6 | **Cook Time:** 7 to 8 hours on LOW | **Slow Cooker Size:** 6-quart (5.7-L)

Fresh vegetables are cooked up into a lovely pie right in your slow cooker. We have listed our favorite mix of vegetables, but feel free to change it up to use whatever you have on hand. This is a great recipe to make when you are cleaning out the produce drawer in the refrigerator and have a handful of this and a handful of that of veggies.

½ cup (120 ml) milk

1 tablespoon (8 g) cornstarch

15 ounces (425 g) ricotta cheese

4 large eggs

¼ cup (25 g) grated Parmesan cheese

¼ cup (25 g) chopped green onion

¼ cup (12 g) chopped fresh basil

½ teaspoon kosher salt

¼ teaspoon freshly ground black pepper

1 medium yellow summer squash, sliced

1 medium zucchini, sliced

1 medium Roma tomato, sliced

1. Spray the slow cooker with nonstick cooking spray, line with parchment paper, and spray the parchment paper with additional cooking spray.

2. In a large bowl, whisk together the milk and cornstarch. Add the ricotta cheese and eggs and continue to whisk.

3. Add the Parmesan cheese, green onion, basil, salt, and pepper and whisk again.

4. Pour into the bottom of the prepared slow cooker and spread around with the back of a spoon.

5. Carefully arrange the vegetables on top of the batter.

6. Place a layer of paper towels between the rim of the slow cooker and the lid.

7. Cook on LOW for 7 to 8 hours, or until the pie is set.

HEALTHY BUTTERNUT SQUASH QUINOA CASSEROLE

Serves: 4 to 6 | **Cook Time:** 4 to 6 hours on LOW or 2 to 4 hours on HIGH
Slow Cooker Size: 4-quart (3.8-L) or larger

This lovely vegetarian casserole combines butternut squash, quinoa, black beans, and subtle Mexican flavors into a lovely dish that you can serve either as a main dish or as a side.

1½ cups (260 g) quinoa, rinsed

2 tablespoons (30 ml) olive oil

6–7 cups (840–980 g) peeled and cubed butternut squash

14.5 ounces (411 g) canned black beans, drained and rinsed

14.5 ounces (411 g) canned corn kernels, drained (or 2 cups fresh or frozen corn)

1 tablespoon (7 g) ground cumin

¼ teaspoon kosher salt

¼ freshly ground black pepper

2 cups (475 ml) water

1 lime, juiced

2 cups (230 g) shredded Cheddar cheese

FOR SERVING (OPTIONAL):

1 medium tomato, chopped

1 medium avocado, chopped

1. Add the rinsed quinoa to the bottom of the slow cooker.

2. Drizzle the olive oil over the top of the quinoa.

3. Layer the butternut squash cubes, black beans, and corn on top of the quinoa.

4. Season the top of the vegetables and beans with the cumin, salt, and pepper.

5. Add the water and the lime juice over everything.

6. Cover the slow cooker. Cook on LOW for 4 to 6 hours or on HIGH for 2 to 4 hours.

7. During the last 30 minutes, add the Cheddar cheese to the top of the casserole.

8. Cover and continue to cook for the last 30 minutes, until the quinoa is cooked.

9. Serve the casserole topped with chopped tomato and avocado (if desired).

PERFECT PARMESAN SPAGHETTI SQUASH

Serves: 4 | **Cook Time:** 5 to 6 hours on LOW | **Slow Cooker Size:** 6-quart (5.7-L)

Spaghetti squash is a great alternative to traditional pasta. In this recipe the squash is cooked in the slow cooker, but it's finished on the stove top to add some great flavor. The hard work is cooking the squash, but the slow cooker takes care of it all for you!

1 small spaghetti squash (about 2–4 pounds, or about 1–1.8 kg)

2 cups (475 ml) water

2 tablespoons (28 g) unsalted butter

⅓ cup (27 g) shredded Parmesan cheese, plus more for optional garnish

¼ cup (65 g) prepared pesto

½ teaspoon kosher salt

24 ounces (680 g) jarred marinara sauce

1. Wash the spaghetti squash and pierce the flesh 4 or 5 times with a sharp knife. Place in the slow cooker with the water.

2. Cover the slow cooker. Cook on LOW for 5 to 6 hours, checking occasionally to add more water if it has evaporated out.

3. Using tongs, carefully remove the cooked squash from the slow cooker.

4. Using a sharp knife, cut the squash lengthwise and scoop out and discard seeds.

5. Use a fork to shred the flesh of the squash to create squash "spaghetti."

6. In a large skillet, heat the butter over medium-low heat until melted. Add the squash flesh, Parmesan cheese, pesto, and salt. Cook while stirring continuously to evaporate some of the moisture from the squash and to mix the cheese and pesto into the "noodles."

7. Warm a jar of your favorite marinara up in a separate pan.

8. Serve the squash topped with the marinara sauce. Top with additional Parmesan cheese (if desired).

ITALIAN EGGPLANT PARMESAN

Serves: 6 | **Cook Time:** 6 to 8 hours on LOW or 4 to 5 hours on HIGH | **Slow Cooker Size:** 6-quart (5.7-L)

Sarah's family grows eggplant in their summer vegetable garden, and this recipe is full of great flavor. It is rather easy to make, too. It is a great vegetarian dinner option to eat in the summer when eggplant is in season!

2 medium fresh eggplants

¼ teaspoon kosher salt

72 ounces (2 kg) jarred marinara sauce

Italian seasoned bread crumbs

4 ounces (115 g) shredded Parmesan cheese

1 medium yellow onion, finely diced

3 cloves garlic, minced

6 ounces (168 g) shredded mozzarella cheese

FOR SERVING:

Pasta

1. Spray the slow cooker with nonstick cooking spray. Set aside.
2. Cut the top off the eggplant and peel the skin off with a potato peeler. Slice into ½-inch (1-cm)-thick slices.
3. Add the slices of eggplant to a large bowl and sprinkle with salt on all sides. Let rest for 10 to 15 minutes to allow the salt to draw out the bitterness from the eggplant.
4. Rinse the salt off of the eggplant under cool running water in the sink and pat each slice dry with paper towels.
5. Add a light layer of marinara sauce to the bottom of the slow cooker and spread it around.
6. Add a layer of sliced eggplant on top of the sauce, covering as much of the crock as possible. You can cut slices of eggplant in half if needed.
7. Add a thin layer of bread crumbs on top of the eggplant.
8. Add a thin layer of Parmesan cheese.
9. Add another layer of marinara sauce as well as a small amount of the onion and garlic.
10. Add a layer of mozzarella cheese.
11. Repeat the layers, starting with a layer of eggplant.
12. You will do 3 to 4 layers total, finishing off with a layer of marinara sauce and mozzarella cheese.
13. Cover the slow cooker. Cook on LOW for 6 to 8 hours or on HIGH for 4 to 5 hours.
14. About 30 minutes before the eggplant is done cooking, start to cook some pasta on the stove top according to the package directions.
15. Serve the eggplant Parmesan over the cooked pasta.

VEGETARIAN ZUCCHINI AND SPINACH LASAGNA

Serves: 6 to 8 | **Cook Time:** 4 hours on LOW
Slow Cooker Size: 3½-quart (3.3-L) casserole or 6-quart (5.7-L) oval or larger

This healthy recipe uses fresh zucchini that has been cut with a mandolin to make flat lasagnalike noodles. Sarah's kids didn't even realize they were eating zucchini! Best of all, this entire recipe is vegetarian and gluten-free! I cooked this recipe in my 3½-quart (3.3-L) casserole slow cooker, but you can totally make it in a 6-quart (5.7-L) or larger oval slow cooker, too!

4 medium zucchini

3 cups (165 g) baby spinach

1 teaspoon olive oil

48 ounces (1.4 kg) jarred marinara sauce

½ cup (80 g) diced yellow onion

32 ounces (905 g) part-skim ricotta cheese

¾ cup (75 g) grated Parmesan cheese

2 eggs

16 ounces (455 g) mozzarella cheese, shredded

1. Using a mandolin, sliced the zucchini into ⅛-inch (3-mm)-thick slices lengthwise. Spray two rimmed baking sheet and lay them on the baking sheet. Broil in the oven for about 6 to 8 minutes, remove from the oven, and let the sliced zucchini rest for a few minutes. Blot the cooked zucchini with paper towels to remove the oil and excess moisture.

2. While the zucchini are broiling, heat a small skillet on the stove top. Add the olive oil and cook the spinach until it is wilted, about 5 minutes or less.

3. In a medium mixing bowl, add the marinara sauce, cooked spinach, and onion.

4. In another medium mixing bowl, combine the ricotta cheese, Parmesan cheese, and eggs.

5. Spray the slow cooker with nonstick cooking spray.

6. Spread a thin layer of the marinara sauce mixture in the bottom of the slow cooker.

7. Add a layer of zucchini "noodles."

8. Add a layer of the ricotta cheese mixture.

9. Add a layer of mozzarella cheese.

10. Repeat the layers, ending with a layer of marinara sauce and mozzarella.

11. Cover the slow cooker. Cook on LOW for 4 hours.

12. Remove the lid, unplug the slow cooker, and let the lasagna stand for 10 to 15 minutes to allow the lasagna to set up.

SAUCY LASAGNA RICOTTA ROLLS

Serves: 6 | **Cook Time:** 4 to 6 hours on LOW | **Slow Cooker Size:** 6-quart (5.7-L)

This is one of Katie's favorite recipes to serve to company because it tastes amazing and really impresses everyone. I always get compliments from guests about how pretty these lasagna rolls are. Serve this with a nice side salad and some crusty Italian bread.

1 pound (455 g) lasagna noodles (about 14 to 15 noodles)

3 cups (345 g) shredded mozzarella cheese

15 ounces (425 g) part-skim ricotta cheese

½ cup (40 g) shredded Parmesan cheese

2 large eggs

48 ounces (1.4 kg) jarred marinara sauce

1. Bring a large stockpot of water to boil on the stove top. Cook the lasagna noodles until they are al dente according to the directions on the package.

2. Drain the noodles and rinse them in cool water to stop the cooking. Set aside.

3. In a medium mixing bowl, mix together 2 cups (230 g) of the mozzarella cheese, the ricotta cheese, Parmesan cheese, and eggs until everything is well combined.

4. Pour ½ of the marinara sauce in the bottom of the slow cooker.

5. Lay one noodle flat on a cutting board and spoon 1 heaping tablespoon of the ricotta cheese mixture onto the bottom half of the noodle. Roll noodle up around the ricotta mixture.

6. Add the roll to the slow cooker on top of the sauce.

7. Repeat with the remaining noodles and ricotta cheese.

8. Add the remaining marinara sauce.

9. Cover the slow cooker. Cook on LOW for 4 to 6 hours.

10. About 15 to 20 minutes before serving, sprinkle the remaining 1 cup (115 g) of mozzarella cheese over the top and allow it to melt.

GARDEN VEGGIE ROTINI WITH TOMATO SAUCE

Serves: 10 to 12 | **Cook Time:** 6 to 7 hours on LOW | **Slow Cooker Size:** 6-quart (5.7-L) or larger

This recipe turned into a super-rich, thick meal with great textures, and it's a fun way to eat various garden veggies. Sarah used vegetables that she knew my family enjoyed and what was in season at the time. You can, of course, play with the vegetables to suit your family's needs.

4 cups (940 ml) vegetable broth

1 small yellow summer squash, diced

1 large yellow onion, diced

1 cup (100 g) fresh green beans, cut in half

2 medium ribs celery, thinly sliced

28 ounces (794 g) canned diced tomatoes, undrained

1 tablespoon (5 g) dried basil

1 teaspoon kosher salt

½ teaspoon freshly ground black pepper

½ teaspoon dried oregano

2–3 cans (10.25 ounce) condensed tomato soup

2 cups (168 g) rotini pasta

Parmesan cheese (optional)

1. Add all the ingredients except for the tomato soup and pasta to the slow cooker.
2. Add 2 cans of tomato soup and add the third can only if you have room. Do not add additional water.
3. Mix well.
4. Cover the slow cooker. Cook on LOW for 6 to 7 hours.
5. About 30 minutes before serving, cook the pasta on the stove top according to the directions on the package until al dente, being careful not to overcook. Strain.
6. Add the cooked pasta to the sauce and stir. Turn off the heat on the slow cooker and eat right away.
7. Top with Parmesan cheese (if desired).

SAVORY ZUCCHINI GRATIN

Serves: 4 to 6 | **Cook Time:** 3½ to 4½ hours on HIGH
Slow Cooker Size: 3½-quart (3.3-L) casserole or 6-quart (5.7-L) oval

A delicious recipe to help use up those overloaded summer gardens full of zucchini and yellow summer squash. The trick with this recipe is to steam the vegetables first so you can squeeze out most of the extra liquid from them. This helps cook it faster, and the vegetables retain their beautiful colors and textures.

3 medium zucchini

½ medium yellow onion

3 small yellow summer squash

¼ cup (25 g) plus 1 tablespoon (5 g) shredded Parmesan cheese, divided

1 tablespoon (3 g) Italian seasoning

½ teaspoon kosher salt

¼ teaspoon freshly ground black pepper

½ teaspoon ground paprika

¼ teaspoon red pepper flakes

1 large egg

2 medium to large Roma tomatoes, sliced ¼-inch (6-cm) thick

1½ cups (about 173 g) shredded cheese (such as Cheddar, jack, mozzarella, etc.)

1. Spray the slow cooker with nonstick cooking spray. Set aside.

2. Wash the zucchini, cut off and discard the ends, and cut in half. Quarter each half of the zucchini lengthwise. Steam the zucchini.

3. Dice the onion half and steam.

4. Wash the yellow squash, cut off and discard the ends, and cut in half. Quarter each half of the squash lengthwise. Steam the squash.

5. Add the steamed vegetables to a large strainer. Use a heavy spoon to squeeze and press out as much of the excess liquid and seeds as possible. Place in a large bowl.

6. In a small bowl, mix together the ¼ cup (25 g) of Parmesan cheese, the Italian seasoning, salt, pepper, paprika, and red pepper flakes. Add the seasonings to the vegetables and mix.

7. Mix in the egg until combined.

8. Spread the mixture into the slow cooker; leave any excess liquid in the bowl if there is any.

9. Arrange the tomato slices over the top of the vegetable mixture, overlapping if necessary so that the entire top is covered in tomato slices.

10. Cover the slow cooker. Cook on HIGH for 3 to 4 hours.

11. Remove the lid, sprinkle the remaining tablespoon (5 g) of Parmesan cheese, and let rest for 10 minutes.

12. Add the shredded cheese and turn the slow cooker back on HIGH and cook uncovered for an additional 30 minutes to allow the cheese to melt.

NOTES: *Sarah uses microwave steaming bags to steam the vegetables in. You can use the steaming function on a rice cooker, electric pressure cooker, or microwave steamer bowl.*

VEGGIE-LOADED SPAGHETTI

Serves: 4 to 6 | **Cook Time:** 3 to 4 hours on LOW plus 30 minutes on HIGH
Slow Cooker Size: 4-quart (3.8-L) or larger

Katie's family loves spaghetti night, and she loves making this healthy, vegetarian spaghetti sauce in the slow cooker. This homemade sauce is full of all sorts of vegetables like green pepper, tomatoes, mushrooms, zucchini, and more. Spaghetti noodles are cooked right in the sauce during the last 30 minutes of cooking.

2 medium tomatoes, diced

1 medium yellow onion, sliced

1 medium green bell pepper, seeded and diced

1 small zucchini, sliced thick

16 ounces (455 g) fresh white button mushrooms, sliced

2 cups (475 ml) water

14 ounces (397 g) canned diced tomatoes

2 cloves garlic, minced

2 tablespoons (6 g) chopped fresh basil

2 tablespoons (8 g) chopped fresh parsley

¼ teaspoon kosher salt

¼ teaspoon freshly ground black pepper

16 ounces (455 g) spaghetti noodles

1. Add everything except for the spaghetti noodles to the slow cooker. Stir to combine.

2. Cover the slow cooker. Cook on LOW for 3 to 4 hours, until the onions and peppers are softened.

3. Add the uncooked spaghetti noodles to the slow cooker. Stir and push the noodles into the sauce until they are covered in the sauce.

4. Cover and cook for an additional 30 minutes on HIGH, or until the noodles are cooked.

MEXICAN BLACK BEAN SPINACH ENCHILADAS

Serves: 4 to 6 | **Cook Time:** 4 hours on LOW
Slow Cooker Size: 3½-quart (3.3-L) casserole or 6-quart (5.7-L) oval

Sarah loves using black beans and spinach in vegetarian meals because they're so versatile and rich in nutrients. This recipe fits well with a 3½-quart casserole (3.3-L) slow cooker or in a 6-quart (5.7-L) or larger oval slow cooker. The casserole crock features nice even sides that fit the enchilada well. If you use an oval-shaped cooker, you will need to adjust the size of the enchilada, and you may need to adjust the folds at the curved ends of the oval slow cooker so they will fit.

Olive oil

12–16 flour tortillas (7–8 inches, or 18–20 cm)

6 ounces (168 g) fresh baby spinach

8 ounces (225 g) chive and onion cream cheese

3 cups (345 g) shredded three-cheese blend

16 ounces (455 g) frozen corn, thawed

15 ounces (425 g) canned black beans, drained and rinsed

1 small yellow onion, diced

2 teaspoons (5 g) ground cumin

2 teaspoons (5 g) chili powder

10 ounces (280 g) canned red enchilada sauce

FOR SERVING (OPTIONAL):

Sour cream

Shredded cheese

Guacamole or diced avocado

Salsa

1. Heat a large skillet on the stove top over medium-high heat. Drizzle a little bit of olive oil in the pan and cook each tortilla until slightly browned to remove a bit of the moisture from the tortillas. Set the tortillas aside.

2. In the same skillet, drizzle a little bit more olive oil and add the baby spinach. Cook until the spinach is wilted. Remove from heat.

3. While the spinach is cooking, remove the foil lid off the chive and onion cream cheese and place it in a microwave-safe bowl. Heat in the microwave at 50 percent power for 30 seconds, stir, and continue heating for an additional 30 seconds.

4. In a medium mixing bowl, combine the spinach, cream cheese, 2 cups (230 g) shredded cheese, the corn, beans, onion, cumin, and chili powder. Mix well.

5. Spray the bottom and sides of the slow cooker with nonstick cooking spray.

6. Pour a small amount of enchilada sauce in the bottom of the slow cooker and spread it to cover the bottom.

7. Evenly divide the bean and cream cheese mixture between the tortillas and roll the tortillas up around the mixture. Place in the bottom of the slow cooker seam side down.

8. Pour the remaining enchilada sauce over the tortillas and sprinkle with the remaining shredded cheese.

9. If you are cooking this in a 6-quart (5.7-L) oval slow cooker, you may have to do layers of rolled tortillas. If so, pour the enchilada sauce and sprinkle a little bit of cheese between the layers.

10. Cover the slow cooker. Cook on LOW for 4 hours.

11. Serve the enchiladas with your choice of toppings (if desired).

VEGETARIAN LENTIL TACOS

Serves: 8 | **Cook Time:** 5 to 6 hours on LOW or 2 to 3 hours on HIGH
Slow Cooker Size: 5-quart (4.7-L) or larger

Lentils are a quick-cooking legume and a great meat alternative if you are vegetarian. These lentils are full of flavor, and you can serve them in taco shells or flour tortillas just like you would with ground beef taco filling.

3½ cups (825 ml) water

2 cups (384 g) dried brown or black lentils

1 medium yellow onion, diced

3–4 cloves garlic, minced

2 tablespoons (16 g) chili powder

2 tablespoons (14 g) ground cumin

½ teaspoon kosher salt

½ teaspoon freshly ground black pepper

FOR SERVING:

Taco shells or tortillas

Shredded lettuce

Shredded cheese

Diced tomatoes

Diced red onion

Sour cream

Diced avocado

1. Add all the ingredients to the slow cooker and stir to combine.
2. Cover the slow cooker. Cook on LOW for 5 to 6 hours or on HIGH for 2 to 3 hours.
3. Serve the lentils in taco shells or tortillas with your favorite taco toppings.

SO-EASY COCONUT QUINOA CURRY

Serves: 6 to 8 | **Cook Time:** 4 to 5 hours on HIGH | **Slow Cooker Size:** 6-quart (5.7-L)

This slow cooker curry is full of a TON of great flavor. You do need to do a little cutting of vegetables as far as prep work goes. But when you have that done, this is just a dump-and-go recipe where you just throw everything in the slow cooker and let it do its thing.

1 cup (235 ml) water

1 medium sweet potato, peeled and diced

1 large crown broccoli, cut into florets

½ medium yellow onion, diced

15 ounces (425 g) canned garbanzo beans, drained and rinsed

28 ounces (794 g) canned diced tomatoes

29 ounces (858 ml) canned coconut milk

¼ cup (43 g) quinoa, rinsed

3 cloves garlic, minced

1 tablespoon (6 g) freshly grated ginger

2 teaspoons (10 ml) soy sauce (or tamari sauce)

1 teaspoon ground turmeric

½ teaspoon red pepper flakes

1. Add all the ingredients to the slow cooker and stir well to combine.
2. Cover the slow cooker. Cook on HIGH for 4 to 5 hours, until the sweet potatoes are fork-tender and the curry has thickened.

VEGETABLE SIDES

SWEET ROOT BEER BAKED BEANS

Serves: 8 | **Cook Time:** 5 to 6 hours on LOW
Slow Cooker Size: 5-quart (4.7-L) or larger

If you need to bring a side dish to a summer cookout, this simple recipe is just the thing to bring. Canned pork and beans are made even better with the addition of root beer, bacon, and a few other ingredients. There won't be any leftovers of this yummy side dish!

Feel free to double this recipe to serve a larger crowd; just add an extra 1 hour to the cooking time.

3 slices bacon

1 small yellow onion, diced

32 ounces (905 g) canned pork and beans

½ cup (120 ml) root beer

¼ cup (57 g) hickory-flavored bottled barbecue sauce

1 teaspoon dried mustard

½ teaspoon freshly ground black pepper

⅛ teaspoon hot sauce

1. Cook the bacon in a large skillet over medium heat until crisp. Remove the bacon and drain on a plate lined with paper towels. Reserve 2 tablespoons (30 ml) of the bacon drippings.

2. Sauté the onion in the hot reserved bacon drippings over high heat, until the onions are tender and starting to turn golden-brown.

3. Crumble the bacon into the slow cooker. Add the remaining ingredients and stir to combine well.

4. Cover the slow cooker. Cook on LOW for 5 to 6 hours, until everything is hot and bubbly.

ULTIMATE PARTY BEANS

Serves: 12 to 16 | **Cook Time:** 8 hours on LOW or 4 hours on HIGH | **Slow Cooker Size:** 6-quart (5.7-L) or larger

This is a great recipe for a barbecue or party where you need a huge pot of beans that will smell and taste delicious. We loved that instead of having hot dogs, this recipe has Little Smokies. The flavor is tart and smooth. You could even make this recipe and freeze part of it if you want it to last you a while.

16 ounces (455 g) beef Little Smokies sausages, cut in half

42 ounces (1.2 kg) canned kidney beans, drained

42 ounces (1.2 kg) canned great Northern beans, drained

42 ounces (1.2 kg) canned pork and beans

2 large yellow onions, diced

1 cup (240 g) ketchup

1 cup (225 g) brown sugar, packed

½ cup (170 g) molasses

2 tablespoons (12 g) prepared yellow mustard

1 tablespoon (12 g) bottled barbecue sauce

1 teaspoon garlic powder

1. Combine all the ingredients in the slow cooker and stir well to combine.

2. Cover the slow cooker. Cook on LOW for 8 hours or on HIGH for 4 hours, stirring occasionally to keep it from getting too hot on the sides.

ZIPPY RANCH-STYLE BEANS

Serves: 8 | **Cook Time:** 8 to 10 hours on LOW | **Slow Cooker Size:** 6-quart (5.7-L)

Ranch-style beans are a great alternative when you want a bean side dish that is not as sweet as your typical baked beans. This recipe is great to serve at a backyard barbecue cookout. It starts with dried pinto beans and has some great flavors with the addition of ancho chile powder, tomatoes, apple cider vinegar, and a little bit of brown sugar. We like these beans served with grilled steak or pork chops in the summer. They are SO good!

1 pound (455 g) dried pinto beans

6 cloves garlic, minced

1 medium yellow onion, diced

10 ounces (280 g) canned diced tomatoes with green chilies

3 bay leaves

1 teaspoon freshly ground black pepper

1 teaspoon ancho chile powder

1 teaspoon ground paprika

1 teaspoon dried oregano

1 teaspoon ground cumin

1 teaspoon brown sugar

1 teaspoon apple cider vinegar

6 cups (1.4 L) low-sodium beef broth, store-bought or homemade (page 311)

Kosher salt, to taste

1. Sort through the dried beans and discard any stones and shriveled beans. Put the beans in a colander in the sink. Rinse well to remove any dust or dirt from the beans. Place the beans in the slow cooker and add cold water to 3 inches (7.5 cm) above the beans. Soak the beans overnight at room temperature.

2. In the morning, drain and rinse the beans in a colander in the kitchen sink. Place the beans back in the slow cooker.

3. Add the remaining ingredients except for the salt to the slow cooker and stir to combine.

4. Add water, if needed, until the liquid in the slow cooker is ½ inch (1 cm) above the beans.

5. Cover the slow cooker. Cook on LOW for 8 to 10 hours, until the beans are tender.

6. Remove and discard the bay leaf.

7. Taste the beans and season with salt to suit your taste.

SUPER CHEESY BROCCOLI

Serves: 4 | **Cook Time:** 2½ hours on HIGH plus 30 minutes on LOW | **Slow Cooker Size:** 4-quart (3.8-L) or larger

Katie's kids will eat just about any vegetable if it is served with a yummy cheese sauce. This super cheesy broccoli does not disappoint in the cheese department, and it is a favorite side dish any night of the week.

20 ounces (567 g) frozen broccoli florets

10.5 ounces (298 g) canned cream of celery soup

½ cup (50 g) chopped green onions

2 cups (230 g) shredded Cheddar cheese

1. Add the broccoli, cream of celery soup, and green onions to the slow cooker.
2. Cover the slow cooker. Cook on HIGH for 2½ hours.
3. Add the shredded Cheddar cheese and stir to combine.
4. Cover and cook for an additional 30 minutes on LOW, or until the cheese is melted.

EASY GREEN BEANS AND BACON

Serves: 10 | **Cook Time:** 8 hours on LOW or 4 to 5 hours on HIGH
Slow Cooker Size: 5-quart (4.7-L)

With just five simple ingredients, this amazingly delicious green bean dish is special enough to serve at any holiday meal but easy enough for every day, too! Green beans are flavored with bacon and a touch of maple syrup, and the combination is just perfect.

12 ounces (340 g) bacon

1 medium yellow onion, diced

29 ounces (822 g) canned green beans, drained

½ cup (161 g) real maple syrup

¼ cup (38 g) brown sugar, packed

1. In a saucepan on the stove top, heat the bacon and onion just until the bacon is cooked but not browned.
2. Add the drained green beans, bacon, onion (including the drippings), maple syrup, and brown sugar. Stir to combine.
3. Cover the slow cooker. Cook on LOW for 8 hours or on HIGH for 4 to 5 hours.

NOTES: *Do not be afraid to substitute fresh green beans or even frozen green beans for the canned green beans in this recipe.*

ORANGE MARMALADE–GLAZED CARROTS

Serves: 6 to 8 | **Cook Time:** 5 to 6 hours on LOW plus 30 minutes on HIGH
Slow Cooker Size: 3-quart (2.8-L)

These marmalade-glazed carrots are a big hit with Heidi's entire family. Tender baby carrots are cooked in the slow cooker with orange marmalade, brown sugar, butter, cinnamon, salt, and pepper for a great side dish that works for dinner any night of the week. Or double the recipe for a great holiday side to serve to company.

2 pounds (about 1 kg) baby carrots

½ cup (160 g) orange marmalade

¼ cup (60 ml) orange juice, divided

2 tablespoons (30 g) light brown sugar

1 tablespoon (14 g) unsalted butter, melted

½ teaspoon ground cinnamon

¼ teaspoon ground nutmeg

¼ teaspoon kosher salt

⅛ teaspoon freshly ground black pepper

1 tablespoon (8 g) cornstarch

1. Combine the carrots, marmalade, 1 tablespoon (15 ml) of orange juice, brown sugar, butter, cinnamon, nutmeg, salt, and pepper in the slow cooker.

2. Cover the slow cooker. Cook on LOW for 5 to 6 hours, or until the carrots are tender.

3. Mix the cornstarch and the remaining 3 tablespoons (45 ml) orange juice; stir until there are no lumps of cornstarch. Add mixture to carrots and stir to combine.

4. Cover and cook for 30 minutes on HIGH, or until the glaze has thickened.

MASHED PESTO CAULIFLOWER

Serves: 4 to 6 | **Cook Time:** 3 hours on HIGH
Slow Cooker Size: 5-quart (4.7-L) or larger

Mashed cauliflower is a great side dish to eat if you are trying to watch your carbs as it can replace mashed potatoes. The basil pesto gives such a fabulous flavor, and a little sour cream makes it extra creamy.

1 large head cauliflower, cut into florets

14.5 ounces (411 g) low-sodium chicken broth (or water)

¼ cup (55 g) unsalted butter, softened

½ cup (115 g) sour cream

¼ cup (65 g) basil pesto

½ teaspoon onion powder

½ teaspoon kosher salt

¼ teaspoon freshly ground black pepper

1. Add the cauliflower and chicken broth to the bottom of the slow cooker.

2. Cover the slow cooker. Cook on HIGH for 3 hours, stirring halfway during the cooking time.

3. With a slotted spoon, scoop out the cauliflower into a large mixing bowl, leaving the liquid in the slow cooker.

4. With an immersion blender (you can also use a food processor or mash by hand), blend the cauliflower until mashed.

5. Add the butter, sour cream, pesto, onion powder, salt, and pepper. Blend those into the mashed cauliflower to mix.

AUTUMN PUMPKIN RISOTTO

Serves: 4 | **Cook Time:** 4 hours on LOW | **Slow Cooker Size:** 3-quart (2.8-L)

Creamy risotto is cooked in the slow cooker with canned pumpkin and earthy herbs for a side dish that is out of this world. And it doesn't require all that stirring a traditional stove-top risotto does.

3 tablespoons (45 ml) extra-virgin olive oil, divided

½ onion, finely diced

1 clove garlic, minced

1⅔ cups (166 g) arborio rice

15 ounces (425 g) canned pumpkin puree

2 fresh sage leaves, minced

1 tablespoon (2 g) minced fresh rosemary

32 ounces (946 ml) low-sodium chicken broth, store-bought or homemade (page 310)

½ cup (50 g) freshly grated Parmesan cheese

1. In a small skillet, sauté the diced onion and garlic in 2 tablespoons (30 ml) of the olive oil until the onion starts to turn translucent and just slightly turning to golden colored.

2. Use the remaining tablespoon (15 ml) of olive oil to oil the inside of the slow cooker.

3. Add the onion mixture, rice, pumpkin puree, herbs, and chicken broth to the slow cooker and stir to combine.

4. Cover the slow cooker. Cook on LOW for 4 hours, stirring once at the 2-hour mark.

5. Stir in the grated Parmesan cheese before serving.

NOTES: *You could easily turn this into a vegetarian side dish by replacing the chicken broth with a good-quality vegetable broth.*

BACON AU GRATIN CAULIFLOWER

Serves: 4 to 6 | **Cook Time:** 4 to 5 hours on LOW | **Slow Cooker Size:** 4-quart (3.8-L) or larger

This cauliflower recipe is sinfully delicious and a bit over the top. Fresh cauliflower is cooked in the slow cooker with cheese and cream and topped with cooked crispy bacon bits. You won't be able to stop eating this out-of-this-world side dish!

1 medium head cauliflower, cut into florets

1 cup (235 ml) heavy cream

1½ cups (115 g) shredded Cheddar cheese

½ cup (120 ml) milk

6 cloves garlic, minced

¼ teaspoon freshly ground black pepper

⅛ teaspoon kosher salt

4–6 slices bacon, cooked and crumbled

1. Add the cauliflower to the bottom of the slow cooker.
2. Add the cream, cheese, milk, garlic, pepper, and salt to a saucepan. Heat on the stove top over medium heat, stirring constantly until the cheese is melted. Pour over the cauliflower in the slow cooker.
3. Cover the slow cooker. Cook on LOW for 4 to 5 hours, until the cauliflower is fork-tender.
4. While the slow cooker is cooking, cook the bacon in a frying pan on the stove top or bake it in the oven and let it cool. Crumble it and sprinkle it over the top of the cauliflower when it is done cooking.

WARM CORN CASSEROLE

Serves: 12 | **Cook Time:** 2 to 3 hours on HIGH
Slow Cooker Size: 4-quart (3.8-L) or larger

A classic family-dinner side dish cooked in the slow cooker. You can also use fresh corn when it is season in the summer instead of the canned corn kernels. Try adding other ingredients such as crumbled cooked bacon, green onions, diced red bell peppers, or even jalapeño peppers to give this a little zip!

29 ounces (822 g) canned cream-style corn

29 ounces (822 g) canned corn kernels, drained

17 ounces (482 g) boxed corn muffin mix

1 cup (230 g) sour cream

1 cup (115 g) shredded Cheddar cheese

½ cup (112 g) unsalted butter, melted

1. Add all the ingredients to the slow cooker and stir to combine.
2. Cover the slow cooker. Cook on HIGH for 2 to 3 hours, until the center of the casserole is set.

AUTUMN BUTTERNUT SQUASH WITH APPLES

Serves: 4 to 6 | **Cook Time:** 5 to 6 hours on LOW or 3 hours on HIGH | **Slow Cooker Size:** 4-quart (3.8-L) or larger

This side dish just screams "autumn" with all the great favors of butternut squash, apples, cranberries, and walnuts, and it's seasoned with fall spices of cinnamon and nutmeg. This recipe is a great healthy side dish to serve any night for dinner, but it is also fancy enough to serve at your Thanksgiving or Christmas dinner, too!

5 cups (700 g) diced fresh butternut squash

4 Gala apples, cored and chopped into chunks

1 cup (120 g) dried cranberries

½ cup (60 g) chopped walnuts

1 tablespoon (7 g) ground cinnamon

1½ teaspoons nutmeg

1. Add the squash, apples, cranberries, and walnuts to the slow cooker.
2. Sprinkle with cinnamon and nutmeg.
3. Cover the slow cooker. Cook on LOW for 5 to 6 hours or on HIGH 3 hours, until the squash is fork-tender.

SUPER EASY BAKED POTATOES

Serves: 6 | **Cook Time:** 6 to 8 hours on LOW or 3 to 4 hours on HIGH
Slow Cooker Size: 3½-quart (3.3-L) casserole or 6-quart (5.7-L) oval

This recipe is so easy that it hardly qualifies as a recipe. But we decided to include it in this book because it's something Heidi cooks at least once a week. Of course, you can serve baked potatoes as a side dish with dinner, but you can also turn them into a hearty lunch or dinner depending on what you top them with.

**6 medium-size potatoes
(russet or Idaho)**

Salt (optional)

**TRY SOME OF THESE
BAKED POTATO TOPPINGS:**

- **Butter**
- **Sour cream**
- **Chives**
- **Chili**
- **Cheese**
- **BBQ pulled pork**
- **Ranch dressing**
- **Salsa**
- **Taco meat**

1. Scrub the potatoes under running water to remove any dirt.
2. Pat the potatoes off with a paper towel to slightly dry them.
3. Place each potato on a sheet of aluminum foil and sprinkle with a little pinch of salt (if desired).
4. Roll each potato in foil and place it in the bottom of the slow cooker.
5. Cover with a lid. Cook on LOW for 6 to 8 hours or on HIGH for 3 to 4 hours, until the potatoes are tender when pierced with a fork.
6. Top the baked potatoes with your favorite toppings and enjoy!

NOTES: *Baked potatoes can be stored in the refrigerator wrapped in foil for up to 1 week. To reheat, unwrap and discard the foil, and place them on a microwave-safe plate. Reheat them in the microwave for 2 minutes.*

CREAMY AU GRATIN POTATOES

Serves: 6 | **Cook Time:** 5 to 6 hours on LOW
Slow Cooker Size: 3½-quart (3.3-L) casserole or 4-quart (3.8-L) oval

This easy and delicious recipe comes out so creamy and cheesy. It's the perfect side dish to serve on Easter, Christmas, Thanksgiving, or any special occasion! It is also a great everyday side dish recipe to serve with roasted chicken, pork chops, or roast beef.

Butter (for pan)

2 pounds (about 1 kg) russet potatoes, peeled, rinsed, and sliced into about ⅙-inch (4-mm) -thick slices

1¼ cups (295 ml) heavy cream

2–3 teaspoons (1–2 g) minced fresh rosemary

3 cloves garlic, minced

¼ teaspoon kosher salt

¼ teaspoon freshly ground black pepper

2 cups (230 g) shredded extra-sharp Cheddar cheese

1. Butter the bottom and sides of the stoneware insert of the slow cooker.

2. Layer half of the sliced potatoes in the bottom of the slow cooker.

3. Drizzle the potatoes with half of the cream, half of the rosemary, garlic, salt, and pepper. Top with half of the cheese.

4. Create another layer of potatoes, cream, rosemary, garlic, salt, pepper, and cheese.

5. Cover the slow cooker. Cook on LOW for 5 to 6 hours, or until the potatoes are fork-tender and the cheese is melted and everything is bubbly.

NOTES: *This recipe can easily be doubled to serve a larger number of people. Just use a 6- to 7-quart (5.7- to 6.6-L) slow cooker and add an additional 1 to 1½ hours cooking time. Be sure to test the doneness of the potatoes on all layers.*

CHEESY BACON RANCH POTATOES

Serves: 4 | **Cook Time:** 4 to 6 hours on LOW | **Slow Cooker Size:** 4- to 4½-quart (3.8- to 4.3-L)

Your family will flip for this easy side dish. Tender chunks of potatoes are cooked in a ranch-flavored sauce with bacon and cheese. Simply amazing!

4 medium potatoes (russet or Idaho), peeled, rinsed, and sliced into about ¼-inch (6-mm) -thick slices

1 medium yellow onion, sliced into rings

1 pound (455 g) bacon, cooked and crumbled

1 packet (28 g) ranch dressing mix, store-bought or homemade (page 318)

2½ cups (285 g) shredded Cheddar cheese, divided

Sliced green onion (optional)

1. Line a slow cooker with aluminum foil, allowing enough extra foil to fold over the potatoes.
2. Spray the foil with nonstick cooking spray (or lightly butter).
3. Layer the ingredients in at least 2 layers in this order: potatoes, onion, cooked bacon, dry ranch dressing mix, and 2 cups (225 g) of cheese.
4. Fold the foil over the top of the potatoes.
5. Cover the slow cooker. Cook on LOW for 4 to 6 hours.
6. Fold back the foil and sprinkle the top of potatoes with the remaining ½ cup (60 g) shredded cheese and the green onion.

ROASTED GARLIC AND HERB MASHED POTATOES

Serves: 4 to 6 | **Cook Time:** 7 to 8 hours on LOW or 4 to 5 hours on HIGH
Slow Cooker Size: 4-quart (3.8-L)

Heidi's husband is a HUGE garlic lover, and these mashed potatoes are hands-down his favorite mashed potatoes ever. Small baby red potatoes are cooked in the slow cooker with fresh thyme and rosemary and roasted garlic that you roast ahead of time. Then, everything is mashed together right in the slow cooker with some heavy cream. When the dish is done, you can serve them right away or set the slow cooker on the WARM setting for up to 3 hours.

2 pounds (about 1 kg) red potatoes, cut into 1-inch (2.5-cm) pieces

½ cup (120 ml) water

1 teaspoon fresh minced thyme

1 teaspoon fresh minced rosemary

1 head roasted garlic (see notes)

¼ cup (55 g) unsalted butter

1½ teaspoons kosher salt

1 teaspoon freshly ground black pepper

½ cup (120 ml) heavy cream

1. Spray the inside of the slow cooker with nonstick cooking spray.

2. Add the potatoes, water, thyme, rosemary, roasted garlic cloves, butter, salt, and pepper.

3. Cover the slow cooker. Cook on LOW for 7 to 8 hours or on HIGH for 4 to 5 hours.

4. Use a hand mixer (or potato masher for lumpier potatoes) on low speed right in the stoneware insert to mash the potatoes. Add the cream and continue mashing until creamy.

NOTES: To roast garlic, preheat the oven to 375°F (190°C, or gas mark 5). Cut off the top of the head of garlic and peel off as much of the papery skin as possible without breaking the garlic head. Place the head of garlic on a sheet of aluminum foil, drizzle the top of the garlic with 2 teaspoons (10 ml) of olive oil, and sprinkle with salt and pepper. Wrap the foil around the garlic and roast in the oven for 1 hour.

SARAH'S FAMOUS FUNERAL POTATOES

Serves: 8 | **Cook Time:** 8 hours on LOW or 4 to 5 hours on HIGH
Slow Cooker Size: 6-quart (5.7-L)

The name for this recipe may sound morbid to some people, but here in the Midwest these are the potatoes that you take to a family that is grieving after a loved one has passed away. The potatoes are rich and cheesy, and they are comfort food at its best. If the name is too much for you, just call them "cheesy potatoes."

1 can (10.75 ounces, or 305 g) cream of celery soup

1 cup (230 g) sour cream

1 medium yellow onion, diced

¼ cup (55 g) unsalted butter, melted

8 ounces (225 g) cream cheese, softened

2 cloves garlic, minced

1 teaspoon kosher salt

¼ teaspoon freshly ground black pepper

32 ounces (905 g) frozen diced hash brown potatoes

2 cups (230 g) shredded Cheddar cheese

1. In a large mixing bowl, mix together the cream of celery soup, sour cream, onion, butter, cream cheese, garlic, salt, and pepper until combined.

2. Add the hash brown potatoes and shredded cheese and stir to combine.

3. Spray the slow cooker insert with nonstick cooking spray.

4. Pour the potato mixture into the prepared slow cooker and spread evenly.

5. Cover the slow cooker. Cook on LOW for 8 hours or on HIGH for 4 to 5 hours, or until the potatoes are tender.

6. Stir once or twice during cooking, then spread the mixture back out evenly in the slow cooker after stirring if your slow cooker tends to cook hot around the edges.

HOLIDAY SWEET POTATOES WITH MARSHMALLOWS

Serves: 8 | **Cook Time:** 6 to 7 hours on LOW or 3 to 4 hours on HIGH plus 20 to 30 minutes on LOW
Slow Cooker Size: 4-quart (3.8-L)

Fresh sweet potatoes are slow-cooked for hours and then topped with miniature marshmallows in this delicious side dish that is perfect for your holiday table. Cooking the sweet potatoes in your slow cooker frees up oven space for your turkey or ham!

5 large sweet potatoes (see note), scrubbed, peeled, and cut into ½-inch (1-cm) pieces

¾ cup (170 g) brown sugar, packed

¼ cup (55 g) unsalted butter, melted

1 teaspoon ground cinnamon

1 teaspoon ground nutmeg

½ teaspoon kosher salt

½ cup (120 ml) orange juice

3 cups (150 g) miniature marshmallows

1. Place the sweet potatoes, brown sugar, butter, cinnamon, nutmeg, and salt in the bottom of the slow cooker.

2. Cover the slow cooker. Cook on LOW for 6 to 7 hours or on HIGH for 3 to 4 hours, or until the sweet potatoes are tender.

3. Using a potato masher, mash the sweet potatoes right in the slow cooker to your desired consistency.

4. Add the orange juice and stir to mix it into the mashed sweet potatoes.

5. Cover the surface with marshmallows. Cover the cooker and cook for an additional 20 to 30 minutes on LOW, until the marshmallows are melted on top.

NOTES: *There is much confusion between a yam and a sweet potato. Here in the United States, the orange-fleshed tubers that are labeled as yams are actually sweet potatoes. A yam, on the other hand, is a white-fleshed tuber with a nonsweet flavor and can usually be found in ethnic grocery stores. In this dish we are looking for orange-fleshed sweet potatoes.*

HOLIDAY PECAN SWEET POTATOES

Serves: 6 | **Cook Time:** 6 to 7 hours on LOW or 3 to 4 hours on HIGH plus 10 to 15 minutes on LOW
Slow Cooker Size: 3½-quart (3.3-L) casserole or 6-quart (5.7-L) oval

Sweet potatoes are cooked in orange juice in the slow cooker, then mashed and topped with a lovely pecan topping, and then the traditional miniature marshmallows for a side dish that is perfect for your Thanksgiving table. If you are not a fan of marshmallows on top of your sweet potatoes, you can simply leave them off because the pecan topping is great on its own!

4 medium sweet potatoes, scrubbed, peeled, and cut into ½-inch (1-cm) pieces

¼ cup (60 ml) orange juice

½ cup (100 g) granulated sugar

¼ cup (60 ml) milk

5 tablespoons (69 g) butter, melted

TOPPING:

4 tablespoons (55 g) butter, melted

½ cup (68 g) all-purpose flour

½ cup (115 g) brown sugar, packed

½ teaspoon kosher salt

¾ cup (83 g) roughly chopped pecans

16 ounces (455 g) miniature marshmallows

1. Place the sweet potatoes in the bottom of the slow cooker. Add the orange juice.

2. Cover the slow cooker. Cook on LOW for 6 to 7 hours or on HIGH for 3 to 4 hours, or until the sweet potatoes are tender.

3. Add the granulated sugar, milk, and melted butter and mash the sweet potatoes with a potato masher.

4. In a medium mixing bowl, mix together the butter, flour, brown sugar, and salt. Pour over the top of the sweet potatoes.

5. Sprinkle the chopped pecans over the top and then the miniature marshmallows.

6. Cover and cook on LOW for 10 to 15 minutes, until the marshmallows are melted.

9

DESSERTS AND SWEET TREATS

BAKED OATMEAL WITH SPICY PEARS

Serves: 6 | **Cook Time:** 3 to 4 hours on LOW | **Slow Cooker Size:** 3- to 4-quart (2.8– to 3.8-L)

One of our favorite things to eat for dessert is oatmeal, because it's so nutritious and healthy. This recipe is super tasty, and to make it feel more like a dessert, top each serving with a little whipped cream or vanilla ice cream. You can of course eat this healthy dessert oatmeal for breakfast, too. But maybe skip the ice cream or whipped cream!

1–2 ripe pears, peeled and diced into bite-size pieces

1 cup (120 g) steel-cut oatmeal

½ cup (125 g) unsweetened applesauce

2 tablespoons (20 g) brown sugar

1 tablespoon (7 g) ground cinnamon

1 teaspoon honey

1 teaspoon pure vanilla extract

⅛ teaspoon ground allspice

⅛ teaspoon ground nutmeg

1½ cups (355 ml) milk

TOPPINGS (OPTIONAL):

Vanilla ice cream

Whipped cream

1. Spray the insert of the slow cooker with nonstick cooking spray. Set aside.
2. In a medium mixing bowl, combine the pear, oatmeal, applesauce, brown sugar, cinnamon, honey, vanilla, allspice, and nutmeg.
3. Add the milk to the mixture and stir gently to combine.
4. Pour the oatmeal mixture into the prepared slow cooker.
5. Cover the slow cooker. Cook on LOW for 3 to 4 hours.
6. Top individual servings with ice cream or whipped cream (if desired).

SNACKABLE CINNAMON-SUGAR ALMONDS

Serves: 6 to 8 | **Cook Time:** 3½ hours on LOW | **Slow Cooker Size:** 5-quart (4.7-L) or larger

These cinnamon-sugar almonds are an easy recipe to make, and they are such a fun and tasty treat. These are great for a party, neighbor gifts, and holiday gatherings. They smell divine, too!

1¼ cups (250 g) granulated sugar

1¼ cups (285 g) brown sugar, packed

2½ tablespoons (19 g) ground cinnamon

⅛ teaspoon ground allspice

⅛ teaspoon ground ginger

⅛ teaspoon kosher salt

1 large egg white

2 teaspoons (10 ml) pure vanilla extract

4 cups (580 g) whole raw almonds

¼ (60 ml) cup water

1. Spray the slow cooker insert with nonstick cooking spray. Set aside.

2. In a medium mixing bowl, combine the granulated sugar, brown sugar, cinnamon, allspice, ginger, and salt until there are no lumps of brown sugar and the spices are mixed in evenly.

3. In another medium mixing bowl, whisk together the egg white and vanilla until foamy.

4. Add the almonds to the egg white mixture and toss to coat.

5. Add the coated almonds to the sugar-and-spice mixture and toss to coat.

6. Pour the almonds into the slow cooker and cover. Cook on LOW for 3 hours, stirring every 30 minutes with a rubber spatula that has been sprayed with nonstick cooking spray.

7. Add the water to the slow cooker and mix well so all the almonds get wet with the water.

8. Cover and cook for an additional 15 to 30 minutes, stirring occasionally with the sprayed spatula, watching that the almonds do not burn.

9. Spread the almonds out on two rimmed baking sheets lined with parchment paper that has been sprayed lightly with nonstick cooking spray.

10. Let the almonds cool for 5 minutes on the baking sheets. Stir the almonds to break them up a little bit.

11. Allow the almonds to cool completely before eating or store them in an airtight container for up to 2 weeks.

NOTES: *You can use any other type of nut in this recipe. Try pecans, almonds, peanuts, cashews, etc.*

CINNAMON SPICE BAKED APPLES

Serves: 6 | **Cook Time:** 6 hours on LOW
Slow Cooker Size: 6-quart (5.7-L)

There is something magical about warm apples all spiced with cinnamon and nutmeg. These apples can be served alone just as they are or spooned over vanilla ice cream. You can even serve them as a side dish at dinner. And, if there are leftovers, spoon them into oatmeal or yogurt the next morning.

3 pounds (1.4 kg) Granny Smith or Fuji apples

½ cup (100 g) granulated sugar

½ cup (115 g) brown sugar, packed

1 teaspoon ground cinnamon

½ teaspoon ground nutmeg

2 tablespoons (28 g) unsalted butter, sliced

1. Wash, peel, core, and slice the apples into ¼-inch (6-mm) wedges and add them to the bottom of the slow cooker insert.
2. Stir in the granulated sugar, brown sugar, cinnamon, nutmeg, and butter until the sugar and spices coat the apple slices.
3. Cover with the lid propped up slightly with a wooden spoon. Cook on LOW for 3 hours.
4. Remove the lid and stir the apples. Cover and continue to cook on LOW for an additional 3 hours.
5. The apples are done when they are fully cooked and juicy.

HOMESTYLE PEACH CRISP

Serves: 6 | **Cook Time:** 2 hours on HIGH
Slow Cooker Size: 6-quart (5.7-L)

Fresh summer peaches are spiced up perfectly with a little bit of cinnamon and cooked into a mouthwatering crisp.

8 medium to large fresh peaches, peeled and sliced

1½ teaspoons ground cinnamon, divided

¼ cup (50 g) granulated sugar

½ cup (112 g) unsalted butter, softened

¾ cup (60 g) old-fashioned oats

¾ cup (94 g) all-purpose flour

¼ cup (38 g) brown sugar

1. In a large mixing bowl, toss together the peaches, 1 teaspoon of cinnamon, and the granulated sugar.
2. Pour the peaches into the bottom of the slow cooker.
3. In a medium mixing bowl, combined the butter, oats, flour, brown sugar, and the remaining ½ teaspoon cinnamon. Cut with a pastry blender or two butter knives until the mixture resembles coarse crumbs.
4. Evenly sprinkle the crumble mixture over the top of the peaches in the slow cooker.
5. Cover the slow cooker. Cook on HIGH for 2 hours.

NOTES: *Serve peach crisp warm, at room temp, or even chilled. It's best served with a little vanilla ice cream for the ultimate indulgence!*

SWEET CARAMEL APPLE CRISP

Serves: 6 to 8 | **Cook Time:** 6 hours on LOW or 4 hours on HIGH | **Slow Cooker Size:** 6-quart (5.7-L)

Warm fall apples are spiced just right with cinnamon and cloves and tossed with caramel candies. Then the whole thing is topped with a great crisp topping and cooked in the slow cooker. When you are ready to serve, drizzle a little store-bought caramel topping and add a scoop of ice cream if desired.

11 ounces (312 g) caramel candies, unwrapped

10 medium Granny Smith apples, peeled and diced

½ cup (68 g) all-purpose flour

¼ cup (38 g) brown sugar

1 teaspoon ground cinnamon

¼ teaspoon ground cloves

CRUMB TOPPING:

1 cup (80 g) old-fashioned oats

½ cup (112 g) unsalted butter, cubed

¼ cup (38 g) brown sugar

½ teaspoon ground cinnamon

1 pinch ground cloves

FOR SERVING (OPTIONAL):

6 ounces (168 g) store-bought caramel ice cream topping

Vanilla ice cream

1. Spray the slow cooker with nonstick cooking spray. Set aside.
2. Cut each caramel candy in half with a sharp knife and add them to a large mixing bowl.
3. Add the apples, flour, brown sugar, cinnamon, and cloves to the bowl. Toss to mix.
4. Pour the apple mixture into the prepared slow cooker.
5. In a small mixing bowl, combine all the ingredients for the crumb topping. Cut up with a pastry blender or two butter knives until the mixture is crumbly.
6. Spread the crumble topping mixture evenly over the top of the apples in the slow cooker.
7. Cover the slow cooker. Cook on LOW for 6 hours or on HIGH for 4 hours.
8. Drizzle the caramel over individual servings and top with a scoop of vanilla ice cream before serving (if desired).

NOTES: *This dessert recipe is sweet. To cut down the sugar content, you can use a sugar substitute in place of the brown sugar. You can also use sugar-free caramels and sugar-free caramel sauce if you can find them.*

SUMMER RHUBARB AND STRAWBERRY CRISP

Serves: 6 | **Cook Time:** 2 to 3 hours on LOW | **Slow Cooker Size:** 5-quart (4.7-L) or larger

Strawberries and rhubarb are the perfect combination in this simple crisp recipe. You can use fresh or frozen rhubarb, but make sure you use fresh strawberries for the best flavor and texture! Vanilla ice cream or whipped cream makes this dessert even better.

½ teaspoon ground cinnamon

⅓ cup (66 g) granulated sugar

3 cups (366 g) fresh or frozen diced rhubarb

1 cup (170 g) fresh sliced strawberries

½ cup (68 g) all-purpose flour

1 teaspoon baking powder

⅛ teaspoon kosher salt

4 tablespoons (55 g) butter, softened

⅔ cup (150 g) brown sugar

⅔ cup (52 g) quick-cooking oats

Whipped cream or vanilla ice cream (optional)

1. In a small bowl, mix together the cinnamon and granulated sugar.
2. Combine the rhubarb and strawberries in the slow cooker and sprinkle with the cinnamon-sugar mixture.
3. In a medium mixing bowl, combine the remaining ingredients, cutting in the butter until you have pea-size crumbs to make the crisp topping.
4. Evenly sprinkle the crisp topping over the fruit in the slow cooker.
5. Cover the slow cooker. Cook on LOW for 2 to 3 hours, or until the crisp topping is cooked.
6. Serve individual servings with whipped cream or a scoop of ice cream (if desired).

CLASSIC APPLE CRISP

Serves: 6 | **Cook Time:** 4 hours on HIGH
Slow Cooker Size: 5-quart (4.7-L) or larger

Nothing says fall like a good old-fashioned apple crisp, and you can make this warm and delicious recipe in your slow cooker with this fabulous recipe! Serve it warm with a scoop of vanilla ice cream!

3 pounds (1.4 kg) apples

2 tablespoons (26 g) granulated sugar

2 tablespoons (16 g) all-purpose flour

1 teaspoon ground cinnamon

1 cup (80 g) old-fashioned oats

1 cup (150 g) brown sugar

½ cup (112 g) unsalted butter, softened and cut into cubes

1. Peel, core, and thinly slice the apples and add them to a large mixing bowl.
2. Add the granulated sugar, flour, and cinnamon to the apples and toss to coat.
3. Pour the apples into the bottom of the slow cooker.
4. In a medium mixing bowl, combine together the oats, brown sugar, and butter. Mix with a fork or pastry cutter until the mixture is crumbly.
5. Sprinkle the mixture on top of the apples in the slow cooker.
6. Cover the slow cooker. Cook on HIGH for 4 hours, or until the apples are fully cooked.

NOTES: *You can serve this apple crisp hot, warm, or cold. Topping it with your favorite ice cream is optional–but highly recommended!*

TART APPLE CRUMBLE

Serves: 6 | **Cook Time:** 4 hours on LOW
Slow Cooker Size: 3½-quart (3.3-L) casserole or 5-quart (4.7-L) or larger oval

Tart baking apples are the star of this apple crumble. We like to use Granny Smith, Ida Red, Cortland, or Baldwin apples, but any other apple that holds up well when cooked will work. Topping the finished apple crumble with vanilla ice cream makes this dessert just perfect!

2 cups (56 g) granola

½ cup (120 ml) apple cider

¼ cup (36 g) shelled unsalted sunflower seeds

¼ cup (38 g) brown sugar

¼ cup (80 g) real maple syrup

1 teaspoon ground cinnamon

1 teaspoon ground nutmeg

2 pinches ground allspice

6 tablespoons (83 g) unsalted butter, melted, divided

5–6 tart baking apples

1. In a large mixing bowl, combine the granola, apple cider, sunflower seeds, brown sugar, maple syrup, cinnamon, nutmeg, allspice, and 4 tablespoons (55 g) melted butter. Mix well until the mixture is crumbly.
2. Peel, core, and cut the apples into bite-size chunks and add them to the crumble mixture.
3. With the remaining butter, butter the sides and bottom of the slow cooker insert.
4. Add the apple and crumble mixture to the slow cooker and spread evenly.
5. Cover the slow cooker. Cook on LOW for 4 hours, checking every hour and stirring if you find the mixture is browning too quickly.

TANGY RHUBARB CRUMBLE

Serves: 8 | **Cook Time:** 4 hours on LOW plus 45 minutes on HIGH | **Slow Cooker Size:** 6-quart (5.7-L)

Rhubarb is in season April through June, and whenever Sarah can get her hands on some, she likes to take full advantage of this tart vegetable that is treated like a fruit. This yummy crisp is easy to whip up, and it tastes amazing!

1 cup (125 g) all-purpose flour

1 cup (150 g) brown sugar

¾ cup (60 g) old-fashioned oats

½ cup (112 g) unsalted
butter, melted

1 teaspoon ground cinnamon

4 cups (488 g) rhubarb, cut into
1-inch (2.5-cm) chunks

1 cup (200 g) granulated sugar

1 cup (235 ml) water

2 tablespoons (18 g) cornstarch

1 teaspoon lemon extract
(see note)

Whipped cream or ice
cream (optional)

1. Spray the slow cooker insert with nonstick cooking spray.
2. In a medium mixing bowl, mix together the flour, brown sugar, oats, butter, and cinnamon until fully combined and the mixture is slightly crumbly.
3. Press half of the crumble mixture into the bottom of the slow cooker.
4. Add the rhubarb pieces to the slow cooker.
5. In a small saucepan, combine the sugar, water, cornstarch, and lemon extract. Cook over high heat until thick and clear, stirring constantly.
6. Pour over the rhubarb in the slow cooker.
7. Sprinkle the remaining crumble topping over the top of the fruit.
8. Place a double layer of paper towels between the lid and slow cooker insert to prevent condensation from dripping on crumble while cooking.
9. Cook on LOW for 4 hours.
10. Change the temperature on the slow cooker to HIGH and cook an additional 45 minutes.
11. Remove the slow cooker insert from the heating element and let sit uncovered until either warm or fully cooled.
12. Serve with whipped cream or ice cream (if desired).

NOTES: *If you do not have lemon extract, use the zest of
1 lemon instead.*

EASY PEACH COBBLER

Serves: 6 | **Cook Time:** 3 to 3½ hours on LOW
Slow Cooker Size: 3½-quart (3.3-L) casserole or 6-quart (5.7-L) oval

Take advantage of the season's fresh peaches with this recipe for peach cobbler made in your slow cooker. This dish is so simple to make, and it tastes amazing plain or served with a scoop of vanilla ice cream! The perfect summer dessert!

1⅛ cups (160 g) brown sugar

¾ cup (60 g) rolled old-fashioned oats

¾ cup (94 g) all-purpose flour

⅜ teaspoon salt

½ teaspoon ground cinnamon

½ teaspoon ground nutmeg

½ teaspoon ground allspice

½ cup (112 g) unsalted butter, melted, divided

20 ounces (567 g) fresh or frozen diced or sliced peaches

1. In a large mixing bowl, combine the brown sugar, oats, flour, salt, cinnamon, nutmeg, and allspice until evenly mixed.

2. Mix 6 tablespoons (83 g) of melted butter into the dry mixture until everything is evenly moistened and the mixture is crumbly.

3. Using the remaining butter, butter the sides and bottom of the slow cooker insert.

4. Add ⅓ of the dry crumble mixture evenly to the bottom of the slow cooker.

5. Add the peaches to the bowl with the remaining crumble mixture. Toss to mix.

6. Pour into the slow cooker and spread evenly.

7. Cover the slow cooker. Cook on LOW for 3 to 3½ hours.

NOTES: *If you are using frozen peaches, there is no need to thaw them first.*

FRESH BLACKBERRY COBBLER

Serves: 6 | **Cook Time:** 4 hours on HIGH | **Slow Cooker Size:** 4-quart (3.8-L) or larger

When fresh blackberries are in season and are the size of your thumb (or bigger!), Heidi likes to purchase a flat or two from the produce stand on the side of the road. Of course, she loves to just eat them fresh, but when she has eaten her fill, she makes a simple cobbler for dessert. She usually serves this with a dollop of freshly whipped cream. It is pure bliss! Freeze extra berries so that you can be transported to summer even in the dark depths of winter.

4 cups (580 g) fresh or frozen blackberries (no need to thaw if using frozen berries)

½ cup (100 g) granulated sugar

2 tablespoons (18 g) cornstarch

COBBLER TOPPING:

2 cups (250 g) all-purpose flour

½ cup (100 g) granulated sugar

¼ cup (55 g) unsalted butter, melted

¼ cup (60 ml) milk

1 teaspoon baking powder

1 pinch kosher salt

Whipped cream or ice cream (optional)

1. Add the berries, ½ cup (50 g) of sugar, and cornstarch to the bottom of the slow cooker and toss to coat.

2. In a medium mixing bowl, mix together all the ingredients for the cobbler topping until the mixture forms a soft and sticky dough.

3. Dot the top of the berries in the slow cooker with spoonfuls of the cobbler dough, making sure to keep the dough off the sides of the slow cooker.

4. Cover the slow cooker. Cook on HIGH for 4 hours, or until the fruit is bubbly and the dough is cooked through.

5. Serve plain or top with whipped cream or ice cream (if desired).

NOTES: *This recipe is best cooked on HIGH for a shorter cooking time rather than on LOW for a longer time. This method better replicates baking in an oven and allows the cobbler topping to cook without disintegrating into the fruit.*

MAPLE BACON BREAD PUDDING

Serves: 6 to 8 | **Cook Time:** 2½ to 3 hours on HIGH | **Slow Cooker Size:** 6-quart (5.7-L)

Heidi's husband loves the flavors of maple and bacon together. Maple bacon donuts are his go-to, and he even likes to pour maple syrup on his morning bacon. So, she decided to create a dessert just for him that combines those flavors—and now she is a maple bacon fan, too!

1 teaspoon unsalted butter

8 ounces (225 g) sliced bacon

7 to 8 cups (350–400 g) day-old French bread, cut into ¾-inch (2-cm) cubes

6 large eggs

5 cups (1.2 L) whole milk

1 cup (322 g) real maple syrup

2 teaspoons (10 ml) pure vanilla extract

MAPLE GLAZE:

¼ cup (55 g) unsalted butter

½ cup (161 g) real maple syrup

1 cup (120 g) powdered sugar, sifted

¼ teaspoon maple extract

1. Butter the bottom and sides of the slow cooker insert.
2. Cook the bacon in a large skillet over medium heat until browned and crispy. Transfer to paper towels to drain.
3. Crumble the bacon into bite-size pieces into the slow cooker. Add the bread cubes and toss to combine.
4. In a large mixing bowl, whisk together the eggs, milk, maple syrup, and vanilla until combined and smooth. Pour over the bread mixture, pressing the bread down into the liquid with the back of a wooden spoon.
5. Cover with plastic wrap and place in the refrigerator for 4 hours or overnight.
6. Remove from the refrigerator and place the insert in the heating element base of the slow cooker.
7. Cover the slow cooker. Cook on LOW for 2½ to 3 hours, or until set.
8. While the bread pudding is cooking, prepare the maple glaze. Combine the butter and maple syrup in a small saucepan and heat over low heat until the butter is melted. Remove from the heat.
9. Add the powdered sugar and maple extract and stir to combine. Set the glaze aside to allow it to cool and thicken.
10. Drizzle the glaze over the entire cooked bread pudding or on individual servings right before you serve it.

LUSCIOUS LEMON CURD BREAD PUDDING

Serves: 8 to 10 | **Cook Time:** 1½ to 2 hours on LOW | **Slow Cooker Size:** 6-quart (5.7-L)

Heidi grew up in a citrus-growing community in Southern California with citrus groves surrounding the neighborhood and three huge lemon trees in the backyard. Even though she has moved far away from home, and citrus doesn't grow at all here in Wyoming, she can still enjoy lemony desserts like this delicious lemon curd bread pudding!

1 tablespoon (14 g) unsalted butter, melted

6 cups (180 g) day-old bread, cubed

2½ cups (570 ml) milk

½ cup (160 g) lemon curd

4 large eggs

½ cup plus 1 tablespoon (113 g) granulated sugar, divided

1 tablespoon (6 g) lemon zest

Whipped cream (optional)

1. Grease the slow cooker insert with the melted butter.
2. Add the bread cubes to the slow cooker.
3. In a medium mixing bowl, whisk together the milk, lemon curd, eggs, ½ cup (100 g) of sugar, and lemon zest until smooth.
4. Pour the mixture over the bread cubes and press the bread into the egg mixture.
5. Evenly sprinkle the top of the bread mixture with the remaining 1 tablespoon (13 g) of sugar.
6. Cover the slow cooker. Cook on LOW for 1½ to 2 hours, or until set.
7. Serve warm or cold with a dollop of whipped cream (if desired).

DRIED CRANBERRY AND MAPLE BREAD PUDDING

Serves: 10 to 12 | **Cook Time:** 3 to 3½ hours on LOW
Slow Cooker Size: 3½-quart (3.3-L) casserole or 5-quart (4.7-L) or larger oval

This delicious bread pudding uses dried cranberries, maple syrup, and day-old bread, and it transforms them into a delicious dessert that goes great with a scoop of vanilla ice cream. This recipe makes a lot of bread pudding, but it is a great way to use up old bread before it goes bad. If you don't have day-old bread, just use your toaster to lightly toast the bread before cutting into cubes or tearing it into bite-size chunks.

½ cup plus 2 tablespoons (140 g) butter, melted, divided

16 cups (480 g) of cubed or torn day-old bread (can use loaves of bread, hot dog or hamburger buns, dinner rolls, etc.)

1 cup (120 g) dried cranberries

4 cups (940 ml) evaporated milk

6 large eggs

½ cup (75 g) brown sugar

2 teaspoons pure vanilla extract

4 teaspoons (9 g) ground cinnamon, divided

½ teaspoon ground nutmeg

¼ cup (50 g) granulated sugar

2 tablespoons (40 g) real maple syrup

Vanilla ice cream (optional)

1. Grease the insert of the slow cooker with 2 tablespoons (28 g) of the melted butter.

2. Place the cubed or torn day-old bread and cranberries in the slow cooker.

3. In a medium mixing bowl, whisk together the remaining ½ cup (112 g) of melted butter, the evaporated milk, eggs, brown sugar, vanilla, 2 teaspoons of cinnamon, and nutmeg until smooth.

4. Pour the egg mixture over the bread in the slow cooker. Toss lightly to coat all the bread. Press bread down into the slow cooker with the back of a spatula or wooden spoon to create an even layer.

5. In a small bowl, mix together the remaining 2 teaspoons cinnamon and the granulated sugar. Sprinkle the cinnamon-sugar mixture evenly over the top of the bread.

6. Drizzle the maple syrup over the top of the cinnamon-sugar mixture on top of the bread.

7. Cover the slow cooker. Cook on LOW for 3 to 3½ hours, or until a toothpick inserted in the center of the bread pudding comes out clean.

8. Serve hot with a scoop of vanilla ice cream (if desired).

PUMPKIN PRALINE BREAD PUDDING

Serves: 8 | **Cook Time:** 6 hours on LOW or 3 hours on HIGH
Slow Cooker Size: 4- to 5-quart (4.7-L)

This is, hands down, one of Heidi's favorite autumn desserts to make when the weather starts cooling off and the leaves are falling off the trees. Warm, pumpkin-spiced bread pudding is drizzled with a gooey pecan praline sauce.

1 loaf day-old French bread, cut into ¾-inch (2-cm) cubes

2 cups (475 ml) fat-free half-and-half

15 ounces (425 g) canned pumpkin puree

¾ cup (150 g) granulated sugar

¾ cup (113 g) brown sugar

4 large eggs

2 tablespoons (30 ml) pure vanilla extract

1 tablespoon (7 g) pumpkin pie spice

PRALINE SAUCE:

1 cup (225 g) unsalted butter

1 cup (235 ml) fat-free half-and-half

1 cup (150 g) brown sugar

¾ cup (83 g) chopped toasted pecans

1. Spray the slow cooker insert with nonstick cooking spray.

2. Add the bread cubes to the prepared slow cooker.

3. In a medium mixing bowl, whisk together the half-and-half, pumpkin puree, granulated sugar, brown sugar, eggs, vanilla, and pumpkin pie spice until smooth.

4. Pour the liquid over the bread cubes. Lightly toss with a wooden spoon or spatula, making sure all the bread is coated with the egg mixture.

5. Press the liquid-soaked bread down lightly with the back of your wooden spoon or spatula to create an even layer in the slow cooker.

6. Cover the slow cooker. Cook on LOW for 6 hours or on HIGH for 3 hours until set.

PRALINE SAUCE:

1. In a heavy-bottomed saucepan set over medium-low heat on the stove top, stir together the butter, half-and-half, and brown sugar and bring to a boil.

2. Reduce the heat to low and stir in the pecans.

3. Simmer the sauce for approximately 5 minutes, or until the sauce thickens.

4. Pour warm praline sauce over the cooked bread pudding and serve.

NOTES: *The praline sauce can be made ahead of time and stored in the refrigerator. To warm it up, put it in a saucepan over low heat or microwave it for about 1 to 2 minutes.*

BIG HIT BANANAS FOSTER BREAD PUDDING

Serves: 6 | **Cook Time:** 2 to 2½ hours on LOW | **Slow Cooker Size:** 4-quart (3.8-L) or larger

If you are looking for a great recipe to use up overripe bananas, look no further than this outstanding bread pudding recipe. The key to this recipe is to use really ripe bananas . . . you want the skins on the bananas to be more spots than yellow. A little bit of spiced rum makes this bread pudding reminiscent of the famous bananas Foster dessert. So good!

5 tablespoons (69 g) butter, melted, divided

2 cups (100 g) day-old bread, cubed

4 overripe bananas, peeled and sliced

2 large eggs

1 cup (235 ml) half-and-half

1 cup (225 g) brown sugar, packed

¼ cup (60 ml) spiced rum

2 teaspoons (10 ml) pure vanilla extract

1 teaspoon ground cinnamon

¼ cup (28 g) chopped pecans

1. Grease the slow cooker insert with 1 tablespoon (14 g) of melted butter.
2. Add the bread cubes to the buttered insert.
3. Layer the sliced bananas on top of the bread.
4. In a medium mixing bowl, whisk together the remaining melted butter, eggs, half-and-half, brown sugar, rum, vanilla, and cinnamon until smooth.
5. Pour the egg mixture over the bread and bananas and press the bread into the egg mixture.
6. Cover the slow cooker. Cook on LOW for 1½ to 2 hours.
7. Sprinkle pecans over the top of the bread pudding and cover. Cook for an additional 30 minutes.

HOMEY CINNAMON RICE PUDDING

Serves: 4 | **Cook Time:** 2½ to 3 hours on HIGH | **Slow Cooker Size:** 5-quart (4.7-L) or larger

Growing up, Heidi's mom used to make rice pudding for dessert about once a week because it was a frugal dessert that she could feed her large family and it wasn't too complicated. This recipe is a take on her mom's recipe, made in a smaller batch and cooked in the slow cooker. It just brings back the flavors of home to Heidi.

¾ cup (140 g) long-grain white rice

2 cups (475 ml) milk

2 cups (475 ml) half-and-half

½ cup (100 g) granulated sugar

1 teaspoon ground cinnamon

½ teaspoon ground nutmeg

1 teaspoon pure vanilla extract or vanilla bean paste

2 tablespoons (28 g) unsalted butter

¾ cup (110 g) raisins

1. Place the rice in a fine-mesh colander. Rinse under cold water in the sink to remove excess starch. Add the rice to the slow cooker.

2. Add the remaining ingredients and stir until the sugar is dissolved.

3. Cover the slow cooker. Cook on HIGH for 2½ to 3 hours, or until the rice is cooked through and everything is creamy.

SHORTCUT CHOCOLATE FUDGE

Serves: 12 | **Cook Time:** 1 to 1½ hours on LOW | **Slow Cooker Size:** 3-quart (2.8-L)

We love how easy this two-ingredient recipe for chocolate fudge comes together. This recipe is so simple that even a child could make it. In fact, the kids and Heidi like to make several batches of this easy fudge for Christmas gifts each year!

16 ounces (455 g) canned prepared chocolate frosting

10 ounces (280 g) chocolate chips (semisweet or milk chocolate)

Topping (optional; see notes)

1. Add the entire can of prepared chocolate frosting and the chocolate chips to the slow cooker and stir to combine.

2. Cover the slow cooker. Cook on LOW for 1 to 1½ hours, or until the chocolate chips are fully melted, stirring every 20 minutes or so while cooking.

3. While the chocolate mixture is cooking, prepare an 8- x 8-inch (20- x 20-cm) baking pan by lining it with parchment or waxed paper, leaving paper overhanging on each side.

4. Give the chocolate mixture in the slow cooker one final stir to make sure the chocolate chips are fully melted and combined with the frosting.

5. Pour the fudge mixture into the prepared pan and spread evenly with an offset spatula.

6. Sprinkle the top of the fudge with the topping of your choice (if desired), pressing the topping lightly with your hand to make sure it sticks to the top of the fudge.

7. Place the baking pan in the refrigerator and let it cool for 2 to 3 hours.

8. Using the parchment or waxed paper that was left overhanging on the sides, lift the cooled fudge out of the pan and cut the fudge into 24 pieces with a sharp knife.

9. Serve or package the fudge for gift giving.

NOTES: *For topping options, try crushed peppermint candies, sprinkles to match your holiday, nuts, dried fruit, or chopped candy bars.*

FUDGY CHOCOLATE BROWNIE PUDDING

Serves: 6 | **Cook Time:** 2 to 3 hours on HIGH | **Slow Cooker Size:** 5- to 6-quart (4.7- to 5.7-L)

This decadent chocolate dessert could not get any easier to make. A boxed brownie mix and instant pudding is cooked together for an ooey gooey dessert!

18 ounces (510 g) boxed brownie mix (plus eggs, water, and oil according to package)

5.9 ounces (167 g) boxed instant chocolate pudding mix

2 cups (475 ml) milk

Whipped cream or ice cream (optional)

1. Spray the slow cooker insert with nonstick cooking spray. Set aside.
2. In a large mixing bowl, prepare the brownie mix according to the directions on the box. Pour the batter into the prepared slow cooker.
3. In a small bowl, whisk together the dry instant pudding mix and the milk. Pour the pudding over the brownie batter in the slow cooker.
4. Cover the slow cooker. Cook on HIGH for 2 to 3 hours.
5. Serve warm plain or topped with whipped cream or ice cream.

NOTES: Depending on your slow cooker, this recipe can take up to 3 hours to cook. The pudding on top will stay wet even though the brownie mix is cooked. Watch the edges. When the brownie mix on the edges looks dry and cooked, then this is complete.

If you want to add in some chopped-up candy bars, such as Hershey's chocolate or even a Snickers bar, drop the candy in on top of the brownie batter before adding the pudding.

SILKY CHOCOLATE FONDUE

Serves: 16 | **Cook Time:** 1 hour on LOW | **Slow Cooker Size:** 3- to 4-quart (2.8- to 3.8-L)

Making chocolate fondue in your slow cooker is super easy, and it's a fun dessert to serve to your family or guests. Make the fondue and set out a selection of strawberries, sliced bananas, cubes of pound cake, angel food cake, marshmallows, pretzels, apple slices, or whatever sounds good dipped in chocolate!

4 cups (700 g) semisweet chocolate chips

1⅓ cups (305 ml) half-and-half

1. Add the chocolate chips and half-and-half in the slow cooker insert and stir to combine.
2. Cover the slow cooker. Cook on LOW for 30 minutes. Open lid and stir with a rubber spatula.
3. Cover and continue to cook on LOW for an additional 30 minutes.
4. Stir once more, and your fondue is ready to serve.

VANILLA BEAN CRÈME BRÛLÉE

Serves: 4 | **Cook Time:** 2 to 3 hours on LOW | **Slow Cooker Size:** 6-quart (5.7-L) oval

Crème brûlée is usually Heidi's go-to dessert whenever it is offered on the menu at a restaurant, and she always thought that it was super hard to make at home. One day she decided to give it a try, and she picked up a small kitchen torch at the local kitchenware store. Little did she know that it was actually rather easy and made even easier when you cook the custard in your slow cooker! This is a great dessert to make when you want to impress your guests or family!

1½ cups (355 ml) heavy cream

½ cup (120 ml) whole milk

6 egg yolks

⅓ cup (66 g) granulated sugar

1½ teaspoons vanilla paste
(or 1 vanilla bean scraped)

¼ teaspoon kosher salt

4 teaspoons (17 g) granulated
sugar (for torching)

1. In a large mixing bowl, whisk together the heavy cream, milk, egg yolks, sugar, vanilla, and salt until the sugar has dissolved. Pour the mixture into a large liquid measuring cup or other container with a spout.

2. Place four 6-ounce (177 g) ramekins in the bottom of the slow cooker insert. Carefully pour about 1½ to 2 cups (355 to 475 ml) of water around the ramekins until the water reaches ¾ of the way up the sides.

3. Carefully pour the custard into the ramekins, filling them almost to the top.

4. Cover the slow cooker. Cook on LOW for 2 to 3 hours, or until the custard is set.

5. Carefully remove the ramekins from the slow cooker and place in the refrigerator uncovered to cool for about 1 to 2 hours. When the custard is chilled, cover with plastic wrap.

6. When ready to serve, remove plastic wrap from chilled custards and sprinkle about ½ to 1 teaspoon of granulated sugar evenly over the top of each custard.

7. Using a kitchen torch, melt and caramelize the sugar on top of the custards until a nice golden crust forms.

8. Serve immediately.

NOTES: *You can prepare the custards up to 4 days in advance and keep them chilled in the refrigerator.*

SWEET MEXICAN CARAMEL FLAN

Serves: 4 | **Cook Time:** 3 to 4 hours on HIGH | **Slow Cooker Size:** 6-quart (5.7-L) or larger

Craving a little something creamy and sweet? This delectable recipe for caramel flan will surely fit the bill. Creamy vanilla custard is cooked inside ramekins with a homemade caramel sauce for a sweet slow cooker dessert!

1 cup (200 g) granulated sugar

¼ teaspoon salt

CUSTARD:

3 large eggs

14 ounces (397 g) canned sweetened condensed milk

½ cup (120 ml) whole milk

1 teaspoon pure vanilla extract

½ teaspoon salt

1. In a small saucepan, combine the 1 cup (100 g) of sugar and ¼ teaspoon salt. Cook over medium-high heat on the stove top while stirring constantly until the sugar melts and turns a medium-brown caramel color.

2. Divide the caramel between four heatproof 4-ounce (118 g) ramekins or cups. CAREFULLY swirl the hot caramel around the sides about ¾ of the way up. Set aside.

CUSTARD:

1. In a large mixing bowl, whisk the eggs until a light lemon-yellow color.

2. Add the sweetened condensed milk, whole milk, vanilla, and salt to the egg mixture and whisk everything together until well combined.

3. Pour the custard mixture into the caramel-coated ramekins or cups. Carefully place them in the bottom of the slow cooker.

4. Carefully pour hot water into the slow cooker to create a water bath. The water should come up about ¾ of the way up the sides of the ramekins. Being careful not to get any of the water in your custards.

5. Place a couple of paper towels or a clean kitchen towel over the top of the slow cooker and cover it with the lid.

6. Cook on HIGH for 3 to 4 hours.

7. Turn the slow cooker off. Let the flans cool for 1 hour in the turned-off slow cooker.

8. To unmold your flans, run a butter knife around the sides of the ramekins or cups. Place a small dessert plate over the top and carefully flip the ramekins over onto the plate.

NOTES: *When swirling the hot caramel in the ramekins, be very careful. The caramel is very hot, and you will burn yourself if it gets on your skin.*

SWEET SUGAR-COOKIE PARTY MIX

Serves: 8 to 10 | **Cook Time:** 30 minutes on HIGH | **Slow Cooker Size:** 5-quart (4.7-L) or larger

Everyone loves a good party mix, and this recipe does not disappoint with a sweet sugar-cookie flavor. This recipe is perfect for snacking on or packaging up for holiday gift giving. The sugar sprinkles can be any color you wish. For Christmas, use red or green; for Valentine's Day, use red or pink; for Halloween, use black or orange. Have fun with it!

2 cups (275 ml) light corn syrup

2 ounces (55 g) vanilla almond bark

¼ cup (55 g) unsalted butter

¼ cup (50 g) granulated sugar

2 teaspoons (10 ml) pure vanilla extract

7 cups (210 g) corn or rice Chex cereal (or a combination of the two)

½ cup (60 g) powdered sugar

Colored sugar sprinkles

1. Add the corn syrup, vanilla almond bark, butter, granulated sugar, and vanilla to the bottom of the slow cooker insert.

2. Cover the slow cooker. Cook on HIGH and allow the butter and white almond bark to melt, about 30 minutes. Stir well.

3. Add the cereal to the melted mixture, 1 cup at a time, and mix well, coating the cereal with the almond bark mixture.

4. Sprinkle the powdered sugar over the mixture gradually and toss. Add the colored sugar sprinkles so that all the cereal is coated in the sugar.

5. Dump the party mix onto a foil- or parchment paper–lined rimmed baking sheet. Spread with a spatula and allow it to cool.

6. Store the party mix for up to 5 days in an airtight container or bag.

SLOW COOKER CHOCOLATE CHIP PAN COOKIES

Serves: 8 | **Cook Time:** 2 to 2½ hours on HIGH
Slow Cooker Size: 3½-quart (3.3-L) casserole or 6-quart (5.7-L) oval

Yes, you can bake a giant cookie in your slow cooker. This recipe is always a hit with the kids because they love helping to make the homemade cookie dough and pressing it into the slow cooker insert. We love this recipe because you don't have to heat up the oven to make cookies for dessert! You can mix the dough without an electric mixer, too. We just use a bowl and a sturdy wooden spoon.

1 cup (225 g) unsalted butter, softened

2 large eggs

½ cup (75 g) brown sugar

½ cup (100 g) granulated sugar

1 tablespoon (15 ml) pure vanilla extract

2 cups (250 g) all-purpose flour

½ teaspoon baking soda

¼ teaspoon salt

1 cup (175 g) semisweet chocolate chips

1. In a large mixing bowl, mix together the butter, eggs, brown sugar, granulated sugar, and vanilla until well combined.

2. Add in the flour, baking soda, and salt. Stir well to create the cookie dough.

3. Gently fold in the chocolate chips until evenly distributed throughout the dough.

4. Line the slow cooker insert with aluminum foil or parchment paper, leaving enough excess on the sides so that you can use it to lift the cookie out of the slow cooker when it is done cooking.

5. Butter or spray the foil or parchment paper with nonstick cooking spray. Add the cookie dough to the slow cooker and press it into the bottom of the lined slow cooker.

6. Cover the slow cooker. Cook on HIGH for 2 to 2½ hours, until the cookie is done in the center.

7. Using the foil or parchment paper, lift out the cookie. Let it cool completely before cutting into 8 pieces.

HAZELNUT AND ALMOND DROP COOKIES

Serves: 12 to 16 | **Cook Time:** 2½ hours on LOW | **Slow Cooker Size:** 6-quart (5.7-L)

These rich chocolatey drop cookies have a great nutty flavor. Use your favorite brands of hazelnut and cocoa spread, almond butter, dark chocolate chips, and crunchy granola to make this easy dessert treat. Kids love to help make this recipe because it is super simple. Just let them measure everything out and dump it in the slow cooker. Then, when everything is melted, they like to scoop it out and make the cookies.

¾ cup (241 g) real maple syrup

½ cup (130 g) hazelnut and cocoa spread

¼ cup (65 g) almond butter

¼ cup (59 ml) olive oil

2 teaspoons (10 ml) pure vanilla extract

5 cups (140 g) plain granola

¼ cup (36 g) shelled unsalted sunflower seeds

¾ teaspoon ground cinnamon

½ teaspoon ground ginger

¼ teaspoon ground nutmeg

¼ teaspoon kosher salt

¾ cup (131 g) dark chocolate chips

1. Spray the slow cooker insert with nonstick cooking spray. Set aside.

2. Add the maple syrup, hazelnut spread, almond butter, olive oil, and vanilla to the slow cooker. Stir to mix well.

3. Add the granola, sunflower seeds, cinnamon, ginger, nutmeg, and salt to the slow cooker. Stir to coat everything evenly in the wet mixture.

4. Cover the slow cooker. Cook on LOW for 2½ hours, stirring the mixture every 30 minutes.

5. Remove the lid and carefully fold in the chocolate chips.

6. Remove the insert from the slow cooker base. Let it sit to allow the mixture to cool slightly, about 10 minutes.

7. While the mixture is cooling, line several baking sheets with waxed paper.

8. Using a spoon, drop the mixture into cookies on the prepared baking sheets. Allow them to set up and fully cool.

9. The cooled cookies can be stored in an airtight container for up to 1 week.

NOTES: *Feel free to use other nuts or add dried fruit to the mixture, if you like.*

GOOEY HOT FUDGE TURTLE BROWNIES

Serves: 10 | **Cook Time:** 3 to 3½ hours on HIGH | **Slow Cooker Size:** 6-quart (5.7-L)

Hot fudge sauce, caramel, pecans, and gooey brownies come together for a warm dessert that is irresistible. Top each serving with a scoop of vanilla ice cream to take it over the top!

1 box fudge brownie mix (approximately 18 to 20 ounces)

⅔ cup (117 g) mini semisweet chocolate chips

⅔ cup (158 ml) vegetable oil

¼ cup (60 ml) water

2 large eggs

11 ounces (312 g) caramel bits

⅓ cup (80 ml) heavy cream

¾ cup (83 g) chopped pecans

12 ounces (340 g) jarred hot fudge sauce

¾ cup (175 ml) hot water

Ice cream (optional)

1. Spray the stoneware insert of the slow cooker with nonstick cooking spray. Set aside.

2. In a large mixing bowl, combine the brownie mix, chocolate chips, oil, ¼ cup (60 ml) of water, and eggs together with a sturdy spoon until just combined. Do not overmix.

3. Pour the brownie batter into the prepared slow cooker.

4. In a medium mixing bowl, add the caramel bits and heavy cream. Microwave on high heat in 30-second intervals, stirring in between, until the caramel is fully melted. Stir in the pecans.

5. Pour the caramel mixture over the top of the brownie batter in the slow cooker. Use a knife to swirl the caramel mixture in.

6. In a small mixing bowl, stir together the hot fudge sauce and hot water together until smooth and melted.

7. Pour over the top of the brownie mixture in the slow cooker.

8. Cover the slow cooker. Cook on HIGH for 3 to 3½ hours, or until the edges of the brownies are set but the center is still gooey.

9. Spoon the fudgy brownie mixture into bowls and serve with ice cream (if desired).

HEALTHY BLACK BEAN BROWNIES

Serves: 16 | **Cook Time:** 3 hours on HIGH
Slow Cooker Size: 3½-quart (3.3-L) casserole or 6-quart (5.7-L) oval

No one will know that these rich and fudgy brownies are gluten-free and packed with fiber from canned black beans. Cocoa powder and chocolate chips pack a double chocolate punch in these tasty brownies! Make these in a rectangular 3½-quart (3.3-L) casserole slow cooker so that the finished brownies look more like their oven-baked counterparts. A 6-quart (5.7-L) or larger oval slow cooker will work as well.

14 ounces (397 g) canned low-sodium black beans, drained and rinsed well (see note)

2 large eggs

½ cup (43 g) unsweetened cocoa powder

¾ cup (150 g) granulated sugar

1 tablespoon (15 ml) milk (can use unsweetened almond or soy milk)

1 teaspoon vegetable oil

1 teaspoon vinegar

1 teaspoon pure vanilla extract

½ teaspoon salt

½ teaspoon baking powder

½ teaspoon baking soda

1 cup (175 g) semisweet chocolate chips, divided

1. Line the slow cooker insert with parchment paper, leaving some paper to overhang the edges so that you can lift the brownies out of the slow cooker when done.

2. Spray the parchment paper with nonstick cooking spray.

3. In a food processor, blend together the black beans, eggs, cocoa powder, sugar, milk, oil, vinegar, vanilla, salt, baking powder, and baking soda, scraping down the sides of the food processor as needed to make sure the beans are fully pureed into the batter.

4. Remove the blade of the food processor from the bowl. Fold in half of the chocolate chips.

5. Pour the batter into the prepared slow cooker and spread evenly.

6. Sprinkle the remaining chocolate chips over the top of the brownie batter.

7. Cover the slow cooker. Cook on HIGH for 3 hours.

8. Remove the lid, turn off or unplug the slow cooker, and let the brownies cool for 15 minutes in the pan.

9. Using the parchment paper, lift out the brownies from the slow cooker and let them fully cool on the countertop before cutting into squares.

NOTES: *You want to really rinse the canned black beans well. Open the can and dump them into a strainer or colander in the sink. Turn on the faucet to warm water and rinse the beans under the warm running water, stirring the beans lightly with your fingertips or a spoon to make sure you rinse off all the liquid from the can.*

APPLE CINNAMON MONKEY BREAD

Serves: 12 | **Cook Time:** 2 to 3 hours on HIGH | **Slow Cooker Size:** 6-quart (5.7-L)

Monkey bread gets its name because it is a finger food that you pick at with your fingers, I guess much like a monkey picking at and grooming another monkey. In this recipe, tart Granny Smith apples are cooked along with the bread dough balls in a sweet-and-sticky glaze that has brown sugar and white sugar, butter, and cinnamon, cloves, and nutmeg. Eat this as a dessert, snack, or even breakfast!

2 loaves frozen bread dough (about 1 pound [455 g] each)

4 medium to larger Granny Smith apples, peeled, cored, and diced

¾ cup (177 g) unsalted butter, melted

1 cup (200 g) granulated sugar

¾ cup (170 g) brown sugar, packed

2 teaspoons (5 g) ground cinnamon

¼ teaspoon ground cloves

¼ teaspoon ground nutmeg

1. Thaw the frozen bread dough according to the package directions.
2. Line the slow cooker insert with parchment paper leaving an overhang of parchment paper so that you can remove the monkey bread by lifting it out with the paper. Spray the paper with nonstick cooking spray.
3. Pull off walnut-size pieces of the bread dough and roll it into balls.
4. Add the dough balls and apples to a large mixing bowl.
5. In a small mixing bowl, combine together the remaining ingredients. Pour it over the bread dough and apples and toss to coat.
6. Add the coated bread dough and apples to the prepared slow cooker.
7. Place a double layer of paper towels between the lid and slow cooker insert to prevent condensation from dripping on the monkey bread while it cooks.
8. Cook on HIGH for 2 to 3 hours.
9. Remove the bread from the slow cooker by lifting it out with the parchment paper and serve.

NOTES: *The monkey bread is best enjoyed the same day it is made, but will keep for up to 4 days stored in an airtight container in the refrigerator.*

PUMPKIN APPLE HARVEST SNACK CAKE

Serves: 12 | **Cook Time:** 3 to 4 hours on HIGH | **Slow Cooker Size:** 3½-quart (3.3-L)

This healthy snack cake has no added fat or oil, and it is full of great autumn pumpkin flavor. Feel free to add nuts (or not), dried cranberries, raisins, or even chocolate chips to change the recipe up.

15 ounces (425 g) canned pumpkin puree

½ cup (170 g) honey

½ cup (75 g) brown sugar

2 large eggs

1 cup (125 g) whole wheat flour

1 cup (80 g) old-fashioned rolled oats

4 teaspoons baking powder

2 teaspoons (5 g) pumpkin pie spice

½ teaspoon kosher salt

2 medium apples, diced

MIX-INS (OPTIONAL; ADD UP TO 1 CUP TOTAL, WEIGHT WILL VARY):

Walnuts or pecans (toasted and chopped)

Sweetened dried cranberries

Raisins

Chocolate chips

1. In a large mixing bowl, mix together the pumpkin, honey, brown sugar, and eggs by hand with a silicone spatula or wooden spoon.

2. Add the flour, oats, baking powder, pumpkin pie spice, and salt. Mix very well by hand.

3. Fold in the apples and up to 1 cup of optional mix-ins (if using).

4. Spread the batter evenly into the lightly oiled slow cooker.

5. Place the lid on the slow cooker with a single layer of paper towels (or a clean, flour sack–type kitchen towel) between the lid and the slow cooker.

6. Cook on HIGH for 3 to 4 hours, or until a toothpick inserted in the middle of the cake comes out clean.

7. Let the cake cool completely uncovered before serving.

GINGER CARROT CAKE WITH CREAM CHEESE FROSTING

Serves: 8 | **Cook Time:** 3 to 4 hours on HIGH | **Slow Cooker Size:** 6- to 7-quart (5.7- to 6.6-L)

This is a flavorful carrot cake with a nice touch of ginger. The ginger is not overpowering and complements the moist cake nicely. A delicious, homemade cream cheese frosting takes this cake over the top!

⅔ cup (83 g) all-purpose flour

½ cup (100 g) granulated sugar

1 teaspoon baking soda

¾ teaspoon baking powder

1 teaspoon ground cinnamon

¼ teaspoon ground nutmeg

1 teaspoon freshly grated ginger

¼ teaspoon salt

⅓ cup (79 ml) vegetable oil

2 large eggs

8 ounces (225 g) canned crushed pineapple, undrained

½ cup (75 g) golden raisins

1 cup (110 g) chopped pecans or walnuts (optional)

1 cup (110 g) finely grated carrot

CREAM CHEESE FROSTING:

4 ounces (115 g) cream cheese, softened

1 cup (120 g) powdered sugar

½ teaspoon pure vanilla extract

1. In a small bowl, combine the flour, sugar, baking soda, baking powder, spices, ginger, and salt. Stir with a whisk to thoroughly mix.

2. In a large bowl, combine the oil, eggs, pineapple, raisins, nuts, and carrot. Whisk to combine well.

3. Add the dry ingredients to the wet ingredients and mix by hand with a spoon or rubber spatula till everything is well mixed.

4. Spray a loaf pan with nonstick cooking spray for baking (or butter and flour).

5. Pour the cake batter into the prepared pan and place it in the bottom of the slow cooker.

6. Cover the top of the slow cooker with four paper towels (in a doubled layer of two unattached sheets) or a thin kitchen towel, making sure the towel is not touching the cake in the slow cooker.

7. Cover the slow cooker. Cook on HIGH for 3 to 4 hours, or until a toothpick inserted into the center of the cake comes out clean.

8. Remove the cake pan from the slow cooker and let the cake cool in the pan on a wire cooling rack for 5 minutes.

9. Invert the cake out of the pan onto the cooling rack and let it cool completely before frosting.

FROSTING:

1. In a mixer, whip the cream cheese until fluffy.

2. Add the powdered sugar a little at a time, scraping down the sides of the bowl as needed.

3. Mix in the vanilla.

4. When the cake is cool, frost with the cream cheese frosting.

TROPICAL PINEAPPLE COCONUT SPOON CAKE

Serves: 8 to 10 | **Cook Time:** 2 to 3 hours on HIGH | **Slow Cooker Size:** 4-quart (3.8-L) or larger

Discover the tastes of the tropics with this fun and delicious dessert recipe. A box of yellow cake mix is jazzed up with crushed pineapple, coconut, and pecans for a delightful tropical dessert that can be served either warm or at room temperature.

1 box (425 g) yellow cake mix

1 cup (235 ml) water

1 cup (155 g) crushed pineapple (from a 15-ounce [425-g] can)

1 cup (80 g) sweetened shredded coconut

½ cup (112 g) butter, melted

3 large eggs

¼ cup (28 g) chopped pecans

GLAZE:

1½ cups (180 g) powdered sugar

½ cup (40 g) sweetened shredded coconut

¼ cup (55 g) butter, melted

¼ cup (28 g) chopped pecans

Remaining crushed pineapple from the can

TOPPINGS (OPTIONAL):

Ice cream or whipped topping

1. In a large mixing bowl, combine the cake mix, water, crushed pineapple, coconut, butter, eggs, and pecans.
2. Spray the insert of the slow cooker with nonstick cooking spray. Pour the cake batter into the slow cooker.
3. Cover the slow cooker. Cook on HIGH for 2 to 3 hours, or until a toothpick inserted in the middle comes out clean.
4. Turn off the slow cooker and remove the insert from the base.
5. In a small bowl, mix together all the ingredients for the glaze. Pour the glaze over the top of the hot cake.
6. Allow the cake to cool for about 10 to 15 minutes before spooning into bowls.
7. Top the cake with ice cream or whipped topping (if desired).

LEMONY LEMON SPOON CAKE

Serves: 6 to 8 | **Cook Time:** 2 to 3 hours on HIGH | **Slow Cooker Size:** 4-quart (3.8-L) or larger

This cake has a bright pop of lemony flavor, which comes from fresh lemon juice and lemon zest. It is the perfect spring or summer dessert when you don't want to turn on the oven! We like to top servings of this cake with fresh berries and a little bit of whipped cream.

15.25 ounce (432 g) box yellow cake mix

½ cup (120 ml) fresh lemon juice

½ cup (112 g) butter, melted (1 stick)

½ cup (120 ml) water

3 large eggs

1 tablespoon (6 g) fresh lemon zest

GLAZE:

1 cup (120 g) powdered sugar

2 tablespoons (28 ml) fresh lemon juice

1 teaspoon fresh lemon zest

TOPPINGS (OPTIONAL):

Whipped cream

Fresh berries

1. In a medium mixing bowl, add the cake mix, lemon juice, butter, water, eggs, and fresh lemon zest. Mix for 2 to 3 minutes with an electric mixer.

2. Spray the bottom of the slow cooker insert with nonstick cooking spray. Pour the cake batter into the slow cooker, spreading it evenly over the bottom.

3. Cover the slow cooker. Cook on HIGH for 2 to 3 hours, or until a toothpick inserted in the middle of the cake comes out clean.

4. While the cake is cooking, prepare the glaze. Mix the powdered sugar, 2 tablespoons (28 ml) of lemon juice, and 1 teaspoon lemon zest in a small mixing bowl. Set aside.

5. When the cake is done cooking, pour the glaze evenly over the top of the cake.

6. Spoon the cake into bowls to serve and top with whipped cream and fresh berries (if desired).

***NOTES:** You will need to purchase 4 to 5 lemons to get the amount of lemon juice needed for this recipe. Each lemon typically yields 4 to 5 tablespoons of fresh lemon juice.*

GERMAN CHOCOLATE SPOON CAKE

Serves: 6 to 8 | **Cook Time:** 2 to 3 hours on HIGH | **Slow Cooker Size:** 5-quart (4.7-L) or larger

This cake is easy to make and tastes amazing. A box of German chocolate cake is combined with coconut, chocolate chips, pecans, and a few other key ingredients. Katie's kids always enjoy the mystery of the end result and getting to spoon the cake into bowls while it is still hot. We like to top our cake with a scoop of ice cream or even frozen whipped topping!

1 box (425 g) German chocolate cake mix

3 large eggs

1 cup (235 ml) water

½ cup (112 g) unsalted butter, melted

1 teaspoon pure vanilla extract

1 cup (80 g) sweetened coconut flakes

1 cup (175 g) dark chocolate chips

½ cup (55 g) chopped pecans

Vanilla ice cream or frozen whipped topping (optional)

1. In a large mixing bowl, mix together the cake mix, eggs, water, butter, and vanilla.

2. Spray the liner of the slow cooker with nonstick cooking spray. Pour the cake batter into the prepared crock.

3. Sprinkle the coconut flakes, chocolate chips, and pecans over the top of the cake batter.

4. Cover the slow cooker. Cook on HIGH for 2 to 3 hours, or until the center of the cake is set and a toothpick inserted in the center comes out clean.

5. Spoon the warm cake into bowls and top with ice cream or whipped topping (if desired).

WARM CHOCOLATE LAVA CAKE

Serves: 8 | **Cook Time:** 2 to 3 hours on HIGH | **Slow Cooker Size:** 3-quart (2.8-L) or larger

Everyone loves chocolate, right? This recipe is ooey and gooey and just to die for! This is a cake you definitely want to eat warm right out of the slow cooker. Serve with some ice cream which gets all melt-y from the heat of the cake and you have one hot chocolaty mess of a dessert.

1 box (425 g) devil's food cake mix

1⅔ cups (395 ml) water

⅓ cup (79 ml) vegetable oil

3 large eggs

3.9 ounces (111 g) boxed chocolate instant pudding mix

2 cups (475 ml) milk

2 cups (350 g) semisweet chocolate chips

1. In a large mixing bowl, mix together the cake mix, water, oil, and eggs until well mixed.

2. In a small bowl, whisk together the pudding mix and milk.

3. Add the cake batter to the bottom of the slow cooker.

4. Carefully pour the pudding mixture over the top of the cake batter, but do not mix them together.

5. Pour the chocolate chips right in the middle of the slow cooker on top of the pudding.

6. Cover the slow cooker. Cook on HIGH for 2 to 3 hours, or until a knife inserted in the center of the cake comes out with a little bit of pudding but no raw cake batter on it.

7. Carefully flip the hot cake out onto a large serving platter or plate.

8. Let the cake cool slightly and serve while still warm.

CHOCOLATE BETTER THAN SEX CAKE

Serves: 12 | **Cook Time:** 2 to 3 hours on HIGH
Slow Cooker Size: 3½-quart (3.3-L) casserole or 6-quart (5.7-L) oval

This decadent dessert recipe is well . . . maybe, just maybe, better than sex. Chocolate, caramel, toffee . . . OH MY!

1 box (425 g) chocolate cake mix

1¼ cups (295 ml) water

14 ounces (397 g) canned sweetened condensed milk, divided

¾ cup (177 ml) vegetable oil

2 large eggs

1 tablespoon (15 ml) pure vanilla extract

2 cups (350 g) semisweet chocolate chips

14 ounces (397 g) caramel ice cream topping, divided

½ cup (120 g) toffee bits

13 ounces (369 g) canned whipped cream

1. In a large mixing bowl, combine the cake mix, water, half of the sweetened condensed milk, oil, eggs, and vanilla until well mixed.

2. Spray the insert of the slow cooker with nonstick cooking spray. Pour the cake batter into the slow cooker.

3. Sprinkle the chocolate chips over the top of the batter.

4. Cover the slow cooker. Cook on HIGH for 2 to 3 hours, until the center of the cake is done and a toothpick inserted in the middle comes out clean.

5. Using the handle of a wooden or plastic spoon, poke holes all over the surface of the top of the cake.

6. In a small mixing bowl, combine together the remaining half of the sweetened condensed milk and ¾ of the caramel ice cream topping.

7. Pour the caramel and condensed milk mixture evenly over the cake, allowing the sauce to fill the holes in the top of cake.

8. Place the cake in the refrigerator until chilled and you are ready to serve.

9. Cut the cake into 12 servings and top each slice of cake with whipped cream, reserved caramel ice cream topping, and toffee bits.

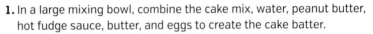

HOT FUDGE PEANUT BUTTER SWIRL CAKE

Serves: 6 to 8 | **Cook Time:** 2 to 3 hours on HIGH | **Slow Cooker Size:** 5-quart (4.7-L) or larger

Creamy peanut butter is mixed into chocolate cake, the top is swirled with hot fudge sauce, and then it's all cooked in the slow cooker. Before serving, top the cake with a delicious peanut butter–fudge glaze. Use a large spoon or ice cream scoop to spoon the cake out. Top with ice cream or whipped cream, and sprinkle some chopped peanut butter cups over the top for a gourmet dessert your family will rave about.

1 box (425 g) yellow cake mix

1 cup (235 ml) water

½ cup (130 g) creamy peanut butter

½ cup (120 g) hot fudge sauce

¼ cup (55 g) softened butter

3 large eggs

GLAZE:

1 cup (120 g) powdered sugar

⅓ cup (86 g) creamy peanut butter

¼ cup (60 ml) milk

⅓ cup (80 g) hot fudge sauce

TOPPINGS (OPTIONAL):

Ice cream or whipped cream

4 to 6 chocolate-covered peanut butter cups, roughly chopped

1. In a large mixing bowl, combine the cake mix, water, peanut butter, hot fudge sauce, butter, and eggs to create the cake batter.

2. Spray the insert of the slow cooker with nonstick cooking spray. Pour half of the cake batter into the slow cooker.

3. Warm the hot fudge sauce slightly in the microwave or on the stove top. Drizzle it over the top of the batter. Using a knife or spatula, swirl the hot fudge sauce into the batter.

4. Top with the remaining cake batter.

5. Cover the slow cooker. Cook on HIGH for 2 to 3 hours, until a toothpick inserted in the middle comes out clean.

6. Remove the insert from the heating base and allow the cake to cool on a rack.

TO MAKE THE GLAZE:

1. While the cake is cooling, prepare the glaze. In a medium mixing bowl, combine together the powdered sugar, peanut butter, and milk.

2. Heat the hot fudge and mix it into the peanut butter mixture.

3. When the cake is fully cooled, spoon the cake into bowls. Drizzle each serving with some of the glaze.

4. Top each serving of cake with ice cream or whipped cream and sprinkle with some chopped peanut butter cups (if desired).

DELIGHTFUL CINNAMON ROLL POKE CAKE

Serves: 6 to 8 | **Cook Time:** 2 to 3 hours on HIGH
Slow Cooker Size: 3½-quart (3.3-L) casserole or 6-quart (5.7-L) oval

Katie has fallen in love with her casserole slow cooker because cakes are super easy to make in them, and they come out looking more like a traditional oven-baked cake. But you can use a 6-quart (5.7-L) oval slow cooker as well if you don't have one. In this recipe, white cake mix is doctored up with a lovely, cinnamon roll filling and topped with icing.

1 box (425 g) white cake mix

3 large eggs

½ cup (120 ml) water

½ cup (120 ml) milk

¼ cup (55 g) butter, melted

FILLING:

¼ cup (55 g) butter, melted

½ cup (115 g) brown sugar, packed

1 tablespoon (7 g) ground cinnamon

1 teaspoon pure vanilla extract

½ cup (120 ml) sweetened condensed milk

GLAZE:

2 cups (240 g) powdered sugar

2 tablespoons (28 g) butter, melted

1 teaspoon pure vanilla extract

1 tablespoon (15 ml) milk

1. In a medium mixing bowl, mix together the cake mix, eggs, water, milk, and butter until combined.
2. Spray inside of slow cooker insert with nonstick cooking spray.
3. Pour the cake batter into the slow cooker and spread to cover the bottom evenly.
4. Cover the slow cooker. Cook on HIGH for 2 to 3 hours, or until a toothpick inserted in the middle comes out clean.
5. In a small mixing bowl, combine all the filling ingredients until well mixed.
6. Using the handle of a wooden spoon or similar instrument, poke holes evenly over the entire surface of the cooked cake.
7. Pour the filling mixture evenly over the cake using a spatula to spread as necessary, being sure to get the filling into the holes you poked into the cake.
8. In another small mixing bowl, combine all the glaze ingredients until well mixed.
9. Pour the glaze over the top of the cake and serve either warm or at room temperature.

EASY RED VELVET LAVA CAKE

Serves: 6 to 8 | **Cook Time:** 2 to 3 hours on HIGH | **Slow Cooker Size:** 4-quart (3.8-L) or larger

This delicious cake is so easy to make with only 10 minutes of prep work involved. It has a chocolate cake base and creates its own molten lava center. Katie loves serving this cake warm right from the slow cooker, topping each serving with a big scoop of vanilla ice cream!

1 box (425 g) red velvet cake mix

1½ cups (355 ml) water

⅓ cup (79 ml) vegetable oil

3 large eggs

1 box (4 serving size) vanilla instant pudding mix

2 cups (475 ml) cold milk

12 ounces (340 g) white chocolate chips

Ice cream or whipped cream (optional)

1. In a large mixing bowl, mix together the cake mix, water, oil, and eggs to create the cake batter.

2. Spray the slow cooker insert with nonstick cooking spray. Pour the cake batter into the slow cooker.

3. In a small mixing bowl, whisk together the pudding mix and cold milk. Pour the pudding mixture over the cake batter in the slow cooker. Do not stir them together.

4. Sprinkle the white chocolate chips over the top of the pudding.

5. Cover the slow cooker. Cook on HIGH for 2 to 3 hours, or until the cake has set.

6. Spoon the cake into bowls while still warm and top with ice cream or whipped cream (if desired).

NOTES: *You can also use chocolate pudding and chocolate chips for a different, delicious flavor profile!*

PINEAPPLE PECAN DUMP CAKE

Serves: 10 | **Cook Time:** 2 to 2½ hours on HIGH
Slow Cooker Size: 3½-quart (3.3-L) casserole or 5-quart (4.7-L) or larger oval

One day Sarah was craving something sweet with pecans, and she decided to find a way to incorporate pecans into a dessert. Dump cakes are fun and easy to make, and this recipe turned out great with the pecans. The butter and brown sugar make a caramel-like texture, and the pecans add a fabulous crunch!

½ cup (112 g) butter, melted

2 cups (224 g) pecan halves, divided

1 cup (225 g) brown sugar, divided

1 box (425 g) yellow cake mix

1 cup (235 ml) pineapple juice

½ cup (120 ml) water

Whipped cream or ice cream (optional)

1. Pour melted butter into the insert of the slow cooker and use a pastry brush or paper towel to spread the butter all around and up the sides of the insert.
2. Sprinkle 1 cup (112 g) of the pecan halves on top of the butter.
3. Sprinkle ½ cup (112 g) of the brown sugar over the pecans and butter.
4. Pour the dry cake mix over the brown sugar as evenly as possible.
5. Sprinkle the remaining brown sugar over the top of the dry cake mix.
6. Combine the pineapple juice and water in a glass liquid measuring cup. Pour it carefully over the top of the cake, covering the entire cake mix, but do not mix.
7. Cover the slow cooker. Cook on HIGH for 2 to 2½ hours, until the sides of the cake begins to brown.
8. Serve warm with whipped cream or ice cream (if desired).

LUSH PIÑA COLADA DUMP CAKE

Serves: 6 | **Cook Time:** 2 hours on LOW
Slow Cooker Size: 6-quart (5.7-L)

Whenever canned pineapple goes on sale, Katie always stocks up because her family really likes to eat pineapple as a snack straight from the can or in recipes, such as this simple dump cake. Shredded coconut makes this yummy cake taste like the tropics.

14 ounces (397 g) canned crushed pineapple in juice

1 cup (80 g) unsweetened shredded coconut

1 box (425 g) yellow cake mix

1 cup (225 g) unsalted butter, melted

1. Add the entire can of pineapple to the slow cooker insert.
2. Sprinkle the shredded coconut over the top of the pineapple.
3. Evenly sprinkle the dry cake mix over the top of the pineapple and coconut.
4. Carefully pour the melted butter over the top of the dry cake mix.
5. Cover the slow cooker. Cook on LOW for 2 hours.

EASY APPLE DUMP CAKE

Serves: 6 | **Cook Time:** 2½ hours on LOW
Slow Cooker Size: 6-quart (5.7-L)

With just five ingredients, this dump cake recipe uses canned apple pie filling as the base. It really is perfect when served warm with a scoop of vanilla ice cream on top!

21 ounces (595 g) canned apple pie filling

1 tablespoon (13 g) granulated sugar

1 teaspoon ground cinnamon

1 box (425 g) yellow cake mix

1 cup (225 g) unsalted butter, melted

Vanilla ice cream (optional)

1. Add the can of apple pie filling into the slow cooker insert and spread evenly.
2. Sprinkle the sugar and cinnamon evenly over the pie filling.
3. Next, evenly sprinkle the dry cake mix over the top of the apple pie filling.
4. Carefully pour the melted butter evenly over the top of the dry cake mix.
5. Cover the slow cooker. Cook on LOW for 2 hours.
6. Serve warm with vanilla ice cream (if desired).

SPICED APPLE DUMP CAKE

Serves: 6 | **Cook Time:** 2 hours on LOW
Slow Cooker Size: 5- to 6-quart (4.7- to 5.7-L)

This dump cake uses a box of spice cake mix instead of the standard yellow cake mix for some cinnamon-and-spice flavor. Oatmeal and walnuts add some great texture. You will want to serve this warm with a scoop of ice cream for sure!

1 box (425 g) spice cake mix

1 cup (80 g) quick-cooking oats

¾ cup (177 g) unsalted butter, melted

29 ounces (822 g) canned apple pie filling

1 cup (120 g) chopped walnuts

Ice cream (optional)

1. In a large mixing bowl, combine the dry cake mix, oats, and melted butter until mixed and crumbly.
2. Add the apple pie filling to the bottom of the slow cooker insert and spread evenly over the bottom.
3. Sprinkle the cake mixture evenly over apple pie filling.
4. Sprinkle the walnuts evenly over cake mixture.
5. Cover the slow cooker. Cook on LOW for 2 hours.
6. Serve warm with ice cream (if desired).

FALL PUMPKIN DUMP CAKE

Serves: 6 | **Cook Time:** 2 hours on HIGH
Slow Cooker Size: 6-quart (5.7-L)

This delicious recipe has all the wonderful flavors of autumn with a great crunch from the pecans. Make sure you use canned pumpkin puree and not pumpkin pie filling, which has sugar and spices already added to the can.

15 ounces (425 g) canned 100% pumpkin puree

12 ounces (355 ml) canned evaporated milk

4 large eggs

1½ cups (300 g) granulated sugar

2 teaspoons (5 g) pumpkin pie spice

½ teaspoon kosher salt

1 box (425 g) yellow cake mix

½ cup (112 g) unsalted butter, melted

1 cup (110 g) chopped pecans

Ice cream or whipped cream (optional)

1. In a large mixing bowl, mix together the pumpkin puree, evaporated milk, eggs, sugar, pumpkin pie spice, and salt until smooth.
2. Pour into the slow cooker insert and spread evenly.
3. Evenly sprinkle the dry cake mix to the top of the pumpkin mixture.
4. Pour melted butter evenly over the top of the dry cake mix.
5. Cover the slow cooker. Cook on HIGH for 2 hours.
6. Serve warm or cold with ice cream or whipped cream (if desired).

JUST PEACHY PEACH DUMP CAKE

Serves: 6 | **Cook Time:** 2 hours on HIGH
Slow Cooker Size: 5-quart (4.7-L) or larger

This is another great easy three-ingredient dump cake using canned peaches. Katie loves that she can go to her pantry and usually find the ingredients on hand to make this simple dessert.

14.5 ounces (411 g) canned peaches in juice

1 box (425 g) yellow cake mix

1 cup (225 g) unsalted butter, melted

Whipped cream (optional)

1. Add the can of peaches with the juice to the insert of slow cooker.
2. Sprinkle the dry cake mix on top of the peaches as evenly as possible.
3. Pour melted butter over the dry cake mix as evenly as possible without mixing.
4. Cover the slow cooker. Cook on HIGH for 2 hours.
5. Serve warm or cold with whipped cream (if desired).

3-INGREDIENT CHERRY DUMP CAKE

Serves: 8 | **Cook Time:** 4 hours on LOW or 2 hours on HIGH | **Slow Cooker Size:** 3- to 5-quart (2.8- to 4.7-L)

You really cannot find an easier dessert to make than this cherry dump cake. With just three ingredients, this comes together in a matter of minutes.

42 ounces (1.2 kg) canned cherry pie filling

16.5 ounces (468 g) yellow cake mix

½ cup (112 g) butter, melted

Ice cream (optional)

1. Add the cherry pie filling to the insert of the slow cooker.
2. In a medium mixing bowl, mix together the dry yellow cake mix and the melted butter until the butter is mixed in and everything is crumbly.
3. Sprinkle all the cake mixture evenly over the surface of the cherry pie filling in the slow cooker.
4. Cover the slow cooker. Cook on LOW for 4 hours or on HIGH for 2 hours.
5. Serve warm or cold with ice cream (if desired).

BEST EVER SLOW COOKER CHEESECAKE

Serves: 6 | **Cook Time:** 2 to 2½ hours on HIGH | **Slow Cooker Size:** 6-quart (5.7-L) or larger

A slow cooker is the perfect way to make a small cheesecake. And this recipe could not be any easier or more delicious. You will, however, need a small heatproof bowl or springform pan that will fit inside your slow cooker.

24 ounces (680 g) cream cheese, softened

¾ cup (150 g) granulated sugar

3 large eggs

1½ teaspoons pure vanilla extract

GRAHAM CRACKER CRUST:

6 whole graham crackers, crushed into crumbs

¼ cup (55 g) butter, melted

NOTES: *Serve the cheesecake plain or with your favorite fruit topping.*

1. In a large mixing bowl, mix together the cream cheese and granulated sugar using a hand mixer until the sugar is well combined and the cream cheese is light and fluffy.

2. Add the eggs to the cheese mixture, one at a time, mixing well after each egg is added.

3. Mix in the vanilla and set the cheesecake mixture aside while you prepare the crust.

4. In a separate bowl, mix together the graham cracker crumbs and butter with a fork until the mixture resembles damp sand.

5. Add the mixture to the bottom of a small heatproof bowl or springform pan that will fit inside the slow cooker.

6. With a spoon or the back of a dry measuring cup, press the graham cracker mixture into the bowl or pan until you have a smooth flat layer of crust.

7. Spoon the cream cheese mixture over the top of the crust and spread it evenly in the bowl or pan.

8. Place the cheesecake inside the slow cooker. Using a liquid measuring cup or a tea kettle with a spout, carefully add water in the space between the cheesecake and the slow cooker insert, making sure not to get any water on the cheesecake itself. The water level should reach halfway up the side of the cheesecake.

9. Place a double layer of paper towels between the slow cooker insert and lid to prevent condensation from dripping on the cheesecake while it cooks.

10. Cook on HIGH for 2 to 2½ hours, or until the center of the cheesecake is no longer runny when you stick a thin knife into the center of it.

11. Turn the slow cooker off and leave the lid off. Let the cheesecake cool in the slow cooker for 30 minutes to 1 hour.

12. Carefully remove the cheesecake from the slow cooker. Cover the top with foil or plastic wrap and place it in the refrigerator for at least 1 hour to chill before eating.

CHOCOLATE MINT CHEESECAKE

Serves: 6 | **Cook Time:** 3 hours on LOW or 2 hours on HIGH | **Slow Cooker Size:** 6-quart (5.7-L)

Inspired by the famous Thin Mint Girl Scout cookie, this delicious cheesecake uses peppermint chocolate cookies as the crust and the cheesecake filling is flavored just right with peppermint extract. You won't want to stop eating this cheesecake!

CRUST:

16 whole chocolate peppermint cookies, pulverized (see note)

¼ cup (55 g) butter, melted

24 ounces (680 g) cream cheese, softened

¾ cup (150 g) granulated sugar

3 large eggs

1 teaspoon peppermint extract

3 drops green food coloring

NOTES: *Many grocery stores now sell a generic version of the Girl Scout cookies. If you cannot find them, use chocolate cream-filled cookies and add ½ of a teaspoon of peppermint extract to the crust mixture.*

1. Prepare the crust by combining the cookie crumbs and butter until the mixture resembles damp sand.
2. Press the crust mixture into a heatproof glass bowl or small 6-inch (15-cm) springform pan with your hands or the back of a dry measuring cup. Set aside.
3. In a medium mixing bowl, add the cream cheese and sugar. Beat with a mixture until the mixture is light and fluffy.
4. Add each egg, one at a time, beating well after the addition of each egg.
5. Add the peppermint extract and food coloring and mix well.
6. Pour the cheesecake batter into the prepared pan and spread evenly over the crust.
7. Place the cheesecake pan in the bottom of the slow cooker. Carefully pour 4 to 6 cups (940 ml to 1.4 L) of water around the sides of the pan so that the water reaches halfway up the sides of the cheesecake. Be very careful not to pour water on or inside your cheesecake. It is best to do this with a liquid measuring cup or tea kettle with a spout.
8. Place a double layer of paper towels between the lid of the slow cooker and the stoneware insert.
9. Cook on LOW for 3 hours or on HIGH for 2 hours, or until you see the sides of the cheesecake start to pull away from the pan and the center of the cheesecake is spongy to the touch.
10. Remove the lid from the slow cooker and unplug it. Allow the cheesecake to cool in the slow cooker for 1 hour.
11. Remove the cheesecake from the slow cooker insert and refrigerate for at least 2 hours before serving.

PUMPKIN SPICE CHEESECAKE IN A JAR

Serves: 8 | **Cook Time:** 6 hours on LOW or 4 hours on HIGH | **Slow Cooker Size:** 6-quart (5.7-L)

Nothing says fall like all things pumpkin spice, and these individual servings of pumpkin spice cheesecake are just the right thing to get you in the mood for autumn. Each cheesecake is baked in a mini mason jar. A little whipped cream on top is the perfect finishing touch!

CRUST:

2 tablespoons (28 g) butter

2 cups (200 g) gingersnap cookie crumbs (plus a little extra for sprinkling on top, if you desire)

16 ounces (455 g) cream cheese, softened

1 cup (200 g) granulated sugar

2 large eggs

15 ounces (425 g) canned pumpkin puree (not pumpkin pie filling)

2 teaspoons (5 g) pumpkin pie spice

Whipped cream (optional)

1. Prepare the crust by adding the butter to a microwave-safe bowl and heating for 30 seconds on HIGH.

2. Add the gingersnap cookie crumbs to the bowl and mix together until the mixture resembles damp sand.

3. Divide the crust mixture evenly between eight 8-ounce (235-ml) jelly canning jars, pressing the mixture down with your fingers or a spoon. Set aside.

4. In a medium mixing bowl, mix the cream cheese and sugar with a mixer until light and fluffy.

5. Add the eggs one at a time, beating well after each addition.

6. Mix in the pumpkin puree and pumpkin pie spice until well combined.

7. Divide the cheesecake mixture between the eight jars and place each jar inside the slow cooker.

8. Carefully pour water between the jars until the water reaches halfway up the sides of the jars, being careful not to get any water inside your cheesecakes.

9. Place a double layer of paper towels between the lid and stoneware insert and cook on LOW for 6 hours or on HIGH for 4 hours.

10. Carefully remove the jars from the slow cooker and let them cool to room temperature.

11. Chill in the refrigerator for at least 2 hours before serving.

12. To serve, add a dollop of whipped cream and sprinkle a little bit of the reserved gingersnap cookie crumbs on top (if desired).

NOT YOUR GRANDMA'S PECAN PIE

Serves: 6 to 8 | **Cook Time:** 2 to 3 hours on HIGH
Slow Cooker Size: 3½-quart (3.3-L) casserole or 5-quart (4.7-L) or larger oval

Katie would never have thought that you could bake a pie in a slow cooker, but she had to give it a try—and this pecan pie is fabulous. This recipe calls for a store-bought refrigerated pie crust, but if you have the time to make a homemade crust, feel free to use that instead. This really is not your grandma's pecan pie!

1 refrigerated pie crust

3 large eggs

1 cup (200 g) granulated sugar

½ cup (120 ml) dark corn syrup

⅓ cup (75 g) unsalted
butter, melted

⅛ teaspoon kosher salt

1 teaspoon pure vanilla extract

¾ cup (83 g) chopped pecans

¾–1 cup (84–112 g) whole pecan
halves, reserved

FOR SERVING (OPTIONAL):

Whipped cream

Vanilla ice cream

HOMEMADE PIE CRUST:

2 cups (250 g) all-purpose flour

1 teaspoon kosher salt

⅔ cup (150 g) butter or
shortening, chilled

5–7 tablespoons (75–105 ml)
ice water

1. Spray the slow cooker insert with nonstick cooking spray.

2. Unroll the pie crust and mold it to fit the bottom and up the sides a little of the slow cooker. The pie crust will be a little uneven, but that is okay. It is going to taste great!

3. In a large mixing bowl, whisk together the remaining ingredients except for the pecans, until combined.

4. Pour the pie filling into the crust in the slow cooker, making sure that the pecan filling does not come up over the pie crust.

5. Arrange the whole pecans nicely on top of the filling.

6. Cover the slow cooker. Cook on HIGH for 2 to 3 hours.

7. Allow the pie to fully cool before serving. Top with whipped cream or vanilla ice cream (if desired).

HOMEMADE PIE CRUST

1. In a large mixing bowl, add the flour and salt.

2. Cut the chilled butter or shortening into the flour using a pastry blender or two butter knives until the mixture resembles coarse crumbs and there are still small pea-size bits of butter/shortening.

3. Slowly add ice water a tablespoon at a time, mixing after each table-spoon of water is added until a dough starts to form.

4. Roll the pie dough out on a floured countertop with a rolling pin until you have a shape that will fit in your slow cooker. Trim the edges, if desired, and place the pie crust dough in the slow cooker.

10

STAPLES: HOMEMADE STOCKS, SAUCES, AND SEASONING MIXES

CHICKEN BROTH OR STOCK

Yield: 4 quarts broth or 2 quarts stock | **Cook Time:** 8 to 10 hours on LOW for broth plus 3 to 4 hours on HIGH for stock | **Slow Cooker Size:** 6-quart (5.7-L) or larger

The slow cooker is the perfect vessel for making your own chicken broth or stock. The difference between broth and stock is that a broth is reduced further to create a richer liquid, which is stock. So, first we will make a beautiful chicken broth. Then, if you want to turn it into stock, you will prop open the slow cooker lid and continue to cook until the liquid is reduced by about half.

Bones and skin from 1 whole roasted chicken OR 1–2 pounds (455 g to about 1 kg) chicken wings

2 medium yellow onions, diced

4 ribs celery, diced

2 medium carrots, peeled and diced

2 cloves garlic, minced

2 bay leaves

1 teaspoon dried thyme

1 teaspoon freshly ground black pepper

½ teaspoon dried oregano

4 quarts (3.8 L) water

1. Place all the ingredients in the slow cooker insert.

2. Cover the slow cooker. Cook on LOW for 8 to 10 hours.

3. Using tongs, remove the larger pieces of chicken bones from the slow cooker and discard them.

4. Place a fine-mesh strainer over a large bowl, pan, or container. Using hot pads to hold the hot slow cooker, carefully strain the chicken broth to remove all solids.

5. To make chicken stock, wipe out the slow cooker insert and add the strained chicken broth back to the slow cooker.

6. Place the lid back on the slow cooker and prop the lid open slightly with a wooden spoon or other heatproof utensil.

7. Cook on HIGH heat for about 3 to 4 hours, or until the liquid has reduced by about half. Pour the hot stock into a bowl, pan, or container.

8. Cover the container that you poured the chicken broth or stock with plastic wrap or a lid and place in the refrigerator overnight to allow the fat to rise to the top and harden.

9. Remove the broth/stock from the refrigerator and remove the solid fat from the surface with a slotted spoon.

10. Your broth or stock is now ready to use. It can be stored in labeled freezer containers in the refrigerator for up to 1 week or in the freezer for up to 3 months.

BEEF BROTH OR STOCK

Yield: 4 quarts broth or 2 quarts stock | **Cook Time:** 8 to 10 hours on LOW for broth plus 3 to 4 hours on HIGH for stock | **Slow Cooker Size:** 6-quart (5.7-L) or larger

Making your own beef broth or stock is made simple when you use your slow cooker to do all the simmering. While you will need to roast your beef bones in the oven, the rest of the work is all done in your slow cooker. Beef stock is just beef broth that has been allowed to reduce by about half until you have rich and flavorful liquid that is perfect for soups and other wonderful dishes.

3–4 pounds (1.4–1.8 kg) mixed beef bones (knuckles, neck bones, oxtail and/or short ribs)

3 medium carrots, peeled and diced

3 stalks celery, diced

3 cloves garlic, minced

2 medium yellow onions, diced

2 tablespoons (30 ml) apple cider vinegar

1 teaspoon freshly ground black pepper

2 bay leaves

4–5 quarts (3.8–4.7 L) water

1. Preheat the oven to 400°F (200°C, or gas mark 6).
2. Place the beef bones on a rimmed baking sheet. Roast in the oven for 1 hour, flipping the bones over halfway through the cooking time.
3. While the bones are roasting, prepare the vegetables and place them in the slow cooker insert.
4. Add the roasted bones and add the water to cover the bones.
5. Cover the slow cooker. Cook on LOW for 8 to 10 hours.
6. Using tongs, remove the larger pieces of beef bones from the slow cooker and set aside. (Feel free to use the meat from the bones in a soup or stew.)
7. Place a fine-mesh strainer over a large bowl, pan, or container. Using hot pads to hold the hot slow cooker, carefully strain the beef broth to remove all solids.
8. To make beef stock, wipe out the slow cooker insert and add the strained beef broth back to the slow cooker.
9. Place the lid back on the slow cooker and prop the lid open slightly with a wooden spoon or other heatproof utensil.
10. Cook on HIGH heat for about 3 to 4 hours, or until the liquid has reduced by about half. Pour hot stock into a bowl, pan, or container.
11. Cover the container that you poured the beef broth or stock with plastic wrap or a lid and place it in the refrigerator overnight to allow the fat to rise to the top and harden.
12. Remove the broth/stock from the refrigerator and remove the solid fat from the surface with a slotted spoon.
13. Your broth or stock is now ready to use. It can be stored in labeled freezer containers in the refrigerator for up to 1 week or in the freezer for up to 3 months.

VEGETABLE BROTH OR STOCK

Yield: 4 quarts broth or 2 quarts stock | **Cook Time:** 6 to 8 hours on LOW for broth plus 3 to 4 hours on HIGH for stock | **Slow Cooker Size:** 6-quart (5.7-L) or larger

Vegetable broth or stock is a great way to use up leftover vegetables and scraps and turn them into a luscious liquid that is perfect for soups and stews. We have even been known to cook rice in vegetable broth instead of water for some added flavor and nutrients. The recipe below is a base recipe and comes out very good, but if you have any vegetable scraps, throw those in the slow cooker too to use them up. In this recipe, grate the carrots on a cheese grater to get more flavor out of the carrots. The beta-carotene also gives the broth or stock a rich color.

4 stalks celery, diced (including the tops)

4 medium carrots, grated

2 cloves garlic, minced

1 large yellow onion, diced

1 red bell pepper, seeded and chopped

1 medium to large tomato, seeded and chopped

1 cup (60 g) fresh roughly chopped parsley (stems and leaves are okay)

6 ounces (168 g) mushrooms, chopped (use whatever kind you like)

2 bay leaves

1 teaspoon freshly ground black pepper

½ teaspoon dried thyme

½ teaspoon dried rosemary

½ teaspoon dried basil

½ teaspoon dried oregano

4–5 quarts (3.8–4.7 L) water

1. Prepare all the vegetables and add them to the slow cooker insert.
2. Add the herbs and spices, and cover everything with the water.
3. Cover the slow cooker. Cook on LOW for 6 to 8 hours.
4. Place a fine-mesh strainer over a large bowl, pan, or container. Using hot pads to hold the hot slow cooker, carefully strain the vegetable broth to remove all solids.
5. To make vegetable stock, wipe out the slow cooker insert and add the strained vegetable broth back to the slow cooker.
6. Place the lid back on the slow cooker and prop the lid open slightly with a wooden spoon or other heatproof utensil.
7. Cook on HIGH heat for about 3 to 4 hours, or until the liquid has reduced by about half. Pour the hot stock into a bowl, pan, or container.
8. Your broth or stock is now ready to use. It can be stored in labeled freezer containers in the refrigerator for up to 1 week or in the freezer for up to 3 months.

NOTES: *Most vegetables can be used in vegetable broth or stock; however, it is best to avoid the following vegetables and herbs:*

- *Beets*
- *Bok choy*
- *Broccoli*
- *Cabbage*
- *Cauliflower*
- *Cilantro*
- *Collard greens*
- *Corn*
- *Hot peppers*
- *Kohlrabi*
- *Potato peels*
- *Radish*
- *Rutabaga*
- *Sweet potatoes*
- *Winter squash (acorn, butternut, pumpkin, etc.)*

MARINARA SAUCE

Serves: 12 | **Cook Time:** 3 hours on LOW | **Slow Cooker Size:** 3- to 4-quart (2.8- to 3.8-L)

Marinara sauce is so versatile and easy to make in your slow cooker. You're going to want to stop buying store-bought sauce and start making your own at home. Make up a big batch and freeze it in quart-size freezer containers so that you always have sauce on hand for spaghetti, lasagna, or many other Italian-style dishes.

8–10 cloves garlic, minced

16 ounces (455 g) canned Italian-style diced tomatoes, lightly pureed in blender

14 ounces (397 g) canned Italian-style tomato sauce

2 tablespoons (32 g) canned tomato paste

2 tablespoons (6 g) fresh basil minced (or 2½ tablespoons dried basil)

1 tablespoon (7 g) onion powder

1 tablespoon (3 g) Italian seasoning

1 teaspoon balsamic vinegar

1. Combine all the ingredients in the slow cooker, stirring until well mixed.
2. Cover the slow cooker. Cook on LOW for 3 hours.
3. Store in airtight container, refrigerated for up to 2 weeks.
4. Freeze portions in freezer-safe containers for up to 3 months.

PIZZA SAUCE

Yield: 4 cups | **Cook Time:** 6 to 8 hours on LOW or 3 to 4 hours on HIGH
Slow Cooker Size: 3- to 4-quart (2.8- to 3.8-L)

This pizza sauce is a standard go-to recipe for whenever you need a yummy sauce for pizza or pizza casseroles. You can quickly toss all the ingredients in a small slow cooker and let it cook while you go about your day. If you want to freeze up several containers, double the batch so that you have plenty of sauce for future meals.

32 ounces (905 g) canned tomato sauce

3 tablespoons (48 g) canned tomato paste

1 tablespoon (5 g) dried basil

1 tablespoon (3 g) dried oregano

1 tablespoon (13 g) granulated sugar or honey

1 teaspoon garlic powder

1 teaspoon fennel seeds

⅛ teaspoon kosher salt

⅛ teaspoon freshly ground black pepper

1. Add all the ingredients to a slow cooker.
2. Cover the slow cooker. Cook on LOW for 6 to 8 hours or on HIGH for 3 to 4 hours.

NOTES: *Feel free to double or even triple this batch. It freezes beautifully. Freeze 1-cup containers to have on hand for 1 pizza.*

PESTO

Yield: 4 to 5 cups

In the summer, growing several basil plants in containers out in your yard makes it easy to cook batches of fresh pesto to freeze and enjoy the flavors of summer all year round. In this frugal recipe, we stretch the basil by using baby spinach along with the fresh basil leaves. This also makes for a milder pesto. If you do not grow your own basil, you can easily find fresh basil in the produce section of most grocery stores.

2 cups (96 g) packed fresh basil leaves

2 cups (110 g) packed fresh baby spinach leaves

6 cloves garlic, peeled

⅔ cup (68 g) pine nuts (or walnuts)

1 cup (236 ml) extra-virgin olive oil

1 cup (100 g) grated Parmesan cheese

⅛ teaspoon kosher salt

⅛ teaspoon freshly ground black pepper

1. Combine the basil, spinach, garlic, and pine nuts in the bowl of a food processor. Pulse a few times.

2. Slowly stream the olive oil through the food processor tube while the processor is running on low speed. About halfway through, stop the food processor to scrape down the sides of the bowl to make sure everything is getting processed.

3. Add the Parmesan cheese, salt, and pepper and pulse a few times to incorporate.

NOTES: *To freeze, spoon finished pesto into freezer-safe bags or containers and store in freezer for up to 8 months. For large families, freeze in 1-cup portions. You may want to do smaller or larger portion sizes depending on your needs. You can also freeze in ice cube trays, pop out your frozen pesto cubes, and freeze in larger freezer bags. Thaw as many cubes as you need. You can add one or two pesto cubes to your favorite marinara sauce or soups in the winter.*

ITALIAN SEASONING SPICE MIX

Yield: 9 tablespoons

3 tablespoons (9 g) dried oregano

4 teaspoons (10 g) garlic powder

2 bay leaf, crushed

2 teaspoons (1 g) dried marjoram

2 teaspoons (1 g) dried thyme

2 teaspoons (1 g) dried rosemary

2 teaspoons (1 g) dried tarragon

1 teaspoon red pepper flakes

1 teaspoon dried basil

1 teaspoon dried rosemary

1 teaspoon dried sage

1 teaspoon celery seeds

1. Place all the ingredients in a small bowl. Mix and crush with the back of a spoon.
2. Store in an airtight container for up to 6 months.

SHAWARMA SEASONING SPICE MIX

Yield: 10 tablespoons

2 tablespoons (14 g) ground cumin

2 tablespoons (12 g) ground coriander

2 tablespoons (14 g) garlic powder

1 tablespoon (7 g) smoked paprika

1 tablespoon (15 g) kosher salt

2 teaspoons (5 g) ground turmeric

1 teaspoon ground cloves

1 teaspoon black pepper

1 teaspoon ground cinnamon

½ teaspoon ground ginger

½ teaspoon ground cardamom

1. Place all the ingredients in a small bowl. Mix and crush with the back of a spoon.
2. Store in an airtight container for up to 6 months.

TACO SEASONING SPICE MIX

Yield: 6 tablespoons

3 tablespoons (24 g) chili powder

2 tablespoons (14 g) ground cumin

1 tablespoon (6 g) freshly ground black pepper

1 teaspoon ground paprika

1 teaspoon kosher salt

½ teaspoon garlic powder

½ teaspoon onion powder

½ teaspoon crushed red pepper

½ teaspoon dried oregano

1. Place all the ingredients in a small bowl. Mix and crush with the back of a spoon.

2. Store in an airtight container for up to 6 months.

BAY SEASONING SPICE MIX

Yield: 8 tablespoons

2 tablespoons (6 g) bay leaf powder

2 tablespoons (12 g) celery salt

1 tablespoon (11 g) ground mustard seed

1 tablespoon (1 g) dried parsley flakes

2 teaspoons (4 g) freshly ground black pepper

2 teaspoons (3 g) ground ginger

2 teaspoons (5 g) smoked paprika

1 teaspoon ground nutmeg

1 teaspoon ground allspice

½ teaspoon ground mace

½ teaspoon ground cardamom

½ teaspoon ground cinnamon

¼ teaspoon crushed red pepper flakes

1. Place all the ingredients in a small bowl. Mix and crush with the back of a spoon.

2. Store in an airtight container for up to 6 months.

GARLIC AND HERB SEASONING AND SPICE MIX

Yield: 14 tablespoons

2 tablespoons (6 g) dried marjoram

2 tablespoons (6 g) dried oregano

2 tablespoons (4 g) dried rosemary

2 tablespoons (9 g) dried basil

2 tablespoons (2 g) dried parsley flakes

1 tablespoon (7 g) onion powder

1 tablespoon (2 g) dried thyme

1 tablespoon (15 g) kosher salt

1 tablespoon (7 g) garlic powder

1 teaspoon lemon pepper

1 teaspoon dried marjoram

1 teaspoon dried sage

½ teaspoon cayenne pepper

1. Place all the ingredients in a small bowl. Mix and crush with the back of a spoon.
2. Store in an airtight container for up to 6 months.

BUTTERMILK RANCH DRESSING MIX

Yield: 10 tablespoons

⅓ cup (40 g) dry buttermilk powder

2 tablespoons (14 g) dried minced onion

2 teaspoons dried parsley flakes

1 teaspoon dried dill

1 teaspoon freshly ground black pepper

1 teaspoon kosher salt

1 teaspoon garlic powder

1 teaspoon dried chives

1. Place all the ingredients in a small bowl. Mix and crush with the back of a spoon.
2. Store in an airtight container for up to 6 months.

ITALIAN DRESSING SPICE MIX

Yield: 7 tablespoons

2 tablespoons (6 g) dried oregano

1 tablespoon (7 g) garlic powder

1 tablespoon (7 g) onion powder

1 tablespoon (13 g) granulated sugar

1 tablespoon (1 g) dried parsley

1 teaspoon freshly ground black pepper

1 teaspoon dried basil

1 teaspoon salt (optional)

¼ teaspoon dried thyme

¼ teaspoon dried celery flakes

1. Place all the ingredients in a small bowl. Mix and crush with the back of a spoon.
2. Store in an airtight container for up to 6 months.

NOTES: *To make Italian salad dressing: Mix together 2 tablespoons (10 g) of dry seasoning mix, ¼ cup (60 ml) of vinegar of your choice, 2 tablespoons (28 ml) of water and ½ cup (118 ml) of good-quality extra-virgin olive oil. Whisk or shake in a covered mason jar.*

ONION SOUP MIX

Yield: 6 tablespoons (equivalent of 2 packets)

3 tablespoons (21 g) dried minced onion

2 tablespoons (30 ml) low-sodium beef bouillon granules

1 teaspoon onion powder

¼ teaspoon parsley flakes

⅛ teaspoon celery seed

⅛ teaspoon ground paprika

⅛ teaspoon kosher salt

⅛ teaspoon freshly ground black pepper

1. Place all the ingredients in a small bowl. Mix and crush with the back of a spoon.
2. Store in an airtight container for up to 6 months.

NOTES: *To make soup: Place 3 tablespoons (15 g) of onion soup mix in a medium saucepan. Stir in 4 cups (940 ml) of water and bring to a boil, stirring occasionally. Reduce the heat and simmer uncovered, stirring occasionally, for 10 minutes.*

To make onion dip: Combine 3 tablespoons (15 g) of onion soup mix with one 16-ounce (454 g) container of sour cream or Greek yogurt.

SAVORY HERB AND GARLIC SOUP MIX

Yield: 15 tablespoons (equivalent of 3 packets)

3 tablespoons (21 g) dried minced onion

2 tablespoons (6 g) dried marjoram

2 tablespoons (6 g) dried oregano

2 tablespoons (6 g) dried rosemary

2 tablespoons (9 g) dried basil

2 tablespoons (2 g) dried parsley flakes

1 tablespoon (2 g) dried thyme

2 teaspoons (5 g) garlic powder

1 teaspoon onion powder

1 teaspoon salt

1 teaspoon black pepper

1. Place all the ingredients in a small bowl. Mix and crush with the back of a spoon.
2. Store in an airtight container for up to 6 months.

NOTES: *To make soup: Place 3 tablespoons (15 g) of onion soup mix in a medium saucepan. Stir in 4 cups (940 ml) of water and bring to a boil, stirring occasionally. Reduce the heat and simmer uncovered, stirring occasionally, for 10 minutes.*

To make onion dip: Combine 3 tablespoons (15 g) of onion soup mix with one 16-ounce (454 g) container of sour cream or Greek yogurt.

AU JUS MIX

Yield: 10 tablespoons (equivalent of 5 packets)

4 tablespoons (60 ml) low-sodium beef bouillon granules

4 tablespoons (36 g) cornstarch

4 teaspoons (9 g) onion powder

2 teaspoons dried parsley flakes

¼ teaspoon freshly ground black pepper

¼ teaspoon garlic

1. Place all the ingredients in a small bowl. Mix and crush with the back of a spoon.
2. Store in an airtight container for up to 6 months.

NOTES: *To make au jus: Measure out 2 tablespoons (28 ml) into a small saucepan. Whisk with 2 cups (475 ml) of water over medium-high heat for 15 minutes, until thickened and bubbly.*

ALL-PURPOSE BAKING MIX

Yield: 7 cups

6 cups (750 g) all-purpose flour

3 tablespoons (42 g) baking powder

2 teaspoons (9 g) granulated sugar

1 tablespoon (18 g) salt

1 cup (225 g) vegetable shortening or butter, cubed

1. Add the flour, baking powder, sugar, and salt to the bowl of a food processor.

2. Pulse the ingredients for about 15 seconds.

3. Add in the vegetable shortening or butter and pulse the processor until the mixture resembles cornmeal.

4. Store the baking mix for up to 3 months. If you are using shortening, you can store the mix in the pantry. If you are using butter, you can store it in the refrigerator.

ABOUT THE AUTHORS

Heid Kennedy is a work-at-home mom living in Wyoming with her husband and five kids. She has a passion for feeding her family and friends delicious food cooked at home as well as running her food blog *Crock-Pot Ladies* (www.crockpotladies.com).

Katie Handing was a founding partner at *Crock-Pot Ladies*. She is a single mother to two gorgeous daughters, Molly and Natalie, and one yellow Labrador retriever, Winnie. She grew up living the big city life where she spent fifteen years working in law enforcement. Having children changed everything for her, and she moved to the country thirty minutes away from the city lights. She works full time at a school for special-education students. Her free time is spent cooking for family, neighbors, and her co-workers and carting her kids to basketball, piano, tumbling, and the local strip mine lake for fishing and swimming. Keep up with what Katie is cooking at her new blog *Frugal Cooking with Friends* (www.frugalcookingwithfriends.com).

Sarah Ince is one of the original *Crock-Pot Ladies*. She lives in idyllic rural Kansas where she has found many excuses to pull out her slow cookers for various organizations that she volunteers with and helps feed, of course! She helps run several science-based groups online and one for her community. She lives her dream of residing among the corn, wheat, soy, and cows—where the towns are small, the past times are golden, and freeways, jets, and traffic don't exist. She lives with her husband, Garth, three children, Corianne, Wesley, and Melissa, and her sister, Jocelyn. They raise five chickens: Betty Lou, Chubby, Fluffernutter, Hedwig, and Duke. They are not the owners of the three cats that reside on their porch: You Don't Live Here, Go Away, and You Don't Like Us Anyways. Follow Sarah's next adventure at her new blog *Frugal Cooking with Friends* (www.frugalcookingwithfriends.com).

INDEX